P9-AOW-835

CRY OF THE THUNDERBIRD

The Civilization of the American Indian Series

CRY OF THE
The American

Edited and with an Introduction and Commentary by

CHARLES HAMILTON

THUNDERBIRD

Indian's Own Story

With paintings by
George Catlin

and sketches by
American Indian Artists

UNIVERSITY OF OKLAHOMA PRESS : NORMAN

By Charles Hamilton

Men of the Underworld: The Professional Criminal's Own Story (New York, 1952)
Braddock's Defeat: The Journal of a British Officer, Halkett's Orderly Book (editor; Norman, 1959)
Collecting Autographs and Manuscripts (Norman, 1961, 1970)
Lincoln in Photographs: An Album of Every Known Pose (with Lloyd Ostendorf; Norman, 1963)
The Robot That Helped to Make a President (New York, 1965)
Scribblers and Scoundrels (New York, 1968)
Cry of the Thunderbird: The American Indian's Own Story (New York, 1950; Norman, 1972)

Library of Congress Cataloging in Publication Data

Hamilton, Charles, 1913– ed.
Cry of the Thunderbird.
(The Civilization of the American Indian Series, v. 119)
Bibliography p. 263–274
1. Indians of North America–Social life and customs. 2. Indians of North America–History.
I. Title. II. Series.
E77.H2 1972 970.1 70–177336
ISBN 0–8061–1003–1

First printing of the new edition 1972. Manufactured in the U.S.A.

Cry of the Thunderbird is Volume 119 in The Civilization of the American Indian Series.

To DORIS

PREFACE TO THE NEW EDITION

When this book was first published, in 1950, it was, I believe, the first and only book in which the Indian told in his own words about his way of life and his view of the white man. Those words are packed with the power and beauty of the Indian dream—his religion, his hopes, his love of nature, his view of battle. Here he tells why he clashed with the whites in a series of bitter wars that he probably knew he could never win.

In today's terms the Indian was a conservationist. He rarely killed for sport, only for sustenance. He believed the white man to be a symbol of extinction and predicted that the day would come when the whites who slaughtered buffaloes, cut down trees, dammed and polluted rivers, and carved up the Great Spirit's land would see nature turn upon him and destroy him. Today those prophecies seem to be coming true.

This book is an indictment of the white man by the "savages" whom he betrayed and virtually destroyed. But it is an indictment tempered with warmth and wisdom and mercy. In the end one sees the hand of the Indian outstretched in friendship and brotherhood.

CHARLES HAMILTON

New York City
January 15, 1972

ACKNOWLEDGMENTS

Acknowledgment is gratefully given to the following publishers or holders of copyright material for permission to reprint selections:

The Caxton Printers, Ltd., for *Yellow Wolf: His Own Story*, by Lucullus Virgil McWhorter, published by the Caxton Printers, Ltd., Caldwell, Idaho, copyright, 1940, by the Caxton Printers, Ltd., and used by special permission of the copyright owners.

The John Day Company, Inc., for *American: The Life Story of a Great Indian*, as he told it to Frank B. Linderman. Copyright, 1930, by Frank B. Linderman.

Dodd, Mead & Company, Inc., for *Flaming Arrow's People*, by James Paytiamo. Copyright, 1932, by Dodd, Mead & Company, Inc.

Mrs. Elaine Goodale Eastman, for *From the Deep Woods to Civilization*, by Ohiyesa (Dr. Charles A. Eastman), copyright, 1916, by Charles A. Eastman, copyright, 1944, by Elaine Goodale Eastman; *Indian Boyhood*, by Ohiyesa, copyright, 1902, by Little, Brown, and Company, copyright, 1930, by Charles A. Eastman; and *Indian Heroes and Great Chieftains*, by Ohiyesa, copyright, 1918, by Little, Brown, and Company, copyright, 1946, by Elaine Goodale Eastman.

Mrs. Minnie-Ellen M. Hastings, for *A Warrior Who Fought Custer*, interpreted by Thomas B. Marquis, published by the Caxton Printers, Ltd., copyright, 1931, by Minnie-Ellen M. Hastings.

Houghton Mifflin Company, for *My People, the Sioux*, by Chief Luther Standing Bear, copyright, 1928, by Luther Standing Bear, and *Land of the Spotted Eagle*, by Chief Luther Standing Bear, copyright, 1933, by Luther Standing Bear, reprinted by permission of and arrangement with Houghton Mifflin Company, the authorized publishers.

William Morrow and Company, Inc., for *Black Elk Speaks*, as told to John G. Neihardt. Copyright, 1932, by John G. Neihardt, by permission of William Morrow and Company, Inc.

Rinehart & Company, Inc., for *Long Lance*, by Chief Buffalo Child Long Lance. Copyright, 1928, by Rinehart & Company, Inc., and reprinted with their permission.

Trail's End Publishing Co., Inc., for *Firewater and Forked Tongues*, by M. I. McCreight. Copyright, 1947, by Trail's End Publishing Co., Inc.

Yale University Press, for *Sun Chief: The Autobiography of a Hopi Indian*, edited by Leo W. Simmons. Copyright, 1942, by Yale University Press.

I wish also to express my gratitude to the Bureau of American Ethnology, Smithsonian Institution, for their invaluable publications on the American Indian; to Mrs. Elaine Goodale Eastman, for information regarding Chief Buffalo Child Long Lance; to Eleanor Daniels, for her understanding and helpful guidance; to my brother Bruce, for his valuable suggestions; and to my wife, Doris, for her advice and encouragement.

Finally I wish to thank the Thomas Gilcrease Institute of American History and Art, Tulsa, Oklahoma, for its generosity in allowing me to reproduce the works of George Catlin included in this new edition of the book.

CONTENTS

ILLUSTRATIONS

COLOR

Paintings by George Catlin

BLACK AND WHITE

MAP

INTRODUCTION

The American Indian is the author of this book. Here the last men of the Stone Age describe their heroic struggle with the first men of the Machine Age, their incredible customs and rites, adventures in hunting and on the warpath, and finally their pathetic efforts to accept the strange ways of the white invader. Their great warriors—Tecumseh, Black Hawk, Sitting Bull, Chief Joseph, Geronimo—speak once more in these pages.

Descriptions of the Indian by white travelers, soldiers, or missionaries seldom show sufficient understanding or knowledge of the red man's character. Reticent in the presence of strangers, the Indian kept his real thoughts to himself and gave out only information which he considered inconsequential. But when he wrote about himself, he told the truth even though it might be unflattering.

The writings of Indian authors are of immense importance because they present a new interpretation of events and bring into sharp focus the true nature of the red man's conflict with the white invader. The Indian explains why he so bitterly contested the white man's advance, and why he often chose to die rather than give up his hunting grounds.

Aside from a few typographical corrections, the texts are exactly as the Indians wrote them. Their spelling is not always uniform because certain words, like Ojibway and tepee, had no standard spelling. Occasionally, repetitious or confusing passages were deleted; but the exact pages quoted from each source are shown in the Notes at the back of the book. A brief biography of each author, and the time and place of the selection will also be found in the Notes.

Only the Indians who lived in what is now the United States are included, for no one book could relate the customs and history of all Indian tribes. Not every tribe is represented, as there were hundreds, each with a different culture, inside the limits of the United States. Many tribes were small and relatively uninteresting. Those Indians who subsisted on fish and berries and gave up their land to the white man without a struggle lacked the qualities which most of us associate with the red man. They are left undisturbed at their peaceful clam digging and berry picking.

Probably the greatest Indian culture in America was that of the Five Civilized Nations—the Cherokees, Creeks, Seminoles, Choctaws, and Chickasaws. These tribes, originally located in the Southeast, were driven west to Oklahoma, where they modeled their civilization after that of the white man. Their cultural achievements set them apart from the elemental world of the fighting Ojibways and Sioux and the great Iroquoian tribes who once held the balance of power in America.

But it is the valiant Plains Indian, with his colorful war bonnet and feathered lance, who has become the symbol of the red man. His long and courageous struggle against the military power of the United States and his nobility in defeat entitle him to a major role in this book.

The different Indian cultures, usually classified by language, geographical location, type of habitation or food, are here grouped together. Tribes in the same area often had many customs in common, but no two tribes were exactly alike. The Sioux were similar to their neighbors, the Cheyennes, but entirely different from more distant tribes like the Hopi or Seneca. To avoid confusion, each author is identified by tribe; and, unless otherwise stated, the custom he describes should be looked upon as applying only to his own tribe.

The Indians are portrayed here not as tribal units but as individuals. If they occasionally cross a boundary without anthropological permission, it is because they are *live* Indians. They are not the sort who fit into neat ethnological rows or stand sedately in front of cigar stores—they are men who lived hard and fought hard, and still found time to philosophize about the beauty and mystery of the earth.

CRY OF THE THUNDERBIRD

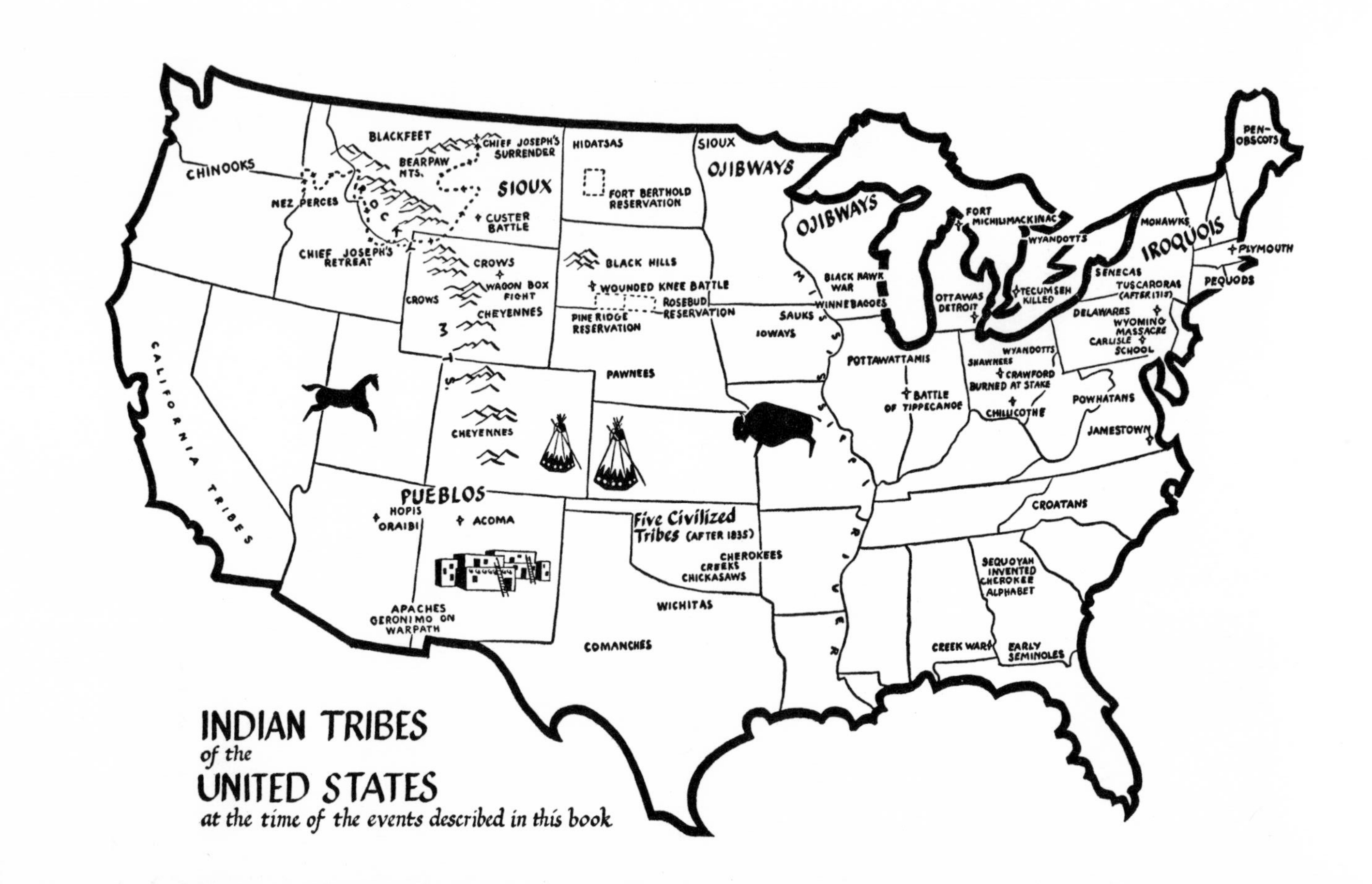

INDIAN TRIBES
of the
UNITED STATES
at the time of the events described in this book

PROLOGUE

CHIEF STANDING BEAR

The feathered and blanketed figure of the American Indian has come to symbolize the American continent. He is the man who through centuries has been moulded and sculped by the same hand that shaped its mountains, forests, and plains, and marked the course of its rivers.

The American Indian is of the soil, whether it be the region of forests, plains, pueblos, or mesas. He fits into the landscape, for the hand that fashioned the continent also fashioned the man for his surroundings. He once grew as naturally as the wild sunflowers; he belongs just as the buffalo belonged.

With a physique that fitteu, the man developed fitting skills—crafts which today are called American. And the body had a soul, also formed and moulded by the same master hand of harmony. Out of the Indian approach to existence there came a great freedom—an intense and absorbing love for nature; a respect for life; enriching faith in a Supreme Power; and principles of truth, honesty, generosity, equity, and brotherhood.

I: AROUND THE CAMPFIRE

The campfire was the center of Indian social life. On festive occasions the fire was built in the dance circle and around it gathered the Indians in their finery. Here the old men talked longingly of the days when arrows were sharper and bows were stronger. Warriors swapped stories of their adventures, and children learned tribal traditions as they listened to the tales of their elders. The women usually sat on one side of the dance circle and the men on the other; few words were exchanged, but there were many shy glances to mark the beginning of courtships.

I: AROUND THE CAMPFIRE

A SIOUX COURTSHIP

BLACK ELK—SIOUX

The following is taken from Black Elk Speaks *by John G. Neihardt, well known authority on Plains Indians, especially the Sioux. It is interesting to note that in his forthcoming novel of Sioux life Neihardt has expanded the character of High Horse in keeping with other stories told by the author's old friends among the Sioux.*

You know, in the old days, it was not so very easy to get a girl when you wanted to be married. Sometimes it was hard work for a young man and he had to stand a great deal. Say I am a young man and I have seen a young girl who looks so beautiful to me that I feel all sick when I think about her. I can not just go and tell her about it and then get married if she is willing. I have to be a very sneaky fellow to talk to her at all, and after I have managed to talk to her, that is only the beginning.

Probably for a long time I have been feeling sick about a certain girl because I love her so much, but she will not even look at me, and her parents keep a good watch over her. But I keep feeling worse and worse all the time; so maybe I sneak up to her tepee in the dark and wait until she comes out. Maybe I just wait there all night and don't get any sleep at all and she does not come out. Then I feel sicker than ever about her.

Maybe I hide in a brush by a spring where she sometimes goes to get water, and when she comes by, if nobody is looking, then I jump out and hold her and just make her listen to me. If she likes me too, I can tell that from the way she acts, for she is very bashful and maybe will not say a word or even look at me the first time. So I let her go, and then maybe I sneak around until I can see her father alone, and I tell him how many horses I can give him for his beautiful girl, and by now I am feeling so sick that maybe I would give him all the horses in the world if I had them.

Well, this young man I am telling about was called High Horse, and there was a girl in the village who looked so beautiful to him that he was just sick all over from thinking about her so much and he was getting sicker all the time. The girl was very shy, and her parents thought a great deal of her because they were not young any more and this was the only child they had. So they watched her all day long, and they fixed it so that she would be safe at night too when they were asleep. They thought so much of her that they had made a rawhide bed for her to sleep in, and after they knew that High Horse was sneaking around after her, they took rawhide thongs and tied the girl in bed at night so that nobody could steal her when they were asleep, for they were not sure but that their girl might really want to be stolen.

Well, after High Horse had been sneaking around a good while and hiding and waiting for the girl and getting sicker all the time, he finally caught her alone and made her talk to him. Then he found out that she liked him maybe a little. Of course this did not make him feel well. It made him sicker than ever, but now he felt as brave as a bison bull, and so he went right to her father and said he loved the girl so much that he would give two good horses for her—one of them young and the other one not so very old.

But the old man just waved his hand, meaning for High Horse to go away and quit talking foolishness like that.

High Horse was feeling sicker than ever about it; but there was another young fellow who said he would loan High Horse two ponies and when he got some more horses, why, he could just give them back for the ones he had borrowed.

Then High Horse went back to the old man and said he would give four horses for the girl—two of them young and the other two not hardly old at all. But the old man just waved his hand and would not say anything.

So High Horse sneaked around until he could talk to the girl again, and he asked her to run away with him. He told her he thought he would just fall over and die if she did not. But she said she would not do that; she wanted to be bought like a fine woman. You see she thought a great deal of herself too.

That made High Horse feel so very sick that he could not eat a bite, and he went around with his head hanging down as though he might just fall down and die any time.

Red Deer was another young fellow, and he and High Horse were great comrades, always doing things together. Red Deer saw how High Horse was acting, and he said: "Cousin, what is the matter? Are you sick in the belly? You look as though you were going to die."

Then High Horse told Red Deer how it was, and said he thought he could not stay alive much longer if he could not marry the girl pretty quick.

Red Deer thought awhile about it, and then he said: "Cousin, I have a plan, and if you are man enough to do as I tell you, then everything will be all right. She will not run away with you; her old man will not take four horses; and four horses are all you can get. You must steal her and run away with her. Then afterwhile you can come back and the old man cannot do anything because she will be your woman. Probably she wants you to steal her anyway."

So they planned what High Horse had to do, and he said he loved the girl so much that he was man enough to do anything Red Deer or anybody else could think up.

So this is what they did.

That night late they sneaked up to the girl's tepee and waited until it sounded inside as though the old man and the old woman and the girl were sound asleep. Then High Horse crawled under the tepee with a knife. He had to cut the rawhide thongs first, and then Red Deer, who was pulling up the stakes around that side of the tepee, was going to help drag the girl outside and gag her. After that, High Horse could put her across his pony in front of him and hurry out of there and be happy all the rest of his life.

When High Horse had crawled inside, he felt so nervous that he could hear his heart drumming, and it seemed so loud he felt sure it would 'waken the old folks. But it did not, and afterwhile he began cutting the thongs. Every time he cut one it made a pop and nearly scared him to death. But he was getting along all right and all the thongs were cut down as far as the girl's thighs, when he became so nervous that his knife slipped and stuck the girl. She gave a big, loud yell. Then the old folks jumped up and yelled too. By this time High Horse was outside, and he and Red Deer were running away like antelope. The old man and some other people chased the young men but they got away in the dark and nobody knew who it was.

Well, if you ever wanted a beautiful girl you will know how sick High Horse was now. It was very bad the way he felt, and it looked as though he would starve even if he did not drop over dead sometime.

Red Deer kept thinking about this, and after a few days he went to High Horse and said: "Cousin, take courage! I have another plan, and I am sure, if you are man enough, we can steal her this time." And High Horse said: "I am man enough to do anything anybody can think up, if I can only get that girl."

So this is what they did.

They went away from the village alone, and Red Deer made High Horse strip naked. Then he painted High Horse solid white all over, and after that he painted black stripes all over the white and put black rings around High Horse's eyes. High Horse looked terrible. He looked so terrible that when Red Deer was through painting and took a good look at what he had done, he said it scared even him a little.

"Now," Red Deer said, "if you get caught again, everybody will be so scared they will think you are a bad spirit and will be afraid to chase you."

So when the night was getting old and everybody was sound asleep, they sneaked back to the girl's tepee. High Horse crawled in with his knife, as before, and Red Deer waited outside, ready to drag the girl out and gag her when High Horse had all the thongs cut.

High Horse crept up by the girl's bed and began cutting at the thongs. But he kept thinking, "If they see me they will shoot me because I look so terrible." The girl was restless and kept squirming around in bed, and when a thong was cut, it popped. So High Horse worked very slowly and carefully.

But he must have made some noise, for suddenly the old woman awoke and said to her old man: "Old Man, wake up! There is somebody in this tepee!" But the old man was sleepy and didn't want to be bothered. He said: "Of course there is somebody in this tepee. Go to sleep and don't bother me." Then he snored some more.

But High Horse was so scared by now that he lay very still and as flat to the ground as he could. Now, you see, he had not been sleeping very well for a long time because he was so sick about the girl. And while he was lying there waiting for the old woman to snore, he just forgot everything, even how beautiful the girl was. Red Deer who was lying outside ready to do his part, wondered and wondered what had happened in there, but he did not dare call out to High Horse.

Afterwhile the day began to break and Red Deer had to leave with the two ponies he had staked there for his comrade and girl, or somebody would see him.

So he left.

Now when it was getting light in the tepee, the girl awoke and the first thing she saw was a terrible animal, all white with black stripes on it, lying asleep beside her bed. So she screamed, and then the old woman screamed and the old man yelled. High Horse jumped up, scared almost to death, and he nearly knocked the tepee down getting out of there.

People were coming running from all over the village with guns and bows and axes, and everybody was yelling.

By now High Horse was running so fast that he hardly touched the ground at all, and he looked so terrible that the people fled from him and let him run. Some braves wanted to shoot at him, but the others said he might be some sacred being and it would bring bad trouble to kill him.

High Horse made for the river that was near, and in among the brush he found a hollow tree and dived into it. Afterwhile some braves came there and he could hear them saying that it was some bad spirit that had come out of the water and gone back in again.

That morning the people were ordered to break camp and move away from there. So they did, while High Horse was hiding in his hollow tree.

Now Red Deer had been watching all this from his own tepee and trying to look as though he were as much surprised and scared as all the others. So when the camp moved, he sneaked back to where he had seen his comrade disappear. When he was down there in the brush, he called, and High Horse answered, because he knew his friend's voice. They washed off the paint from High Horse and sat down on the river bank to talk about their troubles.

High Horse said he never would go back to the village as long as he lived and he did not care what happened to him now. He said he was going to go on the war-path all by himself. Red Deer said: "No, cousin, you are not going on the war-path alone, because I am going with you."

So Red Deer got everything ready, and at night they started out on the war-path all alone. After several days they came to a Crow camp just about sundown, and when it was dark they sneaked up to where the Crow horses were grazing, killed the horse guard, who was not thinking about enemies because he thought all the Lakotas [Sioux] were far away, and drove off about a hundred horses.

They got a big start because all the Crow horses stampeded and it was probably morning before the Crow warriors could catch any horses to ride. Red Deer and High Horse fled with their herd three days and nights before they reached the village of their people. Then they drove the whole herd right into the village and up in front of the girl's tepee. The old man was there, and High Horse called out to him and asked if he thought maybe that would be enough horses for his girl. The old man did not wave him away that time. It was not the horses that he wanted. What he wanted was a son who was a real man and good for something.

So High Horse got his girl after all, and I think he deserved her.

THE MAIDENS' FEAST

OHIYESA—SIOUX

There were many peculiar customs among the Indians of an earlier period, some of which tended to strengthen the character of the people and preserve their purity. Perhaps the most unique of these was the annual "feast of maidens." The casual observer would scarcely understand the full force and meaning of this ceremony.

The last one that I ever witnessed was given at Fort Ellis, Manitoba, about the year 1871.

One bright summer morning, while we were still at our meal of jerked buffalo meat, we heard the herald of the Wahpeton band [of Sioux Indians] upon his calico pony as he rode around our circle.

"White Eagle's daughter, the maiden Red Star, invites all the maidens of all the tribes to come and partake of her feast. It will be in the Wahpeton camp, before the sun reaches the middle of the sky. All pure maidens are invited. Red Star also invites the young men to be present, to see that no unworthy maiden should join in the feast."

The herald soon completed the rounds of the different camps, and it was not long before the girls began to gather in great numbers. The fort was fully alive to the interest of these savage entertainments. This particular feast was looked upon as a semi-sacred affair. It would be desecration for any to attend who was not perfectly virtuous. Hence it was regarded as an opportune time for the young men to satisfy themselves as to who were the virtuous maids of the tribe.

There were apt to be surprises before the end of the day. Any young man was permitted to challenge any maiden whom he knew to be unworthy. But woe to him who could not prove his case. It meant little short of death to the man who endeavored to disgrace a woman without cause.

The youths had a similar feast of their own, in which the eligibles were those who had never spoken to a girl in the way of courtship. It was considered ridiculous so to do before attaining some honor as a warrior, and the novices prided themselves greatly upon their self-control.

From the various camps the girls came singly or in groups, dressed in bright-colored calicoes or in heavily fringed and beaded buckskin. Their smooth cheeks and the central part of their glossy hair was touched with vermilion. All brought with them wooden basins to eat from. Some who came from a considerable distance were mounted upon ponies; a few, for company or novelty's sake, rode double.

The maidens' circle was formed about a cone-shaped rock which stood upon its base. This was painted red. Beside it two new arrows were lightly stuck into the ground. This is a sort of altar, to which each maiden comes before taking her assigned place in the circle, and lightly touches first the stone and then the arrows. By this oath she declares her purity. Whenever a girl approaches the altar there is a stir among the spectators, and sometimes a rude youth would call out:

"Take care! You will overturn the rock, or pull out the arrows!"

Such a remark makes the girls nervous, and especially one who is not sure of her composure.

The whole population of the region had assembled, and the maidens came shyly into the circle. The simple ceremonies observed prior to the serving of the food were in progress, when among a group of Wahpeton Sioux young men there was a stir of excitement. All the maidens glanced nervously toward the scene of the disturbance. Soon a tall youth emerged from the throng of spectators and advanced toward the circle.

At last he stopped behind a pretty Assiniboine maiden of good family and said:

"I am sorry, but, according to custom, you should not be here."

The girl arose in confusion, but she soon recovered her self-control.

"What do you mean?" she demanded, indignantly. "Three times you have come to court me, but each time I have refused to listen to you. I turned my back upon you. Twice I was with Mashtinna. She can tell the people that this is true. The third time I had gone for water when you intercepted me and begged me to stop and listen. I refused because I did not know you. My chaperon, Makatopawee, knows that I was gone but a few minutes. I never saw you anywhere else."

The young man was unable to answer this unmistakable statement of facts, and it became apparent that he had sought to revenge himself for her repulse.

"Woo! woo! Carry him out!" was the order of the chief of the Indian police, and the audacious youth was hurried away into the nearest ravine to be chastised.

The young woman who had thus established her good name returned to the circle, and the feast was served. The "maidens' song" was sung, and four times they danced in a ring around the altar. Each maid as she departed once more took her oath to remain pure until she should meet her husband.

SONGS OF OJIBWAY LOVERS

The Brave to the Maiden:

Awake! flower of the forest, sky-treading bird of the prairie. Awake! awake! wonderful fawn-eyed One. When you look upon me I am satisfied; as flowers that drink dew. The breath of your mouth is the fragrance of flowers in the morning, your breath is their fragrance at evening in the moon-of-fading-leaf. Do not the red

Courtesy of Thomas Gilcrease Institute of American History and Art, Tulsa, Oklahoma

IN-NE-O-COSE
(Blackfoot Brave)
Watercolor on paper
George Catlin
1836

CROW WIGWAM
Oil on canvas
George Catlin
Undated

Courtesy of Gilcrease Institute

streams of my veins run toward you as forest-streams to the sun in the moon of bright nights?

When you are beside me my heart sings; a branch it is, dancing, dancing before the Wind-spirit in the moon of strawberries. When you frown upon me, beloved, my heart grows dark—a shining river the shadows of clouds darken, then with your smiles comes the sun and makes to look like gold furrows the cold wind drew in the water's face. Myself! behold me! blood of my beating heart. Earth smiles—the waters smile—even the sky-of-clouds smiles—but I, I lose the way of smiling when you are not near.

Awake! awake! my beloved.

The Maiden to the Brave:

My love is tall and graceful as the young pine waving on the hill, and as swift in his course as the noble, stately deer; his hair is flowing, and dark as the blackbird that floats through the air, and his eyes, like the eagle's, both piercing and bright; his heart, it is fearless and great, and his arm it is strong in the fight, as this bow made of iron-wood which he easily bends. His aim is as sure in the fight and chase, as the hawk, which ne'er misses its prey. Ah, aid me, ye spirits! of water, of earth, and of sky, while I sing in his praise; and my voice shall be heard, it shall ring through the sky; and echo, repeating the same, shall cause it to swell in the breadth of the wind; and his fame shall be spread throughout the land, and his name shall be known beyond the lakes.

TRADITIONAL ADVICE ON GETTING MARRIED

ANONYMOUS—WINNEBAGO

What Every Young Man Should Know

If you ever get married, my son, do not make an idol of your wife. The more you worship her, the more will she want to be worshipped. Thus the old people said. They warned the young men against the example of those men who always hearken to what the women say, who are the slaves of women.

My son, if you keep on listening to your wife, after a while she will never let you go to any feast at all. All your relatives will scold you and your own sisters will think little of you. Finally, when you have become a real slave to your wife, she might tell you to hit your own relatives, and you would do it. For these reasons, my son, I warn you against the words of women. Steel yourself against them. For if you do not do so you will find yourself different from other men. It is not good to be enslaved by a woman.

My son, this also I will tell you. Women can never be watched. If you try to watch them you will merely show your jealousy and your female relatives will also be jealous. After a while you will become so jealous of your wife that she will leave you and run away. You yourself will be to blame for this. You thought too much of a woman and in worshipping her you humbled yourself, and as a consequence she has been taken away from you. All the other women will know of this, and no one will want to marry you again. Everyone will consider you a very bad man.

What Every Young Woman Should Know

If you marry a man and you want to be certain of always retaining him, work for him. With work you will always be able to retain your hold on men. If you do your work to the satisfaction of your husband, he will never leave you. Remain faithful to your husband. Do not act as though you are married to a number of men at the same time. Lead a chaste life. If you do not listen to what I am telling you and you are unfaithful to your husband, all the men will jeer at you. They will say whatever they wish to [and no one will interfere].

Do not act haughtily to your husband. Whatever he tells you to do, do it. Kindness will be returned to you if you obey your husband, for he will treat you in the same manner.

If a wife has no real interest in her husband's welfare and possessions she will be to him no more than any other woman, and the world will ridicule her. If, on the other hand, you pay more attention to your husband than to your parents, your parents will leave you. Let your husband likewise take care of your parents, for they depend on him. Your parents were instrumental in getting you your husband, so remember that they expect some recompense for it, as likewise for the fact that they raised you.

When you visit your husband's people do not go around with a haughty air or act as if you considered yourself far above them. Try to get them to like you. If you are good-natured, you will be placed in charge of the home at which you happen to be visiting. Then your parents-in-law will tell your husband that their daughter-in-law is acting nicely to them.

HOME AND FAMILY

CHIEF STANDING BEAR—SIOUX

The home was the center of Lakota society—the place where good social members were formed and the place whence flowed the strength of the tribe. Here it was that offspring learned duty to parents, to lodge, to band, to tribe, and to self.

Woman's work, generally, was to cook for the family, keep the tipi in order, and sew the clothing of the household members. The good wife never allowed one of the family to run low in clothing. There were garments to be made, and moccasins, robes and blankets, and sometimes gloves, caps and scarfs. Buttonholes were never made, probably never thought of, but very pretty buttons were fashioned of rawhide and either painted or covered with porcupine quills. Sinew was split for thread, coarse strands for heavy work and medium fine or very fine strands for decorative work, then folded into little bundles and placed in a sewing kit. When the men came home from the hunt there were skins to be cleaned and tanned. New tipis were made and old ones, for the sake of frugality, made into clothing for children. From rawhide were made moccasin soles, bags and trunks for holding ceremonial garments, headdresses, and other articles to be kept in neatness and order.

The good wife always kept plenty of food stored and cooked so that it could be served at any moment. The thought was to not only meet the food requirements of the family, but to be able to serve any one who came to the tipi, strangers or relatives, children who came in from other tipis, or any old people whom the children might bring in. If the husband brought home friends unexpectedly, he could be sure that his wife would receive them hospitably without any request from him.

Many of the courtesies of Indian social life included the preparation and serving of food, and among the Lakota it was a custom of good will just as it is with the white man. When a white friend wishes to extend a courtesy it is usually by asking one to dine. A feast in honor of my father was sometimes given in this way: Some of my mother's relations would invite her over to their tipi. At once the women would begin preparing food for a number of people. When all was ready, they would tell mother to ask father to come to the feast and bring with him some of his friends. Father would gladly accept the invitation and would bring with him, as a rule, some of the old men of the village and there would be singing, eating, storytelling, and a general good time. The meal which the relations offered to father was their good will expressed in their most generous way. All his relations wished him to remain on good terms with his people, so if father could ask a number of old men to share good food with him, his chances for remaining popular would be better. The feast tended to strengthen the ties between father and the headmen of his band and also between him and his wife's relations.

Visiting bands were often received with a feast of welcome. As soon as the visitors stopped and began putting up their tipis, our women and girls built fires and cooked great quantities of food. They then carried the food over and spread the feast for the visitors, waiting upon them with every attention. The visitors ate and enjoyed themselves, but were never allowed to help in clearing away the remains of the feast. This was done by the women after the visitors had departed.

Sometimes a lone stranger came to our village for a visit. He was usually taken from tipi to tipi for a round of feasting and gossip, for the visitor was sure to have news to tell and he was encouraged to tell of his travels and of the people of his band. When the round of visits began, the stranger was given a long stick, pointed at one end, which he carried with him from tipi to tipi, each family putting on his stick some dried meat until it was full and sometimes more. This meat was to supply the visitor with food on his return or continued journey.

The serving of a family meal was a quiet and orderly affair. Mother placed the food in front of her while we children all sat quietly about, neither commenting on the food nor asking for any favors. Father, if at home, sat in his accustomed place at the side of the tipi. He, too, remained perfectly quiet and respectful, accepting the food that mother offered to him without comment. The serving was done on wooden plates, the soup being passed in horn spoons of different sizes, some of them holding as much as a large bowl. The food was portioned to each one of us as mother saw fit, her judgment being unquestioned, for we never asked for more. Before serving us, however, mother put a small portion of the food in the fire as a blessing for the meal.

Grandmother, next to mother, was the most important person in the home. Her place, in fact, could be filled by no one else. It has been told and written that old people among the Indians were sacrificed when they became useless. If this is the case with other tribes, I do not know of it, but I do know that it was never done among the Lakotas. Most old people were revered for their knowledge, and were never considered worthless members to be got rid of. Parental devotion was very strong and the old were objects of care and devotion to the last. They were never given cause to feel useless and unwanted, for there were duties performed only by the old and because it was a rigidly-kept custom for the young to treat their elders with respect. Grandmother filled a place that mother did not fill, and the older she got the more, it seemed, we children depended upon her for attention. I can never forget one of my grandmothers, mother's mother, and what wonderful care she took of me. As a story-teller, she was a delight not only to me but to other little folks of the village. Her sense of humor was keen and she laughed as readily as we.

Mother's and grandmother's tipis were quite close together and they saw a good deal of each other, working together and visiting back and forth. The men folks of the family were, for the most part, away from home during the day on hunting or scouting parties. But whenever father was at home and he chanced to walk out of the tipi, he covered his face with his blanket until he was sure that he would not see his mother-in-law. In this way he showed his respect for her, and had he not observed this courtesy she would have had every right to be affronted. She, too, avoided him, and if by chance they met, she hid her face. Had she allowed him to look upon her, it would have been an unforgivable breach of manners. In order to show her great respect for my father, grandmother often cooked some meat in her tipi, and calling my mother over would give her the meat saying, "Take this to my son-in-law." In this way she let him know that she thought highly of him.

The men, when at home, were shown a good deal of attention by the women. This was but natural, as it was the hunters, scouts and warriors who bore the greatest dangers, and consequently were the recipients of much care and consideration. Young warriors bearing for the first time the hardships of life were specially considered by the women. I remember one winter a party of young hunters returned home exhausted and near starvation, having seen no game. On reaching the village, they entered the first tipi they came to, which happened to be that of an old woman. Without a word, these young men began putting the meat, which was strung on a pole inside the tipi, on the fire to cook, and feeding themselves until it was gone. All the while the old woman ran about crying, not with anger or sorrow, but with joy for the return of the young men, and with gladness for the supply of meat that she was able to furnish. Had a white man witnessed this occurrence, it would probably have been interpreted in a manner far from correct.

Women and children were the objects of care among the Lakotas and as far as their environment permitted they lived sheltered lives. Life was softened by a great equality. All the tasks of women—cooking, caring for children, tanning and sewing—were considered dignified and worth while. No work was looked upon as menial, consequently there were no menial workers. Industry filled the life of every Lakota woman.

The first thing a dutiful husband did in the morning, after breakfasting, was to arrange his wife's hair and to paint her face. The brush was the tail of the porcupine attached to a decorated handle, and in place of a comb a hair parter was used—a slender pointed stick, also with a decorated handle. The husband parted his wife's hair, then carefully brushed and plaited it into two braids which were tied at the ends with strings of painted buckskin. These hair-strings were sometimes works of art, being wrapped with brightly colored porcupine quills and either tipped with ball tassels of porcupine quills or fluffs of eagle feathers. Bead hair-strings were later made, and they, too, are very pretty. When the hairdressing was finished, the part in the hair was sometimes marked with a stripe of red or yellow paint. Next, the husband applied red paint to his wife's face, sometimes just to the cheeks, sometimes covering the entire face. If the woman was to be exposed to the wind and sun all day, she usually had her face covered with a protective coat of paint mixed with grease. It was "style" for the Lakota woman to use much red paint, but the custom was very likely a necessary and comfortable one before it became a mere matter of style. Many Lakota women had skins quite fine in texture and in childhood were light in color. Such skins, of course, burned easily in the hot wind and sun, consequently children were often painted with the red paint and grease, both boys and girls, the mother performing this duty and not the father.

If the man of the family was to be home for several days, he busied himself in many ways, lightening the work of the woman. He cut down trees for the ponies and for wood, made and repaired her saddles, cut up meat conveniently for drying, and, when there was nothing else to be done, gladly amused the baby of the family. A man who unduly scolded his wife or who beat her or his children was not considered a good man. A man who would inflict punishment upon the women and children was considered a weakling and a coward. Whenever it was said about a man, "He ought not to have a wife," that was expressing strong disapproval of him.

As soon as the wife realized that she was to become a mother, she withdrew from the society of her husband, though at all times he had her in his care. But the husband immediately found duties that occupied his time—the hunt, the war-party, or ceremonies. With the knowledge that a child was about to be born the thought of the couple was for its welfare, and both father and mother were willing to sacrifice for the sake of the health of the child and mother. Not till a child was five or six years of age did the parents allow themselves another offspring. As a consequence Lakota families were not large, four or five children being the rule. But disabled mothers were a rarity and many a grandmother was as strong as her granddaughter. And with all the demands placed by parenthood, seldom was the relationship between husband and wife weakened. Children were influential beings with parents also. I remember my stepmother's uncle, Horse Looking, who fell a victim to the habit of drinking. It made of him a terrible man when under its influence, though in his right mind he was the kindest of men. When he was in a drunken frenzy, the only way to curb him was to get his youngest child and present it to him. He would at once forget his temper and begin to pet and fondle the child.

With the nearing event much preparation took place. Sisters, aunts, and other relatives made clothes of the finest and softest doeskin. A cradle was decorated and paints and powders prepared. But to grandmother fell the honor of officiating as supervisor and adviser on all matters pertaining to the occasion. She had, in fact, started her preparations and arrangements for the event of birth from the day of the wedding. During the waiting period grandmother had baked a red earth clay and pounded it to a fine powder to mix with the buffalo fat which she had rendered into a creamy paste. This mixture served as a cleanser and also as a protector to the tender skin of the child. Then grandmother had gathered the driest of buffalo chips and ground them between stones to a powder as fine and soft as talcum. This powder was a purifier, and soothing to an irritated skin.

Perhaps the hardest duty in the performance of parenthood was not so much to watch the conduct of their children as to be ever watchful of their own—a duty placed upon parents through the method used in instructing their young—example. Children, possessors of extreme vigor of health, with faculties sensitized by close contact with nature, made full use of eyes and ears; and Lakota parents and elders were under scrutiny for conduct and conversation. They were consequently bound to act in as kind and dignified a manner as possible.

EDUCATION OF CHILDREN

OHIYESA—SIOUX

It is commonly supposed that there is no systematic education of their children among the aborigines of this country. Nothing could be farther from the truth. All the customs of this primitive people were held to be divinely instituted, and those in connection with the training of children were scrupulously adhered to and transmitted from one generation to another.

The expectant parents conjointly bent all their efforts to the task of giving the new-comer the best they could gather from a long line of ancestors. A pregnant Indian woman would often choose one of the greatest characters of her family and tribe as a model for her child. This hero was daily called to mind. She would gather from tradition all of his noted deeds and daring exploits, rehearsing them to herself when alone. In order that the impression might be more distinct, she avoided company. She isolated herself as much as possible, and wandered in solitude, not thoughtlessly, but with an eye to the impress given by grand and beautiful scenery.

The Indians believed, also, that certain kinds of animals would confer peculiar gifts upon the unborn, while others would leave so strong an adverse impression that the child might become a monstrosity. A case of hare-lip was commonly attributed to the rabbit. It was said that a rabbit had charmed the mother and given to the babe its own features. Even the meat of certain animals was denied the pregnant woman, because it was supposed to influence the disposition or features of the child.

Scarcely was the embryo warrior ushered into the world, when he was met by lullabies that speak of wonderful exploits in hunting and war. Those ideas which so fully occupied his mother's mind before his birth are now put into words by all about the child, who is as yet quite unresponsive to their appeals to his honor and ambition. He is called the future defender of his people, whose lives may depend upon his courage and skill. If the child is a girl, she is at once addressed as the future mother of a noble race.

In hunting songs, the leading animals are introduced; they come to the boy to offer their bodies for the sustenance of his tribe. The animals are regarded as his friends, and spoken of almost as tribes of people, or as his cousins, grandfathers and grandmothers. The songs of wooing, adapted as lullabies, were equally imaginative, and the suitors were often personified, while pretty maidens were repsented by the mink and the doe.

Very early, the Indian boy assumed the task of preserving and transmitting the legends of his ancestors and his race. Almost every evening a myth, or a true story of some deed done in the past, was narrated by one of the parents or grandparents, while the boy listened with parted lips and glistening eyes. On the following evening, he was usually required to repeat it. If he was not an apt scholar, he struggled long with his task; but, as a rule, the Indian boy is a good listener and has a good memory, so that the stories were tolerably well mastered. The household became his audience, by which he was alternately criticized and applauded.

This sort of teaching at once enlightens the boy's mind and stimulates his ambition. His conception of his own future career becomes a vivid and irresistible force. Whatever there is for him to learn must be learned; whatever qualifications are necessary to a truly great man he must seek at any expense of danger and hardship. Such was the feeling of the imaginative and brave young Indian. It became apparent to him in early life that he must accustom himself to rove alone and not to fear or dislike the impression of solitude.

Our manners and morals were not neglected. I was made to respect the adults and especially the aged. I was not allowed to join in their discussions, nor even to speak in their presence, unless requested to do so. Indian etiquette was very strict, and among the requirements was that of avoiding the direct address. A term of relationship or some title of courtesy was commonly used instead of the personal name by those who wished to show respect. We were taught generosity to the poor and reverence for the "Great Mystery." Religion was the basis of all Indian training.

I recall to the present day some of the kind warnings and reproofs that my good grandmother was wont to give me. "Be strong of heart—be patient!" she used to say. She told me of a young chief who was noted for his uncontrollable temper. While in one of his rages he attempted to kill a woman, for which he was slain by his own band and left unburied as a mark of disgrace—his body was simply covered with green grass. If ever I lost my temper, she would say:

"Control yourself, or you will be like that young man I told you of, and lie under a *green blanket!*"

In the old days, no young man was allowed to use tobacco in any form until he had become an acknowledged warrior and had achieved a record. If a youth should seek a wife before he had reached the age of twenty-two or twenty-three, and been recognized as a brave man, he was sneered at and considered an ill-bred Indian. He must also be a skillful hunter. An Indian cannot be a good husband unless he brings home plenty of game.

These precepts were in the line of our training for the wild life.

A HOPI CHILDHOOD

DON C. TALAYESVA—HOPI

The peaceful life of the Hopi has changed little since the Spanish conquest. Most of the Hopi are farmers and herders who raise corn and beans and tend flocks of sheep and goats. Their textiles are still prized by neighboring tribes, just as they were generations ago, and their strange rituals are famous for colorful pageantry and for the weird masks worn by the dancers.

Everybody appeared happy after a rain. We small boys rolled about naked in the mud puddles, doused each other with water, and built little irrigated gardens. In this way we used too much of the water from the little pond on the west side of the village where the women went to wash their clothes and the men to water their stock. Our parents scolded us for wasting water and once my mother spanked me on account of my dirty shirt.

During droughts we had strict rules for the use of water. Even small children were taught to be careful, and I saw mothers bathe their babies by spitting a little water upon them. By watching the old people I learned to wash my face with a mouthful of water—it is the safest way to wash without waste.

Sometimes water gave out. Then the men went with their burros to distant springs while the women stayed up all night taking turns to catch a little trickle that came from the Oraibi spring. My grandfather told me about the cistern that he had chiseled out of the solid rock to catch the rain that fell on the mesa shelf. He said that he had done this hard work when he married my grandmother in order that his children and his grandchildren might not suffer from thirst. My mother went daily to this well to fetch water. In winter she cut out chunks of ice from the rock ledges and brought them in on her back.

Whenever it rained, we were told to take our little pots and go out on the ledges, scoop up puddles, and fill the cisterns. There were about one hundred of these hewn out of the solid rock by our ancestors. The people pointed out that water is essential to life and taught us what to do out in the desert whenever we became so dry and thirsty that we could neither spit nor swallow. Then one should cut twigs off a cottonwood tree and chew them, eat the inner bark of the cedar, or hold dried peaches in his mouth.

The importance of water was impressed upon us by the way the old men prayed for rain and planted pahos [ceremonial prayer sticks] in the springs to please the water serpents and to persuade them to send larger streams to quench our thirst. We were reminded that all the dances and ceremonies were for rain, not for pleasure. They were held in order to persuade the Six-Point-Cloud-People [dead ancestors who live in the clouds and control the rain] to send moisture for our crops. Whenever we had a good rain, we were told to show our happy faces and consider ourselves in favor with the gods. We made it a point never to praise the weather on fair, dry days. Whenever it rained during or just after a dance, the people praised highly those who had taken part in the performance. If a strong wind followed the dance, it was a sign that the people who had invited the Katcinas [priest-dancers] to come and dance had a bad heart or had done some evil.

We were told that there is health-giving power in water, and that it is a good practice to bathe in cold water, to wash our hands and faces in snow, and to rub it upon our bodies to make them tough. The old people said that warm water made wrinkles and shortened life. I saw them setting bowls of water outside to become ice-cold before using it for a bath. Some old men would go out naked and rub snow all over their bodies. My grandfathers often took me outside and rolled me in the snow on winter mornings.

Another important business was to keep track of the time or the seasons of the year by watching the points on the horizon where the sun rose and set each day. The point of sunrise on the shortest day of the year was called the sun's winter home and the point of sunrise on the longest day its summer home. Old Talasemptewa, who was almost blind, would sit out on the housetop of the special Sun Clan house and watch the sun's progress toward its summer home. He untied a knot in a string for each day. When the sun arose at certain mesa peaks, he passed the word around that it was time to plant sweet corn, ordinary corn, string beans, melons, squash, lima beans, and other seeds. On a certain date he would announce that it was too late for any more planting. The old people said that there were proper times for planting, harvesting, and hunting, for ceremonies, weddings, and many other activities. In order to know these dates it was necessary to keep close watch on the sun's movements.

My great-great-uncle Muute, who lived south of the Howeove kiva, was the Special Officer of the Sun Clan, and was called Tawamongwi [Sun Chief]. He would sit at a certain place and watch the sun in order to know when it reached its summer home. When the sun had arrived at its summer home, my uncle would say to the Sun Clan people, "Well, our great-uncle, the Sun god, has reached his summer home and now we must butcher a sheep and make prayer offerings for the sun, moon, and stars. We will pray hard to our Sun god, asking him to send rain and to keep away the bad winds that destroy our crops."

BLANKET SIGNALS

CHIEF STANDING BEAR—SIOUX

The Indian had many ways of communicating. The plains warrior could relay a simple message by smoke a hundred or more miles in a few minutes, for on a clear day smoke signals were nearly as fast as the "talking wires" of the white men. Mirror signals, often used in battle, could flash a message instantly five or ten miles.

When warriors of different tribes met, they talked in the sign language. Far from being crude, this method of communicating was nearly as fluent and accurate as speech. A skilled sign talker could tell a subtle joke or a complicated story, and even the most abstract thoughts could be put into gestures.

The sign language was picture writing in action, and its symbolism was often beautiful and poetic. The sign for "spring" was made by placing the right hand close to the ground, back downward, with the thumb and fingers extended upward. Then the hand was raised slowly several times to indicate the growing grass. The sign for "autumn" was made by picturing leaves falling from a tree. The idea of "falsehood" was conveyed by making the sign for "talk," followed by the sign for "different ways."

Among the Plains Indians the blanket was in almost daily use as a means of conversation, especially distant conversation, as across the village or from a hilltop. When the scout came in sight of the village and had given his signal call, he announced the nearness of the enemy or the rapid coming of the buffalo herd by rolling up his blanket and throwing it up in the air several times quickly, catching it like a ball. This signal meant, "Hurry up." The hunters and warriors got their weapons and prepared for either a hunt or a battle.

If the scout waved his blanket up and down slowly a number of times, then spread it on the ground and jumped over it, that notified the watchers that plenty of buffalo were near. The hunters then waited for the scout to tell them how many buffalo were near. If he walked, say, a quarter of a mile one way, then returned to the blanket and walked a similar distance in the opposite way and back to the blanket, that meant a very large herd was near. But if he walked just a few yards each way and back to his starting point, it meant that not so large a herd had been sighted. In either case preparations were made—the hunters filled quivers with arrows, knives were sharpened, wood was brought for fires, and general activity began.

The blanket was also used for summoning. It was waved in an outward motion from the body and back again. The man used the right arm and the woman the left arm.

Smoke was used for distant communication and was always watched for by those in the village if the hunters, warriors, or scouts were expected. This sort of signaling was usually begun when within a couple of days' travel from home. Smoke meant victory, and if a war-party returned without making smoke there would be no victory to relate.

Of the various modes of communication, perhaps the most dramatic were the mime dances of the braves—hunters, scouts, or warriors, and sometimes, the dances of the women in full male regalia. The Lakota was an actor, in some cases exhibiting splendid ability in the performance of tribal presentation. A close observor of animal life, his imitations of walk, manner and behavior of animals were most artful. Characteristics, through body motion, facial expression, intricate steps, symbolical dress, and even muscle contortion, were brought out with faithful portrayal. Animals like the turtle were imitated and this would call, naturally, for muscle control and subtle suggestion.

When the braves got together for their dances, it was a time for much feasting and social intercourse. The warrior danced his exploits;

the scout his adventures; the hunter his fortunes, and the medicine-man his experiences. Story-telling, no matter how conducted, will always delight a people. Furthermore, history was repeated and kept alive.

The Plains people have always been distinguished from other native people by the beautiful and expressive use of the hands in what is known as the "sign language"—it being the communicating gesture most often seen and noted by the European.

OJIBWAY PICTURE WRITING

CHIEF KAH-GE-GA-GAH-BOWH—OJIBWAY

The Indians did not have an alphabet, so they wrote in pictures. Sometimes these pictographs were etched on copper, but more often they were painted on birch bark or animal skins. The most famous of all Indian picture writings is the Walam Olum, or "painted tally" of the Delawares, their tribal history scratched upon tablets of wood. Another well known Indian manuscript is Lone-Dog's Winter Count, a calendar of winter events in Sioux history painted on a buffalo robe. It covers the period from 1800 to 1871, and for each winter there is a painting. Oddly enough, Lone-Dog and other buffalo robe historians overlooked most of the events that would seem important to us. A horse-stealing foray might be used to describe the year instead of a great battle, or a successful hunt might take the place of an important peace treaty.

Many tribes, especially those living near the sea, used wampum for picture writing. These bits of colored shell were pierced and woven into belts so that the design conveyed a message. Treaties were often preserved on wampum belts. Peter D. Clarke, a Wyandott author, wrote that "every wampum belt representing some international compact was placed in the archives of the Wyandott nation. Each belt bore some mark, denoting the nature of a covenant or contract entered into between the parties, and the hidden contents of which were kept in the memory of the Chiefs."

There is a place where the sacred records are deposited in the Indian country. These records are made on one side of bark and board plates, and are examined once in fifteen years, at which time the decaying ones are replaced by new plates.

Most Indian Nations of the West have places in which they deposit the records which are said to have originated their worship. The Ojibways have three such depositories near the waters of Lake Superior. Ten of the wisest and most venerable of the Nation dwell near these, and are appointed guardians over them.

Fifteen years intervene between each opening. At the end of this time, if any vacancies have been caused by death, others are chosen in the spring of the year, who, about the month of August, are called to witness the opening of the depositories. As they are being opened, all the information known respecting them is given to the new members; then the articles are placed before them. After this, the plates are closely examined, and if any have begun to decay they are taken out; an exact facsimile is made and placed in its stead.—The old one is divided equally among the wise men. It is very highly valued for having been deposited; as a sacred article, every fibre of it is considered sacred, and whoever uses it may be made wise. It is considered efficacious for any good purpose to which it may be put.

These records are written on slate rock, copper, lead, and on the bark of birch trees. The record is said to be a transcript of what the Great Spirit gave to the Indians after the flood, and by the hands of wise men has been transmitted to other parts of the country ever since. Here is a code of moral laws which the Indian calls "a path made by the Great Spirit." They believe that a long and prosperous life will be the result of obeying that law. The records contain certain emblems which transmit the ancient form of worship, and the rules for the dedication of four priests who alone are to expound them. In them is represented how man lived happy in his wigwam, before death was in the world, and the path he then followed marked out an example for those of the present time.

Chief Oreille ("Moose Tail"), in the spring of 1836, related to my uncle an account of one of these depositories.

He said he had been chosen as one of the guardians about five years previous, and that the guardians had for a long time selected as the places of deposit the most unsuspected spot, where they dug fifteen feet, and sunk large cedar trees around the excavation. In the centre was placed a large hollow cedar log, besmeared at one end with gum. The open end is uppermost, and in it are placed the records, after being enveloped in the down of geese or swan, which are changed at each examination. These feathers are afterwards used in war, being supposed to have a protective power. When camping, a few of these feathers are left near each place where the warriors dance.

These are some of the figures used by us in writing. With these, and from others of a similar class, the Ojibways can write their war and hunting songs.

An Indian well versed in these can send a communication to another Indian, and by them make himself as well understood as a pale-face can by letter.

There are over two hundred figures in general use for all the purposes of correspondence. Material things are represented by pictures of them.

The Characters Used in Picture Writing

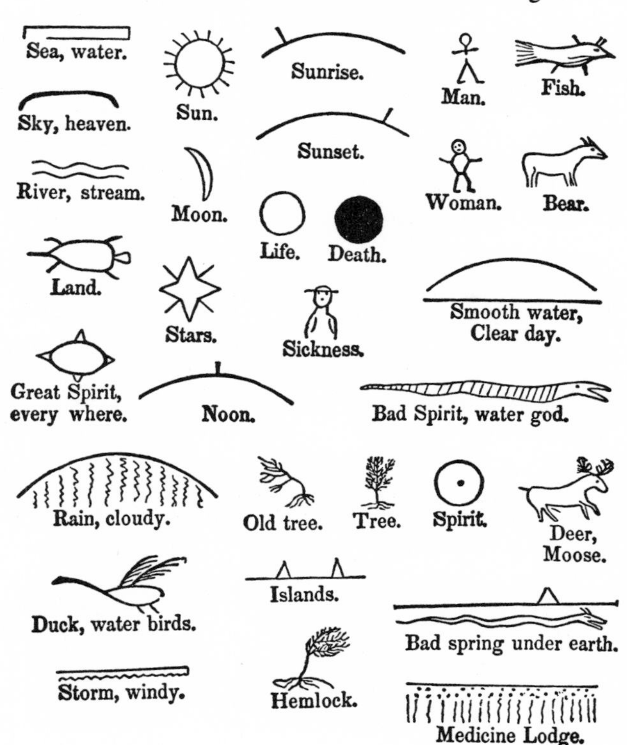

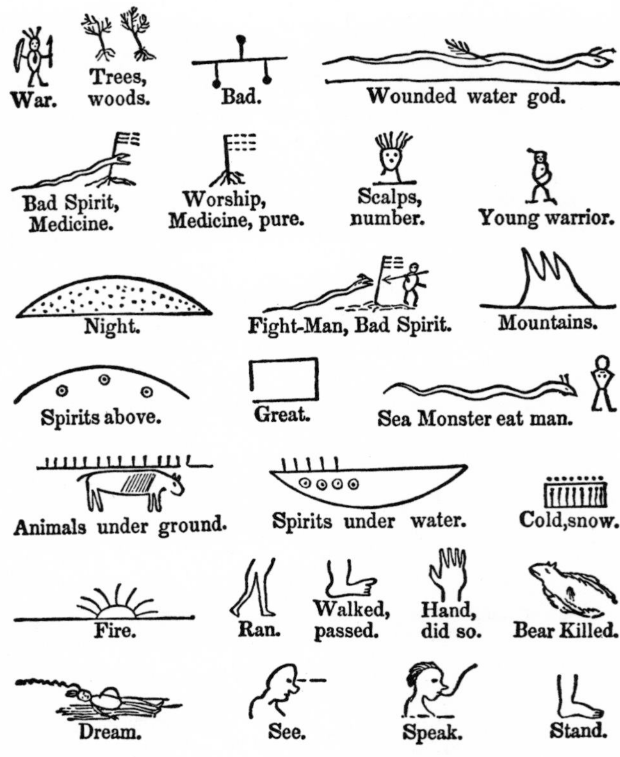

Invitations to Indians to come and worship in the spring are made in the following form:—

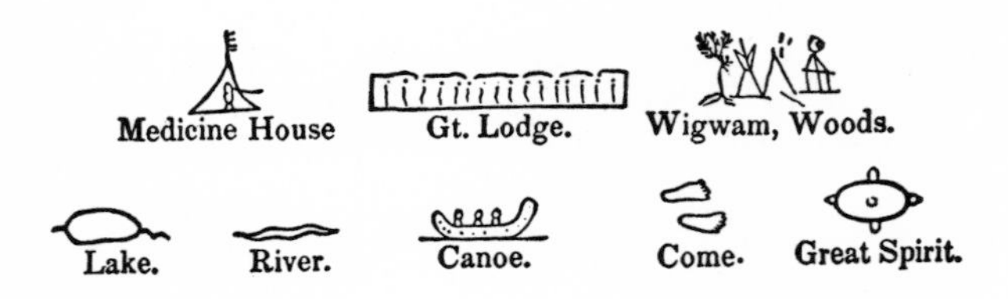

The whole story would thus read:—

"Hark to the words of the Sa-ge-mah."

"The Great Medicine Lodge will be ready in eight [?] days."

"Ye who live in the woods and near the Lakes and by streams of water, come with your canoes or by land to the worship of the Great Spirit."

In the above, the wigwam and the medicine pale [Great Lodge] represent the depositories of medicine, record and work. The Lodge is represented with men in it; the dots above indicate the number of days.

These picture representations were used by the Ojibways until the introduction of European manners among them. When this occurred, they neglected in a great degree their correspondence with other nations, except by special messengers, and became very cautious in giving information respecting their religious worship to the whites, because they, the whites, ridiculed it.

In times of danger or in the progress of a war, beads and shells were used for the purpose of conveying a message, and this custom is yet in vogue [1850].

These beads and shells were colored, and each had a meaning, according to its place on the string. *Black* indicated war or death—*White*, peace and prosperity—*Red*, the heart of the enemy would represent—*Partial white* or *red*, or both intermixed, the beginning of peace or the commencement of war.

Numerals are marked on the shell. The knot gives information of its starting point, or the name of the person sending it. In stringing the shell or beads, the end of the sentence is strung first, so that the first word of the message is in the person's hand. This manner of correspondence is the most common.

Three hundred years ago the Delawares sent communications in this way to the Shawnees in Sandusky, Lake Erie; and they to the Ojibways in Superior and Huron.

This mode was practised by Pontiac in his appeals to the Indians of Michigan, Huron, and the prairies of the West, during the wars. The Indians say that these beads cannot give false stories, for it is not possible for the man who takes it to alter or add to them, during his journey.

TELLING OF LEGENDS

CHIEF ELIAS JOHNSON—TUSCARORA

On long winter evenings the Indian hunters gathered around their fireside, to listen to the historical traditions, legends of war and hunting, and fairy tales which had been handed down through their fathers and fathers' fathers, with scarcely any variation for centuries, kindling the enthusiasm of the warrior and inspiring the little child some day to realize similar dreams, and hand his name down to posterity as the author of similar exploits.

They have superstitious fears of relating fables in summer; not until after snow comes will they relate of snakes, lest they should creep into their beds, or of evil genii, lest they in some way be revenged.

It is very difficult for a stranger to rightly understand the morals of their stories, though it is said by those who know them best, that to them the story was always an illustration of some moral or principle.

To strangers they offer all the rites of hospitality, but do not open their hearts. If you ask them they will tell you a story, but it will not be such a story as they tell when alone. They will fear your ridicule and suppress their humor and pathos; so thoroughly have they learned to distrust pale faces, that when they know that he who is present is a friend, they will still shrink from admitting him within the secret portals of their heart.

And when you have learned all that language can convey, there are still a thousand images, suggestions and associations recurring to the Indian, which can strike no chord in your heart. The myriad voices of nature are dumb to you, but to them they are full of life and power.

II: GAME TRAILS

The Indian was a master of woodcraft. He knew the calls of birds and animals and could imitate them perfectly. He understood wild creatures and their ways because he himself had the wariness and sensitivity of an animal.

When game was plentiful, a skilled hunter could supply enough food for a dozen families. An Ojibway named No-ka started at Crow Wing River near the upper Mississippi and killed in one day's hunt sixteen elk, four buffalo, five deer, three bears, one lynx, and a porcupine.

The Indian hunter did not kill for sport but to provide food and clothing for his family. "The Indian was frugal in the midst of plenty," wrote Chief Standing Bear. "When the buffalo roamed the plains in multitudes he slaughtered only what he could eat and these he used to the hair and bones."

II: GAME TRAILS

BOYHOOD TRAINING IN WOODCRAFT

OHIYESA—SIOUX

It seems to be a popular idea that all the characteristic skill of the Indian is instinctive and hereditary. This is a mistake. All the stoicism and patience of the Indian are acquired traits, and continual practice alone makes him master of the art of woodcraft.

My uncle, who educated me up to the age of fifteen years, was a strict disciplinarian and a good teacher. When I left the teepee in the morning, he would say: "Look closely to everything you see"; and at evening, on my return, he used often to catechize me for an hour or so.

"On which side of the trees is the lighter-colored bark? On which side do they have most regular branches?"

It was his custom to let me name all the new birds that I had seen during the day. I would name them according to the color or the shape of the bill or their song or the appearance and locality of the nest—in fact, anything about the bird that impressed me as characteristic. I made many ridiculous errors, I must admit. He then usually informed me of the correct name. Occasionally I made a hit and this he would warmly commend.

He went much deeper into this science when I was a little older, that is, about the age of eight or nine years. He would say, for instance:

"How do you know that there are fish in yonder lake?"

"Because they jump out of the water for flies at mid-day."

He would smile at my prompt but superficial reply.

"What do you think of the little pebbles grouped together under the shallow water? and what made the pretty curved marks in the sandy bottom and the little sand-banks? Where do you find the fish-eating birds? Have the inlet and the outlet of a lake anything to do with the question?"

He did not expect a correct reply at once to all the voluminous questions that he put to me on these occasions, but he meant to make me observant and a good student of nature.

He would say to me, "You ought to follow the example of the shunktokecha (wolf). Even when he is surprised and runs for his life, he will pause to take one more look at you before he enters his final retreat. So you must take a second look at everything you see.

"It is better to view animals unobserved. I have been a witness to their courtships and their quarrels and have learned many of their secrets in this way. I was once the unseen spectator of a thrilling battle between a pair of grizzly bears and three buffaloes—a rash act for the bears, for it was in the moon of strawberries, when the buffaloes sharpen and polish their horns for bloody contests among themselves.

"I advise you, my boy, never to approach a grizzly's den from the front, but to steal up behind and throw your blanket or a stone in front of the hole. He does not usually rush for it, but first puts his head out and listens and then comes out very indifferently and sits on his haunches on the mound in front of the hole before he makes any attack. While he is exposing himself in this fashion, aim at his heart. Always be as cool as the animal himself." Thus he armed me against the cunning of savage beasts by teaching me how to outwit them.

"In hunting," he would resume, "you will be guided by the habits of the animal you seek. Remember that a moose stays in swampy or low land or between high mountains near a spring or lake, for thirty to sixty days at a time. Most large game moves about continually, except the doe in the spring; it is then a very easy matter to find her with the fawn. Conceal yourself in a convenient place as soon as you observe any signs of the presence of either, and then call with your birchen doe-caller.

"Whichever one hears you first will soon appear in your neighborhood. But you must be very watchful, or you may be made a fawn of by a large wild-cat. They understand the characteristic call of the doe perfectly well.

"When you have any difficulty with a bear or a wild-cat—that is, if the creature shows signs of attacking you—you must make him fully understand that you have seen him and are aware of his intentions. If you are not well equipped for a pitched battle, the only way to make him retreat is to take a long sharp-pointed pole for a spear and rush toward him. No wild beast will face this unless he is cornered and already wounded. These fierce beasts are generally afraid of the common weapon of the larger animals—the horns, and if these are very long and sharp, they dare not risk an open fight.

"There is one exception to this rule—the grey wolf will attack fiercely when very hungry. But their courage depends upon their numbers; in this they are like white men. One wolf or two will never attack a man. They will stampede a herd of buffaloes in order to get at the calves; they will rush upon a herd of antelopes, for these are helpless; but they are always careful about attacking man."

Of this nature were the instructions of my uncle, who was widely known at that time as among the greatest hunters of his tribe.

THE BOY HUNTER

OHIYESA—SIOUX

It will be no exaggeration to say that the life of the Indian hunter was a life of fascination. From the moment that he lost sight of his rude home in the midst of the forest, his untutored mind lost itself in the myriad beauties and forces of nature. Yet he never forgot his personal danger from some lurking foe or savage beast, however absorbing was his passion for the chase. His moccasined foot fell like the velvet paw of a cat—noiselessly; his glittering black eyes scanned every object that appeared within their view. Not a bird, not even a chipmunk, escaped their piercing glance.

There was almost as much difference between the Indian boys who were brought up on the open prairies and those of the woods, as between city and country boys. The hunting of the prairie boys was limited and their knowledge of natural history imperfect. They were, as a rule, good riders, but in all-round physical development much inferior to the red men of the forest.

Our hunting varied with the season of the year, and the nature of the country which was for the time our home. Our chief weapon was the bow and arrows, and perhaps, if we were lucky, a knife was possessed by some one in the crowd. In the olden times, knives and hatchets were made from bone and sharp stones.

We hunted in company a great deal, though it was a common thing for a boy to set out for the woods quite alone, and he usually enjoyed himself fully as much. Our game consisted mainly of small birds, rabbits, squirrels, and grouse. Fishing, too, occupied much of our time. We hardly ever passed a creek or a pond without searching for some signs of fish. When fish were present, we always managed to get some. Fish-lines were made of wild hemp, sinew or horse-hair. We either caught fish with lines, snared or speared them, or shot them with bow and arrows. In the fall we charmed them up to the surface by gently tickling them with a stick and quickly threw them out. We have sometimes dammed the brooks and driven the larger fish into a willow basket made for that purpose.

It was part of our hunting to find new and strange things in the woods. We examined the slightest sign of life; and if a bird had scratched the leaves off the ground, or a bear dragged up a root for his morning meal, we stopped to speculate on the time it was done. If we saw a large old tree with some scratches on its bark, we concluded that a bear or some raccoons must be living there. In that case we did not go any nearer than was necessary, but later reported the incident at home. An old deer-track would at once bring a warm discussion as to whether it was the track of a buck or a doe. Generally, at noon, we met and compared our game, noting at the same time the peculiar characteristics of everything we had killed. It was not merely a hunt, for we combined with it the study of animal life. We also kept strict account of our game, and thus learned who were the best shots among the boys.

I am sorry to say that we were merciless toward the birds. We often took their eggs and their young ones. My brother Chatanna and I once had a disagreeable adventure while bird-hunting. We were accustomed to catch in our hands young ducks and geese during the summer, and while doing this we happened to find a crane's nest. Of course, we were delighted with our good luck. But, as it was already midsummer, the young cranes—two in number—were rather large and they were a little way from the nest; we also observed that the two old cranes were in a swampy place near by; but, as it was moulting-time, we did not suppose that they would venture on dry land. So we proceeded to chase the young birds; but they were fleet runners and it took us some time to come up with them.

Meanwhile, the parent birds had heard the cries of their little ones and come to their rescue. They were chasing us, while we followed the birds. It was really a perilous encounter! Our strong bows finally gained the victory in a hand-to-hand struggle with the angry cranes; but after that we hardly ever hunted a crane's nest. Almost all birds make some resistance when their eggs or young are taken, but they will seldom attack man fearlessly.

We used to climb large trees for birds of all kinds; but we never undertook to get young owls unless they were on the ground. The hooting owl especially is a dangerous bird to attack under these circumstances.

I was once trying to catch a yellow-winged woodpecker in its nest when my arm became twisted and lodged in the deep hole so that I could not get it out without the aid of a knife; but we were a long way from home and my only companion was a deaf mute cousin of mine. I was about fifty feet up in the tree, in a very uncomfortable position, but I had to wait there for more than an hour before he brought me the knife with which I finally released myself.

Our devices for trapping small animals were rude, but they were often successful. For instance, we used to gather up a peck or so of large, sharp-pointed burrs and scatter them in the rabbit's furrow-like path. In the morning, we would find the little fellow sitting quietly in his tracks, unable to move, for the burrs stuck to his feet.

Another way of snaring rabbits and grouse was the following: We made nooses of twisted horse-hair, which we tied very firmly to the top of a limber young tree, then bent the latter down to the track and fastened the whole with a slip-knot, after adjusting the noose. When the rabbit runs his head through the noose, he pulls the slip-knot and is quickly carried up by the spring of the young tree. This is a good plan, for the rabbit is out of harm's way as he swings high in the air.

Perhaps the most enjoyable of all was the chipmunk hunt. We killed these animals at any time of year, but the special time to hunt them was in March. After the first thaw, the chipmunks burrow a hole through the snow crust and make their first appearance for the season. Sometimes as many as fifty will come together and hold a social reunion. These gatherings occur early in the morning, from daybreak to about nine o'clock.

We boys learned this, among other secrets of nature, and got our blunt-headed arrows together in good season for the chipmunk expedition.

We generally went in groups of six to a dozen or fifteen, to see which would get the most. On the evening before, we selected several boys who could imitate the chipmunk's call with wild oat-straws and each of these provided himself with a supply of straws.

The crust will hold the boys nicely at this time of the year. Bright and early, they all come together at the appointed place, from which each group starts out in a different direction, agreeing to meet somewhere at a given position of the sun.

My first experience of this kind is still well remembered. It was a fine crisp March morning, and the sun had not yet shown himself among the distant tree-tops as we hurried along through the ghostly wood. Presently we arrived at a place where there were many signs of the animals. Then each of us selected a tree and took up his position behind it. The chipmunk caller sat upon a log as motionless as he could, and began to call.

Soon we heard the patter of little feet on the hard snow; then we saw the chipmunks approaching from all directions. Some stopped and ran experimentally up a tree or a log, as if uncertain of the exact direction of the call; others chased one another about.

In a few minutes, the chipmunk-caller was besieged with them. Some ran all over his person, others under him and still others ran up the tree against which he was sitting. Each boy remained immovable until their leader gave the signal; then a great shout arose, and the chipmunks in their flight all ran up the different trees.

Now the shooting-match began. The little creatures seemed to realize their hopeless position; they would try again and again to come down the trees and flee away from the deadly aim of the youthful hunters. But they were shot down very fast; and whenever several of them rushed toward the ground, the little red-skin hugged the tree and yelled frantically to scare them up again.

Each boy shoots always against the trunk of the tree, so that the arrow may bound back to him every time; otherwise, when he had shot away all of them, he would be helpless, and another, who had cleared his own tree, would come and take away his game, so there was warm competition. Sometimes a desperate chipmunk would jump from the top of the tree in order to escape, which was considered a joke on the boy who lost it and a triumph for the brave little animal. At last all were killed or gone, and then we went on to another place, keeping up the sport until the sun came out and the chipmunks refused to answer the call.

When we went out on the prairies we had a different and less lively kind of sport. We used to snare with horse-hair and bow-strings all the small ground animals, including the prairie-dog. We both snared and shot them. Once a little boy set a snare for one, and lay flat on the ground a little way from the hole, holding the end of the string. Presently he felt something move and pulled in a huge rattlesnake; and to this day, his name is "Caught-the-Rattlesnake." Very often a boy got a new name in some such manner. At another time, we were playing in the woods and found a fawn's track. We followed and caught it while asleep; but in the struggle to get away, it kicked one boy, who is still called "Kicked-by-the-Fawn."

It became a necessary part of our education to learn to prepare a meal while out hunting. It is a fact that most Indians will eat the liver and some other portions of large animals raw, but they do not eat fish or birds uncooked. Neither will they eat a frog, or an eel. On our boyish hunts, we often went on until we found ourselves a long way from our camp, when we would kindle a fire and roast a part of our game.

Generally we broiled our meat over the coals on a stick. We roasted some of it over the open fire. But the best way to cook fish and birds is in the ashes, under a big fire. We take the fish fresh from the creek or lake, have a good fire on the sand, dig in the sandy ashes and bury it deep. The same thing is done in the case of a bird, only we wet the feathers first. When it is done, the scales or feathers and skin are stripped off whole, and the delicious meat retains all its juices and flavor. We pulled it off as we ate, leaving the bones undisturbed.

Our people had also a method of boiling without pots or kettles. A large piece of tripe was thoroughly washed and the ends tied, then suspended between four stakes driven into the ground and filled with cold water. The meat was then placed in this novel receptacle and boiled by means of the addition of red-hot stones.

HUNTING LAWS

CHIEF KAH-GE-GA-GAH-BOWH—OJIBWAY

The hunting grounds of the Indians were secured by right, a law and custom among themselves. No one was allowed to hunt on another's land, without invitation or permission. If any person was found trespassing on the ground of another, all his things were taken from him, except a handful of shot, powder sufficient to serve him in going *straight* home, a gun, a tomahawk, and a knife; all the fur, and other things, were taken from him. If he were found a second time trespassing, all his things were taken away from him, except food sufficient to subsist on while going home. And should he still come a third time to trespass on the same, or another man's hunting grounds, his nation, or tribe, are then informed of it, who take up his case. If still he disobey, he is banished from his tribe.

My father and another Indian, by the name of Big John, and myself, went out hunting. While we were out on the hunting grounds, we found out that some Indians had gone before us on the route up the river, and every day we gained upon them: their tracks were fresh. The river and the lakes were frozen, and we had to walk on the ice. For some days together we did not fire a gun, for fear they would hear it and go from us, where we could not find them. At length we found them by the banks of the river, they were Nah-doo-ways or Mohawks, from Bay Quinty; they were seven of them, tall fellows. We shook hands with them: they received us kindly. My father had determined to take all they had, if we should overtake them. After they gave us a good dinner of boiled beaver, my father stepped across the fire and ripped open two packs of beaver furs, that were just by him. He said to them "We have only one custom among us, and that is well known to all; this river, and all that is in it are mine: I have come up the river behind you, and you appear to have killed all before you. This is mine, and this is mine," he said, as he touched with the handle of his tomahawk each of the packs of beaver, otter, and muskrat skins. I expected every moment to see my father knocked down with a tomahawk, but none dared touch him; he counted the skins and then threw them across the fire-place to us. After this was done, the same thing took place with the guns; only one was left them to use on their way home. They left, and we took possession of the temporary wigwam they had built. We never saw them afterwards on our hunting grounds.

DEER HUNTING RITUAL

FLAMING ARROW—PUEBLO

Let me take you to an Indian deer hunt.

First we get our men together. Four is enough in a bunch. We start out from home with a song. The song is translated:

> "From Acoma I am going to put the sewed-up moccasins on my feet. I, the man, do put on the moccasin heel-piece.
> Painting my body with yellow, red, blue and white clay color,
> Then clothing myself with an apron round my waist with designs on,
> Then round my knee the colored yarn,
> Then the colored yarn around my wrist,
> Then around my arm green bands with fir tree branches stuck in them.
> Next I paint my face red and black.
> I tie an eagle feather on top of my hair.
> I pick up my arrows. The bow made of a rainbow, and the arrows representing the lightning flash.
> I travel sometimes with song to attract deer with my singing."

After a whole day's travel we camp. For a whole day's trip I travel south from Acoma, and reach a place for my prayer-sticks [ceremonial twigs, painted and decorated with feathers, which are believed to possess magical powers]. I lay them down carefully, and bury them, as if there were strange gods near to hear my prayers; and each one of the party does the same. After we bury our prayer-sticks, we all gather round the campfire.

We have started out with a supply of food and ready baked bread to last us for two weeks, the same amount of blue cornmeal to make our gravy, and such things as lard, onions, potatoes, coffee and sugar. We do not need any meat, as we will be killing rabbits on our way.

When we reach our camp, the first evening after dark, each one goes off in some direction by himself, to pray to strange gods. We pray towards any direction in which we think there may be some god listening to hear our prayers. We pray to the mountain lion, eagles, hawks, wolves, and other wild beasts. Then we bury our prayer-sticks and pick up a piece of log and sprinkle it with cornmeal, and say to it: "You be the deer which I expect to bring into camp," and then we carry this piece of wood in and place it on the campfire, and blow our breath on a pinch of cornmeal in our hands and throw it on the flames. Doing so we receive power, and hunt well.

Then each is seated on his rolled-up blanket around the campfire. The next thing we do is to choose our officers. First we choose the field chief, *Tsa-ta-ow-ho-tcha*. He has to see that all the hunters get their deer. If one of the hunters is unlucky enough not to get a deer, he has to divide up with him. Next we elect our governor, *Dta-po-po*. He is to see that the camp is in order, and keep peace in the camp. The youngest one is always elected as the cook, and also has to look after the horses and burros, and get wood for the fire. If he has any time, after the dishes are washed, and there is plenty of wood and water, and the stock has been watered, he can hunt right around the camp.

After these officers are elected, the field chief gives orders to put down as an altar, between us and the fire, the flint and other stone animals which every hunter carries with him to the hunt, and which are handed down in each family. After all of these little animals are placed on the level ground, they sprinkle white cornmeal over them, and around them, forming a circle of cornmeal. Then a song is sung which means: "We welcome this altar into our camp. Come and take a place with us." Then they sing to the mountain lion to take its place, then the wolf, then the man himself, then the owls, then the hawks. Song after song continues through the night until dawn. In the morning, each one picks up his little hunting animal, and ties it in the handkerchief around his neck, and takes his cornmeal from the little bag at his side. Praying to the strange gods, and breathing his breath on the cornmeal, he sprinkles it out to the east to the sun.

The hunters are ordered to pack up for another day's trip. All are feeling happy, and they are not supposed to make one complaint about anything, which is strict orders. They sing softly all the way they travel.

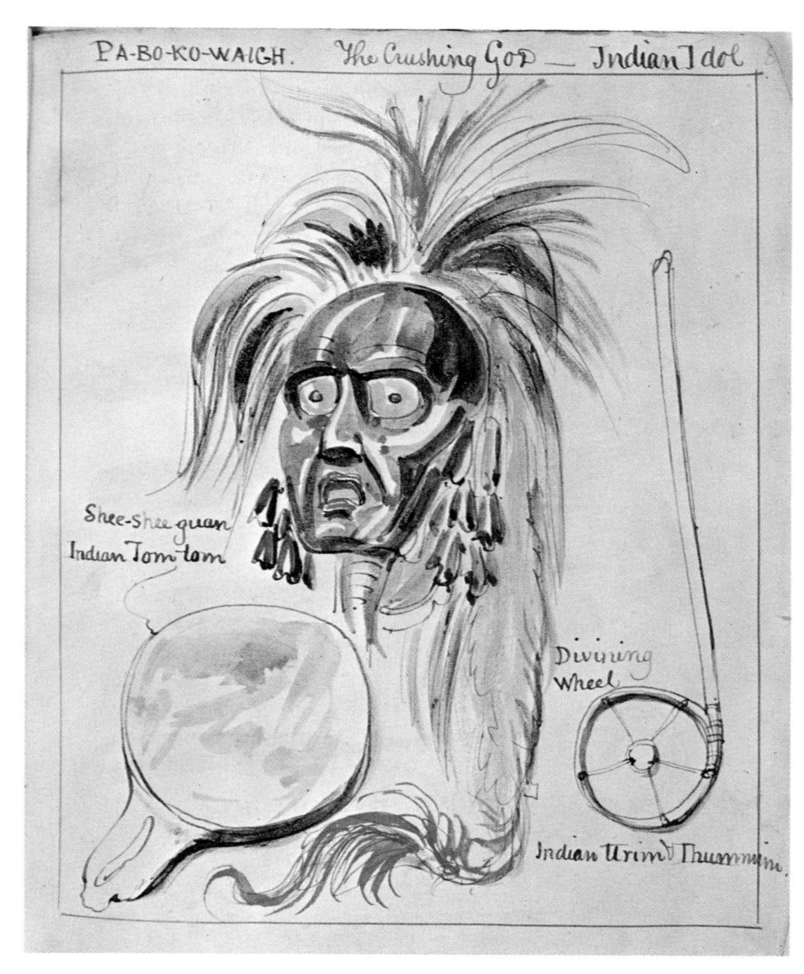

PA-BO-KO-WAIGH, the Crushing God
Indian Idol
George Catlin
ca. 1830–40

From Catlin Sketchbook
Courtesy of Gilcrease Institute

When an Indian has hit a deer, he runs to the fallen animal. First he takes a small branch of a tree and brushes him off, as he has a religious belief that the deer is made of sheets of clouds, and he has to brush off the clouds to get at him. Then he reaches down in his pocket for some yellow pollen he has collected from flowers, takes it between his thumb and forefinger, drops a little on the deer's mouth, then carries it to his own breath, and makes a sign with the pollen towards the hunter's camp, which is supposed to lead the spirit of the deer to the camp.

Then he pulls the deer around by the forelegs, until he lies with his head towards the camp. The next thing is to take the little flint animals in the shapes of lions, wolves and bears, as many as he carries, and place them on the deer to feed and get back the power they gave him. They always come first. While these animals are on the deer, the hunter rolls a cigarette of cornhusks, and while he smokes he talks to the dead creature just as if he were telling a human where to go. When he finishes he gathers his flint animals, carefully places them in his bag, and talks to them while he puts them in the bag, telling them that he hopes for the good luck of another deer. Then he ties the bag with these animals round his neck under his shirt.

He pulls out of his pocket a flint arrowhead, and, starting from the deer's neck pretends to cut it. In older days, they really cut with the spear head, instead of knives. Then he cuts off juniper pine twigs and lays them as thick as he can alongside of the deer, ready to be placed upon it after it is skinned, to keep the blood off the hide and the dirt off the meat.

After skinning the deer and placing the meat on these juniper twigs, the hunter starts to cut the animal into parts like a beef. He is always sure that he takes the entrails out first. He digs in the ground a shallow hole, and washes his hands. If there is no water nearby, he wipes his hands on a cloth. He reaches down with his hands into the blood and dips it up four times, and places it in the shallow hole on the earth. This is to feed the mother earth. Then he takes out the spleen, and places it nearby on a twig of a tree to feed the crow. Then he cuts him up.

The hind legs are taken off first, then the front quarters. Then he strips the meat off the bone from the hoofs to the first joint, and ties these muscles together, front and hind legs, so as to hang the deer over the saddle without any rope. Next the ribs are taken off in such a way as to hang over the saddle without being separated. This leaves the breast connected with the meat of the stomach, and in this way all the parts will balance on a burro's back, and the backbone and fur and head are still together, and are easily balanced on the saddle.

After each hunter gets one deer, they agree on a day to start home. Coming home they will all join in on their new songs, singing as loudly as they can, and if they camp again before reaching home, the burdens of the burros and horses are placed in line, so as to be easy to repack in line in the morning.

When they are within a mile from home, each of the hunters loads his gun with one shot, and they are fired off, one by one, so that each family by counting the shots, can tell which group of hunters is returning. As they come home each hunter makes a round circle from fir trees, to fit his head, puts evergreens on his horse's bridle, and around the deer heads. Even the burros' heads are decorated with fir twigs.

When they arrive home there will be relatives there to take charge of the meat, and see to the unsaddling and feeding of the animals. All the hunter does is to tell his wonderful story.

WAYS OF HUNTING THE DEER

CHIEF KAH-GE-GA-GAH-BOWH—OJIBWAY

The deer was killed in four different ways before the introduction of fire-arms. The first was by a snare formed of a rope of wild hemp, and so placed that when the deer's neck was caught, the more stir he made the more he couldn't stir. At every movement the cord would wind about the neck tighter and tighter, until he was choked. When they wish to get through soon, they placed these snares all around for half a day, then drive the deer all over the snares until some are caught.

The second was by driving sharp spikes of wood into the ground on the deer path, just the other side of a log over which they would be expected to jump. In jumping the logs, they must fall upon these sharp spikes, which would pierce them through, and thus kill them.

The third way was to drive the deer with dogs into the water, when, being out of their element, they could be captured. In winter, instead of driving them into the water, a short chase in the deep snow would soon tire them, and they were soon at the disposal of the hunter.

The fourth and last manner of killing them was by means of bow and arrow. Bows were made of a power to enable them to shoot through the side of a deer without any difficulty. The Indian watched at the "Salt Licks," or at the borders of lakes or rivers, to which the deer often go to feed on the grass. An Indian can shoot a deer in the woods at a distance of fifty paces.

The bow was generally made of iron-wood or red cedar; sometimes of hickory, well seasoned. The arrows were made like spikes at the end. Before they had iron, they used bone and shell for the ends: the shells were carved in such a manner as to admit of being pointed at the end of the arrow.

In the spring but few deer were killed, because they were not in good order, the venison being poor, and the skin so thin, that it was no object to kill them. To hunt deer in the summer was my great delight, which I did in the following manner:—During the day I looked for their tracks, as they came on the shore of the lake or river during the night; they came there to feed. If they came on the bank of the river, I lighted pitch pine, and the current of the river took the canoe along the shore. My lantern was so constructed that the light could not fall on one spot, but sweep along the shore. The deer could see the light, but were not alarmed by it, and continued feeding on the weeds. In this way, I have approached so close that I could have reached them with my paddle. In this manner our forefathers shot them, not with a gun, as I did, but with the bow and arrow.

Another mode of hunting on the lakes, preferred by some, is shooting without a light. Many were so expert, and possessed such an accuracy in hearing, that they could shoot successfully in the dark, with no other guide than the noise of the deer in the water; the position of the deer being well known, in this way, the darkest night. I will here relate an occurrence which took place in 1834. My father and I were hunting on the river Trent, in the night; after we had shot two deer, and while returning homewards, we heard the noise of a deer's footsteps. The night was dark as pitch. We approached the deer. I asked my father at what part of the animal I should aim. He replied, "At the head or neck." I poised my gun and fired; hearing no noise, I concluded that my game was sure. I lighted some pitch pine and walked towards the spot from which the noise had come. The deer lay dead and bleeding. On examination I found that I had shot it just below the ear.

A BUFFALO HUNT

CHIEF STANDING BEAR—SIOUX

A scout had been sent out, and one morning, very early, he reported that there were some buffalo near. Everybody, including myself, began to get ready. While one of my stepmothers was helping me, she said, "Son, when you kill a buffalo, save me the kidney and the skin." I didn't know whether she was trying to poke fun at me or to give me encouragement. But it made me feel proud to have her talk like that to me.

But my father always talked to me as if I were a man. Of course I now felt that I was big enough to do a man's work. The night before the hunt, my father instructed me as follows:

"My son, the land on which these buffalo have been found is reported not to be rough, and you will not have to chase the buffalo into dangerous places, as the land is very level. Whatever you do, watch the buffalo closely. If the one you are after is running straight ahead and not turning, then you can get in very close, and you will stand a good chance to shoot it in the heart. But if you observe the buffalo to be looking at you from the corner of its eye, then look out! They are very quick and powerful. They can get their horns under your horse and toss him high in the air, and you might get killed.

"If you hit in the right spot, you may kill the buffalo with only one arrow, but if not, you will have to use more. If your pony is not fast enough to catch up with the buffalo, the best thing you can do is to shoot an arrow right behind the small ribs. Perhaps it will reach the heart. If the buffalo runs down a hill or into a bank, then you have another chance. Shoot at the joint of the hips, then your buffalo will sit down and you can take your time to kill it.

"Keep your eyes open! In the beginning there will be lots of dust, but after you pass through that, it will be clear, and you will be able to see where you are going."

This was the first time I was to go on a hunt after such large animals. I had killed several small animals, but a buffalo is far from being a small creature, and you can imagine that I was greatly excited.

Early the next morning every one was ready for the start. I carried my bow in my hand, as there was not room for it in my quiver where I kept my arrows. I rode a little black mare, a very fine runner that could cover the ground like a deer.

Two men on beautiful horses rode in front of us. This was for the purpose of keeping order in the party. There was no chance of one man getting ahead of the others and scaring the game. We all had to keep together and stay behind these men.

They rode to the top of a hill where they could get a good look at the herd and figure if there was any better place from which to approach it. We always got as close to the buffalo as possible, because it makes the meat tough to run an animal any farther than necessary.

After looking at the herd from various positions, they chose what was considered the most advantageous spot. Here they cautioned the hunters to change to their running-horses and be all ready. I did not have to make any change, as the little black mare was all the animal I had. I saw some of the men tying their two braids of hair back, and others, who wore shirts, began rolling up their sleeves. They wanted their arms free once they began shooting. They fixed their quivers on the side instead of carrying them on the back. Nobody wore any feathers or carried any spears or lances.

The extra horses were hobbled and left in the charge of an old man. When the two riders gave the command, everybody started right up. Of course I was right at the front with them. I wanted to do something brave. I depended a great deal on my pony, as I knew she was sure-footed and could run as I wanted her to.

At the top of the hill, all the hunters turned their horses loose, and the animals started in running like the wind! I whipped up my little black mare and nearly got ahead of the others. Soon I was mixed up in the dust and could see nothing ahead of me. All I could hear was the roar and rattle of the hoofs of the buffalo as they thundered along. My pony shied this way and that, and I had to hold on for dear life.

For a time I did not even try to pull an arrow from my quiver, as

I had all I could do to take care of myself. I knew if my pony went down and one of those big animals stepped on me, it would be my last day on earth. I then realized how helpless I was there in all that dust and confusion, with those ponderous buffalo all around me. The sound of their hoofs was frightening. My pony ran like the wind, while I just clung to her mane; but presently we came out of the dust.

Then I observed what my father had told me previously. I was quite a bit ahead of the buffalo now, and when they caught sight of me, they started running in two different directions. When I looked at those big animals and thought of trying to kill one of them, I realized how small I was. I was really afraid of them. Then I thought about what my stepmother had said to me about bringing her a kidney and a skin, and the feeling that I was a man, after all, came back to me; so I turned my pony toward the bunch which was running north. There was no dust now, and I knew where I was going.

I was all alone, and I was determined to chase them, whether I killed one or not. By this time I could hear shots fired by some of the hunters who carried guns, and I knew they were killing some. So I rode on after this small bunch, and when I dashed behind them, I pulled out one of my arrows and shot into the middle of them. I did not even know where my arrow went, and was just thinking of quitting when I observed a young heifer running slower than the others.

This encouraged me, so I whipped up my pony again and took after her. As I came in close, she stopped and turned. Then she started running in another direction, but I saw she was losing fast. She was not as big as the others, so I was not afraid. I made up my mind I was going to kill that buffalo if it took all the arrows in my quiver.

I rode right up alongside the buffalo, just as my father had instructed me. Drawing an arrow from my quiver, and holding to my pony with all the strength of my legs, I fitted the arrow and let drive with all my strength. I had expected to kill the buffalo right quick, but the arrow went into the neck—and I thought I had taken such good aim! But the buffalo only shook her head and kept on running. I again caught up with her, and let another arrow loose, which struck near the heart. Although it was not fired with sufficient strength to kill at once, I saw that she was fast weakening and running much slower. Then I pulled my third arrow and fired again. This went into the heart. I began to think that buffalo had all the nine lives of a cat, and was going to prove about as hard as a cat to kill, when I saw blood running from her nose. Then I knew she would have to drop pretty soon. I shot my fourth arrow into her, and she staggered and dropped over on her side, and was soon dead. So I had killed my first buffalo.

When I examined the fallen animal and noted that I had shot five arrows into her, I felt that this was too many arrows for just one buffalo. Then I recalled that my father had once killed two buffalo with only a single arrow. He knew he had hit the first one in the right spot, as the arrow penetrated very deeply and he simply rode up alongside, drew the arrow through, pulled it out again and used it to kill the second one.

As I stood there thinking of this, it made me feel ashamed of my marksmanship. I began to think of pulling all the arrows out but one. In fact, I had started to do this, when a remark that my father had once made to me came into my head. It was, "Son, always remember that a man who tells lies is never liked by anybody." So, instead of trying to cheat, I told the truth; and it made me feel happier.

I took all the arrows out and started in to skin the buffalo. I was doing splendidly until I tried to turn the animal over. Then I discovered that it was too heavy a task for me. As I had but one side skinned I began to think of removing the kidney and cutting out a nice piece of meat for my stepmother. Just then I heard someone call me. I got on my pony and rode to the top of the hill. There I saw my father, who had been looking for me. He called to me, but I just rode back to my buffalo. He knew something had happened, so came over, and then I pointed to the dead buffalo, lying there half-skinned.

He was so pleased that I had tried to do my best. Then I told him about the number of arrows I had had to use, and where each one had struck. I even told him how I had shot my first arrow into the whole bunch, not knowing where it had landed. He laughed, but he was proud of me. I guess it was because I had told the truth, and not tried to cheat or lie, even though I was just a youngster.

Then Father started in on my buffalo. He soon had it all skinned and butchered. He said he had been all ready to go home when he discovered I was missing. He had thought I was with my grandfather, while Grandfather thought I was with him. All that time I was having a hard job all by myself. When we reached home it made me very proud to be able to give my stepmother the skin and kidney. And she was pleased that I had done so well.

My father called the old man of the camp, who always acted as herald, to announced that "Ota Kte" ["Plenty Kill," the boyhood name of Chief Standing Bear] had shot his first buffalo, and that "Standing Bear," his father, was giving away a horse.

KILLING A BEAR

CHIEF KAH-GE-GA-GAH-BOWH—OJIBWAY

Of all animals the bear is the most dangerous to hunt. I had heard so many stories about its cunning that I dreaded to meet one. One day a party of us were going out to hunt the bear. After we had made a temporary place to stay for several days, we marched in file. After a while we halted, each took a different direction. My father said, "My son, you had better loiter behind the rest. Do not go far, for you may lose yourself." We parted—I took my course, and the rest theirs. I trembled for fear I should see what I was hunting for! I went only where I least expected to see a bear, and every noise I heard in the woods, I thought must be one. As I stood on an old mossy log, there was such a crack on the side of the hill that my heart leaped within me. As I turned and looked, there was a large bear running towards me! I hid myself behind a tree; but on he came; I watched him; he came like a hogshead rolling down hill; there were no signs of stopping; when a few feet from me, I jumped aside, and cried *Yah!* (an exclamation of fear). I fired my gun without taking sight; in turning suddenly to avoid me, he threw up the earth and leaves; for an instant I was led to believe that the bear was upon me. I dropped my gun and fell backwards, while the bear lay sprawling just by me. Having recovered, I took up my gun and went a few feet from where I fell, and loaded my gun in a hurry. I then sought for a long pole, and with it, I poked it on its side, to see if it was really dead. It did not move, it was dead; but even then I had not courage to go and touch it with my hands. When all was over, and I had told my father I had killed a bear, I felt as though my little leggings could hardly contain me. In examining it, I found the ball had gone through its heart.

III: WILDERNESS SPORTS

The Indians excelled in competitive sports which demanded alertness and athletic skill. When not hunting or on the warpath, they gave much time to wrestling, target practice with arrows and knives, shinny, and intertribal ball play and pony racing. Once a group of army officers at Fort Chadbourne in Texas pitted their three finest race horses against a shaggy Comanche pony. The little pony won the first two races only by a neck, and the army officers, not realizing that the Comanches were leading them on, wagered large sums on the third race. Their fastest horse, a thoroughbred Kentucky mare, was running. At the starting signal, the shaggy pony got away like the wind and left the mare far behind. The Comanche rider galloped the last fifty yards of the course facing his pony's tail and beckoning to the army officer to hurry.

Although the Indians had no games of mental agility, they played many kinds of guessing games on which both players and spectators often placed heavy bets. Sometimes in the fever of gambling a plains warrior would stake his tepee or even his wife on a single toss of the dice. The loser paid his debts without grumbling, for the Indians put a high value on good sportsmanship.

III: WILDERNESS SPORTS

GAMES OF SIOUX CHILDREN

OHIYESA—SIOUX

The Indian boy was a prince of the wilderness. He had but very little work to do during the period of his boyhood. His principal occupation was the practice of a few simple arts in warfare and the chase. Aside from this, he was master of his time.

Whatever was required of us boys was quickly performed: then the field was clear for our games and plays. There was always keen competition among us. We felt very much as our fathers did in hunting and war—each one strove to excel all the others.

It is true that our savage life was a precarious one, and full of dreadful catastrophes; however, this never prevented us from enjoying our sports to the fullest extent. As we left our teepees in the morning, we were never sure that our scalps would not dangle from a pole in the afternoon! It was an uncertain life, to be sure. Yet we observed that the fawns skipped and played happily while the gray wolves might be peeping forth from behind the hills, ready to tear them limb from limb.

Our sports were molded by the life and customs of our people; indeed, we practiced only what we expected to do when grown. Our games were feats with the bow and arrow, foot and pony races, wrestling, swimming and imitation of the customs and habits of our fathers. We had sham fights with mud balls and willow wands; we played lacrosse, made war upon bees, and coasted upon the ribs of animals and buffalo robes.

No sooner did the boys get together than, as a usual thing, they divided into squads and chose sides; then a leading arrow was shot at random into the air. Before it fell to the ground a volley from the bows of the participants followed. Each player was quick to note the direction and speed of the leading arrow and he tried to send his own at the same speed and at an equal height, so that when it fell it would be closer to the first than any of the others.

It was considered out of place to shoot by first sighting the object aimed at. This was usually impracticable in actual life, because the object was almost always in motion, while the hunter himself was often upon the back of a pony at full gallop. Therefore, it was the off-hand shot that the Indian boy sought to master.

The races were an every-day occurrence. At noon the boys were usually gathered by some pleasant sheet of water and as soon as the ponies were watered, they were allowed to graze for an hour or two while the boys stripped for their noonday sports. A boy might say to some other whom he considered his equal:

"I can't run; but I will challenge you to fifty paces."

A former hero, when beaten, would often explain his defeat by saying: "I drank too much water."

Last of all came the swimming. A little urchin would hang to his pony's long tail, while the latter, with only his head above water, glided sportively along. Finally the animals were driven into a fine field of grass and we turned our attention to other games.

Lacrosse was an older game and was confined entirely to the Sisseton and Santee Sioux. Shinny, such as is enjoyed by white boys on the ice, is still played on the open prairie by the western Sioux. The "moccasin game" [a guessing game, similar to our pea-and-shell game], although sometimes played by the boys, was intended mainly for adults.

The "mud-and-willow" fight was rather a severe and dangerous sport. A lump of soft clay was stuck on the end of a limber and springy willow wand and thrown as boys throw apples from sticks, with considerable force. When there were fifty or a hundred players on each side, the battle became warm; but anything to arouse the bravery of Indian boys seemed to them a good and wholesome diversion.

Wrestling was largely indulged in by us all. It may seem odd, but wrestling was done by a great many boys at once—from ten to any number on a side. It was really a battle, in which each one chose his opponent. The rule was that if a boy sat down, he was let alone, but as long as he remained standing within the field, he was open to attack.

No one struck with the hand, but all manner of tripping with legs and feet and butting with the knees was allowed. Altogether it was an exhausting pastime—fully equal to the American game of football and only the young athlete could really enjoy it.

One of our most curious sports was a war upon the nests of wild bees. We imagined ourselves about to make an attack upon the Ojibways or some tribal foe. We all painted and stole cautiously upon the nest; then, with a rush and war-whoop, sprang upon the object of our attack and endeavored to destroy it. But it seemed that the bees were always on the alert and never entirely surprised, for they always raised quite as many scalps as did their bold assailants! After the onslaught upon the nest was ended, we usually followed it by a pretended scalp dance.

On the occasion of my first experience in this mode of warfare, there were two other little boys who were also novices. One of them particularly was too young to indulge in an exploit of that kind. As it was the custom of our people, when they killed or wounded an enemy on the battle field, to announce the act in a loud voice, we did the same. My friend, Little Wound (as I will call him, for I do not remember his name), being quite small, was unable to reach the nest until it had been well trampled upon and broken and the insects had made a counter charge with such vigor as to repulse and scatter our numbers in every direction. However, he evidently did not want to retreat without any honors; so he bravely jumped upon the nest and yelled:

"I, the brave Little Wound, to-day kill the only fierce enemy!"

Scarcely were the last words uttered when he screamed as if stabbed to the heart. One of his older companions shouted:

"Dive into the water! Run! Dive into the water!" for there was a lake nearby. This advice he obeyed.

When we had reassembled and were indulging in our mimic dance, Little Wound was not allowed to dance. He was considered not to be in existence—he had been killed by our enemies, the Bee tribe. Poor little fellow! His swollen face was sad and ashamed as he sat on a fallen log and watched the dance. Although he might well have styled himself one of the noble dead who had died for their country, yet he was not unmindful that he had *screamed*, and this weakness would be apt to recur to him many times in the future.

We had some quiet plays which we alternated with the more severe and warlike ones. Among them were throwing wands and snow-arrows. In the winter we coasted much. We had no "double-rippers" or toboggans, but six or seven of the long ribs of a buffalo, fastened together at the larger end, answered all practical purposes. Sometimes a strip of bass-wood bark, four feet long and about six inches wide, was used with considerable skill. We stood on one end and held the other, using the slippery inside of the bark for the outside, and thus coasting down long hills with remarkable speed.

The spinning of tops was one of the all-absorbing winter sports. We made our tops heart-shaped of wood, horn or bone. We whipped them with a long thong of buckskin. The handle was a stick about a foot long and sometimes we whittled the stick to make it spoon-shaped at one end.

We played games with these tops—two to fifty boys at one time. Each whips his top until it hums; then one takes the lead and the rest follow in a sort of obstacle race. The top must spin all the way through. There were bars of snow over which we must pilot our top in the spoon end of our whip; then again we would toss it in the air on to another open spot of ice or smooth snow-crust from twenty to fifty paces away. The top that holds out the longest is the winner.

Sometimes we played "medicine dance." This, to us, was almost what "playing church" is among white children, but our people seemed to think it an act of irreverence to imitate these dances, therefore performances of this kind were always enjoyed in secret. We used to observe all the important ceremonies and it required something of an actor to reproduce the dramatic features of the dance. The real dances occupied a day and a night, and the program was long and varied, so that it was not easy to execute all the details perfectly; but the Indian children are born imitators.

Occasionally, we also played "white man." Our knowledge of the pale-face was limited, but we had learned that he brought goods whenever he came and that our people exchanged furs for his merchandise. We also knew that his complexion was pale, that he had short hair on his head and long hair on his face and that he wore coat, trousers, and hat, and did not patronize blankets in the daytime. That was the picture we had formed of the white man.

So we painted two or three of our number with white clay and put on them birchen hats which we sewed up for the occasion; fastened a piece of fur to their chins for a beard and altered their costumes as much as lay within our power. The white of the birch-bark was made to answer for their white shirts. Their merchandise consisted of sand for sugar, wild beans for coffee, dried leaves for tea, pulverized earth for gun-powder, pebbles for bullets and clear water for the dangerous "spirit water." We traded for these goods with skins of squirrels, rabbits and small birds.

When we played "hunting buffalo" we would send a few good runners off on the open prairie with a supply of meat; then start a few equally swift boys to chase them and capture the food. Once we were engaged in this sport when a real hunt by the men was in progress; yet we did not realize that it was so near until, in the midst of our play, we saw an immense buffalo coming at full speed directly toward us. Our mimic buffalo hunt turned into a very real buffalo scare. Fortunately, we were near the edge of the woods and we soon disappeared among the leaves like a covey of young prairie-chickens and some hid in the bushes while others took refuge in tall trees.

We loved to play in the water. When we had no ponies, we often had swimming matches of our own and sometimes made rafts with which we crossed lakes and rivers. It was a common thing to "duck" a young or timid boy or to carry him into deep water to struggle as best he might.

I remember a perilous ride with a companion on an unmanageable log, when we were both less than seven years old. The older boys had put us on this uncertain bark and pushed us out into the swift current of the river. I cannot speak for my comrade in distress, but I can say now that I would rather ride on a swift bronco any day than try to stay on and steady a short log in a river. I never knew how we managed to prevent shipwreck on that voyage and to reach the shore.

We had many curious wild pets. There were young foxes, bears, wolves, raccoons, fawns, buffalo calves and birds of all kinds, tamed by various boys. My pets were different at different times, but I particularly remember one. I once had a grizzly bear for a pet and so far as he and I were concerned, our relations were charming and very close. But I hardly know whether he made more enemies for me or I for him. It was his habit to treat every boy unmercifully who injured me. He was despised for his conduct in my interest and I was hated on account of his interference.

HOPI CHILDREN AT PLAY

DON C. TALAYESVA—HOPI

We learned to catch beetles and put them in circles; we called them our "wild horses," but we were warned never to hurt them, for the old people said they were good in treating some diseases. I never played with spiders because of their mother, the Spider Woman. I never teased the hawks and eagles staked out on the housetops [captured birds used in religious ceremonies], for we were told that they were spirit people.

We made necklaces out of horned toads and strung them around our necks. The old people said, "Don't tease toads too much; they are spirits and can help us." I could pick up a lizard or a horned toad in my hands and not feel afraid. One time I was too rough with a toad, and it bit me. This taught me a lesson. I never tied a string to a toad and hung it around another fellow's neck; he might have slung the toad away roughly, angering it, and this would have been a disgrace. At first I used to pick up small snakes, but later I learned that this was not right. One day I killed a very small one, which was an awful thing to do.

We chased the chickens, threw corncobs at them, and shot them with our toy arrows. We encouraged roosters to fight for our amusement. My grandfather cautioned me that chickens are the chosen pets of the Sun god. "The crowing of the cocks in the early morning is important," he said. "The Sun god put them here to wake up the people. He rings a little bell telling the roosters when to announce the coming dawn. They crow four times before daylight."

GAMES OF THE EASTERN TRIBES

CHIEF KAH-GE-GA-GAH-BOWH—OJIBWAY

The plays I am about to describe are the principal games practised by the people of my nation. One of the most popular games is that of ball-playing [*lacrosse*, now the national game of Canada], which oftentimes engages an entire village. Parties are formed of from ten to several hundred. Before they commence, those who are to take a part in the play must provide each his share of staking, or things which are set apart; and one leader for each party. Each leader then appoints one of each company to be stake-holder.

Each man and each woman (women sometimes engage in the sport) is armed with a stick, one end of which bends somewhat like a small hoop, about four inches in circumference, to which is attached a net work of raw-hide, two inches deep, just large enough to admit the ball which is to be used on the occasion. Two poles are driven in the ground at a distance of four hundred paces from each other, which serve as goals for the two parties. It is the endeavor of each to take the ball to his hole. The party which carries the ball and strikes its pole wins the game.

The warriors, very scantily attired, young and brave, fantastically painted—and women, decorated with feathers, assemble around their commanders, who are generally men swift on the race. They are to take the ball either by running with it or throwing it in the air. As the ball falls in the crowd the excitement begins. The clubs swing and roll from side to side, the players run and shout, fall upon and tread upon each other, and in the struggle some get rather rough treatment.

When the ball is thrown some distance on each side, the party standing near instantly pick it up, and run at full speed with three or four after him at full speed. The others send their shouts of encouragement to their own party. "Ha! ha! yah!" "A-ne-gook!" and these shouts are heard even from the distant lodges, for children and all are deeply interested in the exciting scene. The spoils are not all on which their interest is fixed, but is directed to the falling and rolling of the crowds over and under each other. The loud and merry shouts of the spectators, who crowd the doors of the wigwams, go forth in one continued peal, and testify to their happy state of feeling.

The players receive blows whose marks are plainly visible after the scuffle. The hands and feet are unincumbered, and they exercise them to the extent of their power; and with such dexterity do they strike the ball that it is sent out of sight. Another strikes it on its descent, and for ten minutes at a time the play is so adroitly managed that the ball does not touch the ground,

No one is heard to complain, though he be bruised severely, or his nose come in close communion with a club. If the last mentioned catastrophe befell him, he is up in a trice, and sends his laugh forth as loud as the rest, though it be floated at first on a tide of blood.

It is very seldom, if ever, that one is seen to be angry because he has been hurt. If he should get so, they would call him a "coward," which proves a sufficient check to many evils which might result from many seemingly intended injuries.

The Moccasin play is simple, and can be played by two or three. Three moccasins are used for the purpose of hiding the bullets which are employed in the game. So deeply interesting does this play sometimes become, that an Indian will stake first his gun; next his steel-traps; then his implements of war; then his clothing; and lastly, his tobacco and pipe, leaving him, as we say, "*Nah-bah-wan-yah-ze-yaid;*" a piece of cloth with a string around his waist.

The "Tossing Play" is a game seldom seen among the whites. It is played in the wigwam. There is used in it an oblong knot, made of cedar boughs, of length, say about seven inches. On the top is fastened a string, about fifteen inches long, by which the knot is swung. On the other end of this string is another stick, two and a half inches long, and sharply pointed. This is held in the hand, and if the player can hit the large stick every time it falls on the sharp one he wins.

"Bone Play," is another in-door amusement, so called, because the articles used are made of the hoof-joint bones of the deer. The ends are hollowed out, and from three to ten are strung together. In playing it, they use the same kind of sharp stick, the end of which is thrown into the bones.

Doubtless the most interesting of all games is the "Maidens' Ball Play," in the Ojibway language, *Pah-pah-se-Kah-way*.

The majority of those who take part in this play are young damsels, though married women are not excluded. The ball is made of two deer skin bags, each about five inches long and one in diameter. These are so fastened together as to be at a distance of seven inches from the other. It is thrown with a stick five feet long.

This play is practiced in summer beneath the shade of wide-spreading trees, beneath which each strives to find their homes, *tahwin*, and to run home with it. These having been appointed in the morning, the young women of the village decorate themselves for the day by painting their cheeks with vermillion, and disrobe themselves of as much unnecessary clothing as possible, braiding their hair with colored feathers, which hang profusely down to the feet.

At the set time the whole village assemble, and the young men, whose loved ones are seen in the crowd, twist and turn to send sly glances to them, and receive their bright smiles in return.

The same confusion exists as in the game of ball played by the men. Crowds rush to a given point as the ball is sent flying through the air. None stop to narrate the accidents that befall them, though they tumble about to their no little discomfiture; they rise making a loud noise, something between a laugh and a cry, some limping behind the others, as the women shout. "*Ain goo*" is heard sounding like the notes of a dove, of which it is no bad imitation. Worked garters, moccasins, leggings and vermillion are generally the articles at stake. Sometimes the Chief of the village sends a parcel before they commence, the contents of which are to be distributed among the maidens when the play is over.

OUTDOOR SPORTS OF THE PLAINS INDIANS

WOODEN LEG—CHEYENNE

Competitive sports used to interest us. Horse races, foot races, wrestling matches, target shooting with guns or with arrows, tossing the arrows by hand, swimming, jumping and other like contests were entered upon. In the tribe such competition usually was between men representing the three warrior societies. These were the Elk warriors, the Crazy Dog warriors and the Fox warriors. If any Sioux tribe or big band camped jointly with us the matches were between representative members of the two tribes. Bets were made on every kind of contest. The stakes were of guns, ammunition, bows and arrows, blankets, horses, robes, jewelry, shirts, leggings, moccasins, everything in the line of personal property. The betting always was on even terms. Articles were piled upon a blanket, matched articles in apposition to each other. The winners took all and shouted over the victory.

The Elk warriors, the society to which I belonged, had the best runners. Our speediest man on foot was named Apache. He was almost as tall as I was and he was much heavier. He had remarkably big thighs. One time at a double camping with the Ogallalas on upper Powder river a foot race was arranged between the two tribal champions. The Ogallala fast man was tall and slender. His name was

Black Legs. The distance they were to run was about a mile, I believe, although at that time we had no measurements for distance. Four friends of each man accompanied the two racers to the starting point. A revolver shot told them when to go. Near the finish, the Sioux fell exhausted. Our man Apache was very tired, but he ran on to the end of the route. Of course, the Cheyennes took all of the stakes, let out a chorus of cheers and fired their guns into the air. "The Cheyenne medicine broke his legs," the Sioux said when their man collapsed.

The old Chief Little Wolf had been a great runner when he was a young man. The longer the distance the better it suited him. As the Cheyennes and the Ogallalas were traveling together in moving camp there was much bantering such as, "I think the Sioux can travel faster than the Cheyennes can," or, "It appears the Cheyennes must go a little more slowly in order not to run away from their friends the Sioux." Finally a young Sioux jokingly challenged Little Wolf to a foot race.

"How," assented Little Wolf, "I'll run with you."

The caravan was stopped and arrangements were made for the race. Little Wolf then was past fifty years of age, while his Sioux challenger was just entering young manhood. Nevertheless, the Cheyennes backed their chief heavily. A great pile of bets were placed upon the containing blankets. Four Cheyennes and four Sioux went with the two men to the agreed starting point, which must have been three or four miles away. At the crack of a revolver shot the race began. Up to the last mile the young Sioux kept well in the lead. Then he began to move more slowly. It appeared Little Wolf never changed his pace. So he closed up toward the leader. In the last part of the last mile he went ahead, still running at what appeared to be his same rate while the other man's speed continued to lessen. By a broad hundred yards Little Wolf won the contest. Many of the Sioux, even some who had lost bets, joined the Cheyennes in cheering for the old man.

A good wrestler and general strong man was Little Hawk. He and Buffalo Hump and Brave Wolf made up a playful raiding group in the camp one time after a great hunting party had brought in lots of buffalo beef. All about the camp circle there were drying poles loaded with meat. The three young men had not been fortunate in the chase, so they decided to borrow from their friends. They went to a certain tepee.

"We need meat," they announced. "Your drying poles are too full, and we think our wants can be supplied there. But Little Hawk wants to wrestle for it. If anybody here can throw him we will not take any food from this lodge."

Nobody there wanted to accept this challenge. The young men took some meat and went on to another tepee. There they made the same kind of announcement and proposition. There likewise all of the men present feared to grapple with Little Hawk, and there also the three joking robbers helped themselves from the bountiful store. At the next tepee the transaction was more complex. After some exchange of talk the spokesman of the lodge said: "Big Thigh is here. He says he will wrestle you."

The conditions of the match were agreed upon. The two men stripped to their breechcloths. A group of onlookers assembled. The group soon became a great crowd. Big Thigh and Little Hawk appeared equally confident. Both of them rushed into the grapple. They tugged and shoved and tripped. The advantage seemed to shift back and forth. The throng of spectators whooped and danced. There was some partisan cheering, but most of it was merely the expression of delight at witnessing this tribal championship battle. After several minutes of fierce and continuous struggling Little Hawk began to weaken and wilt. Big Thigh pinioned the arms of his antagonist and bore him face downward to the ground. The victor sat astride the back of the vanquished and sprinkled handfuls of dirt upon him. He also picked up a folded blanket lying near by and used this as a soft club in pretense at beating into complete submission the defeated Little Hawk. Shouts of congratulation greeted the conqueror while jeers were heaped upon the under dog and his two confederates. Brave Wolf and Buffalo Hump, ridiculed to complete embarrassment and compelled to replace their looted buffalo meat, quickly took themselves into hiding.

Our target shooting was with rifles, revolvers and arrows. For the arrow contests an erect wooden figure of a man was the customary mark. Sometimes the arrows were shot from the bow, sometimes they were tossed by hand. Both accuracy and extent of penetration counted in either form of this archery. Shooting arrows for long distance was another test of capability. Here a strong bow and a powerful arm and hand were important elements for success. In all of these games the regular rule allowed four successive shots for each contestant. Fine points in the manipulation of arrows were brought out in the sidewise tossing of them at short distances, each toss being made in attempt at the exact crossing of another arrow thrown out by an opponent.

Most of our few rifles were muzzle loaders and our revolvers usually were of the kind using caps and moulded bullets. The target for practice with them ordinarily was a black ring as broad as a large hand marked upon an animal's dried shoulderblade or upon a barked tree. Teams of three or more men on each side often were arrayed against each other for either the arrow or gun contests. Usually the teams represented their respective warrior societies. On many occasions, though, there were personal engagements. In these there might be sought only an honorable distinction or there might be betting added as an incentive to achievement.

WHISKY SPREES

CHIEF KAH-GE-GA-GAH-BOWH—OJIBWAY

There was a custom among us that when the Ojibways intended to take a general whisky "spree," several young men were appointed by the head chief to collect all the fire arms, knives, war-clubs and other weapons, and keep them in a secret place, till the Indians had completed their frolic. This was done to prevent them from murdering each other when intoxicated. By this means many lives have been saved; although many have been killed during their drunken fights.

They would walk very far for a dram of liquor. I once heard of an individual, whom I had seen many times, who would travel all day for a single drink of fire-water. When he arrived at the trading post, he obtained and guzzled down a cup full of whisky. When the poison had operated, he said, that he felt as if his head was going down his throat; and added, "Whah! I wish my neck was a mile long, so that I might feel and hear the whisky running all the way down!"

A certain Indian once teased a Mrs. F. for whisky, which he said was to cure his "*big toe*," that had been badly bruised the preceding night. Mrs. F. said, "I am afraid you will drink it." He declared he would not drink it; and after much pleading, she handed him some; he took it, and looking first at his toe, and then at the liquor, alternately, all of a sudden he slipped the whisky down his gullet, at the same time exclaiming, as he pointed to his toe, "There, *whisky*, go down to my poor big toe."

TEMPERANCE LESSONS

CHIEF SIMON POKAGON—POTTAWATTAMI

Most Indian leaders disapproved of drinking sprees and appealed to the American government to pass prohibition laws. In 1802 Little Turtle, a Miami chief, addressed the legislatures of Ohio and Kentucky urging that laws be passed to stop the whisky traffic. Of the whisky traders, Little Turtle said: "They stripped the poor Indian of skins, gun, blanket, everything—while his squaw and the children dependent on him lay starving and shivering in his wigwam."

Despite the efforts of Little Turtle and other chiefs, the government made no serious attempt to stop the liquor traders who were enriching themselves at the Indian's expense. One well known whisky recipe called for "two gallons of common whisky, or unrectified spirits, to thirty gallons of water, add red pepper enough to make it fiery, and tobacco enough to make it intoxicating."

Ash-taw was a woman among the Ottawas renowned as a temperance worker. She traveled from place to place, and wherever she found a few families in a neighborhood, she called the children together to hold a little "pow-wow" of their own. She always managed to keep on hand a stock of snakes' eggs. She would hold her meetings at such times as some of the egg litters were about to hatch. She stained them a beautiful red color, placing them on green moss in "wig-was-si ma-kak-ogons" (small, white birch-bark boxes) so as to have them appear to the children as charming as possible. After the children were assembled, she called them about her; then opened the boxes one by one in their presence; and when their admiration was sufficiently excited so they all began to inquire what kind of eggs they were, she would make reply, "These are ish-kot-e-waw-bo wan-an-og (whisky eggs);" then she would add, "Would you like to take some of them?" She would then carefully put into each extended hand some of the charming-colored little eggs.

On receiving them, childlike they would feel of the little beauties with the tips of their fingers, when to their great surprise, the frail egg shells would crumble away, and from each come forth a little snake squirming and wriggling in their hands. Then with a shriek of horror they would let the young reptiles drop, and scatter like leaves in a whirlwind. The cruel joke impressed their youthful minds with such a loathsome hate against ish-kot-e-waw-bo that their very souls ever after would revolt at the sight, smell, or even thought of the deceptive curse.

This shrewd woman would then make an application of the strong object-lesson, convincing the children that what they had witnessed was but a slight foretaste of the awful reality, and that they who drank, after a while would be tormented with "mi-chi-gin-e-big" (great big snakes), which they could not escape, or even let go of.

FIRESIDE HUMOR

OHIYESA—SIOUX

There is scarcely anything so exasperating to me as the idea that the natives of this country have no sense of humor and no faculty for mirth. This phase of their character is well understood by those whose fortune or misfortune it has been to live among them day in and day out at their homes. I don't believe I ever heard a real hearty laugh away from the Indians' fireside. I have often spent an entire evening in laughing with them until I could laugh no more. There are evenings when the recognized wit or story-teller of the village gives a free entertainment which keeps the rest of the community in a convulsive state until he leaves them. However, Indian humor consists as much in the gestures and inflections of the voice as in words, and is really untranslatable.

Matogee (Yellow Bear) was a natural humorous speaker, and a very diffident man at other times. He usually said little, but when he was in the mood he could keep a large company in a roar.

"I am a believer in dreams," one remarked.

"Yes, certainly, so are we all. You know Hachah almost lost his life by believing in dreams," commented Matogee.

"Let us hear that story," was the general request.

"You have all heard of Hachah, the great medicine man, who did many wonderful things. He once dreamed four nights in succession of flying from a high cliff over the Minnesota river. He recollected every particular of the scene, and it made a great impression upon his mind.

"The next day after he had dreamed it for the fourth time, he proposed to his wife that they go down to the river to swim, but his real purpose was to see the place of his dream.

"He did find the place, and it seemed to Hachah exactly like. A crooked tree grew out of the top of the cliff, and the water below was very deep."

"Did he really fly?" I called impatiently from the doorway, where I had been listening and laughing with the rest.

"Ugh, that is what I shall tell you. He was swimming about with his wife, who was a fine swimmer; but all at once Hachah disappeared. Presently he stood upon the very tree that he had seen in his dream, and gazed out over the water. The tree was very springy, and Hachah felt sure that he could fly; so before long he launched bravely forth from the cliff. He kicked out vigorously and swung both arms as he did so, but nevertheless he came down to the bottom of the water like a crow that had been shot on the wing."

"Ho, ho, ho! Ho, ho, ho!" and the whole company laughed unreservedly.

"His wife screamed loudly as Hachah whirled downward and went out of sight like a blue heron after a fish. Then she feared he might be stunned, so she swam to him and dragged him to the shore. He could not speak, but the woman overwhelmed him with reproaches.

" 'What are you trying to do, you old idiot? Do you want to kill yourself?' she screamed again and again.

" 'Woman, be silent,' he replied, and he said nothing more. He did not tell his dream for many years afterward. Not until he was a very old man and about to die, did Hachah tell any one how he thought he could fly."

And at this they all laughed louder than ever.

IV: THE GREAT SPIRIT

The Indian religion was designed to bring happiness in this world, and when the Indian prayed or made sacrificial offerings he demanded immediate results. If the results were not forthcoming from one god, the Indian tried another, for the number of gods—friendly and hostile—was legion.

Most Indians believed that the world was pervaded by a strange, magical force which was possessed by every god and could even be attained by man. Control of this force could make a warrior invulnerable to the weapons of his enemy, successful in hunting, or irresistible to women. Each tribe had a different name for the mysterious power. The Algonquians called it Manito, the Sioux called it Wakan Tanka, and the early missionaries, confusing this force with their own idea of God, named it the Great Spirit.

IV: THE GREAT SPIRIT

SEARCHING FOR A SPIRITUAL GUIDE

EDWARD GOODBIRD—HIDATSA

We Hidatsas believed that this world and everything in it was alive and had spirits; and our faith in these spirits and our worship of them made our religion.

My father explained this to me. "All things in this world," he said, "have souls, or spirits. The sky has a spirit; the clouds have spirits; the sun and moon have spirits; so have animals, trees, grass, water, stones, *everything*. These spirits are our gods; and we pray to them and give them offerings, that they may help us in our need."

We Indians did not believe in one Great Spirit, as white men seem to think all Indians do. We did believe that certain gods were more powerful than others. Of these was *It-si-ka-ma-hi-di*, our elder creator, the spirit of the prairie wolf; and *Ka-du-te-ta*, or Old-woman-who-never-dies, who first taught my people to till their fields. Long histories are given of these gods.

Any one could pray to the spirits, receiving answer usually in a dream. Indeed, all dreams were thought to be from the spirits; and for this reason they were always heeded, especially those that came by fasting and suffering. Sometimes a man fasted and tortured himself until he fell into a kind of dream while yet awake; we called this a vision.

Believing as he did that the world was full of spirits, every Indian hoped that one of them would come to him and be his protector, especially in war. When a lad became about seventeen years of age, his parents would say, "You are now old enough to go to war; but you should first go out and find your god!" They meant by this, that he should not risk his life in battle until he had a protecting spirit.

Finding one's god was not an easy task. The lad painted his body with white clay, as if in mourning, and went out among the hills, upon some bluff, where he could be seen of the gods; and for days, with neither food nor drink, and often torturing himself, he cried to the gods to pity him and come to him. His sufferings at last brought on delirium, so that he dreamed, or saw a vision. Whatever he saw in this vision was his god, come to pledge him protection. Usually this god was a bird or beast; or it might be the spirit of some one dead; the bird or beast was not a flesh-and-blood animal, but a spirit.

The lad then returned home. As soon as he was recovered from his fast, he set out to kill an animal like that seen in his vision, and its dried skin, or a part of it, he kept as his sacred object, or medicine, for in this sacred object dwelt his god. Thus if an otter god appeared to him, the lad would kill an otter, and into its skin, which the lad kept, the god entered. The otter skin was now the lad's medicine; he prayed to it and bore it with him to war, that his god might be present to protect him.

Indians even made offerings of food to their sacred objects. They knew the sacred object did not eat the food; but they believed that the god, or spirit, in the sacred object, ate the spirit of the food. They also burned cedar incense to their sacred objects.

My grandfather once told me of a man who had a vision of four buffalo skulls that became alive.

Many years ago when our villages were on Knife River [North Dakota] a man named Bush went to find his god. He sought a vision from the buffalo spirits; and he thought to make himself suffer so that the spirits might pity him. He tied four buffalo skulls in a train, one behind another, and as Bush walked he dragged the train of skulls behind him.

He made his way painfully up the Missouri, mourning and crying to the gods. The banks of the Missouri are much cut up by ravines, and Bush suffered greatly as he dragged the heavy skulls over this rough country.

Fifty miles north of the villages, he came to the Little Missouri, a shallow stream, but subject to sudden freshets; he found the river flooded, and rising.

He stood on the bank and cried: "O gods, I am poor and I suffer! I want to find my god. Other men have suffered, and found their gods. Now I suffer much, but no god answers me. I am going to plunge into this torrent. I think I shall die, yet I will plunge in. O gods, if you are going to answer me, do it now and save me!"

He waded in, dragging the heavy skulls after him. The water grew deeper. He could no longer wade, he had to swim; he struck out.

He wondered that he no longer felt the weight of the skulls, and that he did not sink. Then he heard something behind him cry, "*Whoo-oo-ooh!*" He looked around. The four buffalo skulls were swimming about him, buoying him up; but they were no longer skulls! Flesh and wooly hair covered them; they had big, blue eyes; they had red tongues. They were alive!

Bush himself told this story to my grandfather.

It should not be thought that Bush was trying to deceive when he said he saw these things. If one had been with him when he sprang into the torrent, and had cried, "Bush, the skulls are not alive; it is your delirium that makes you think they live!" he would have answered, "Of course you cannot see they are alive! The vision is to me, not to you. The flesh and hair and eyes are spirit flesh. I see them; you see only the skulls!"

THE GODS OF THE OJIBWAYS

CHIEF KAH-GE-GA-GAH-BOWH—OJIBWAY

The Ojibway Nation believed in a Great Good Spirit, and in a Bad Spirit. They had also "gods innumerable," among which was "the god of war," "the god of hunting," and "the god of the fowls of the air."

The skies were filled with the deities they worshipped, and the whole forest awakened with their whispers. The lakes and streams were the places of their resort, and mountains and valleys alike their abode. All the remarkable spots in the country were considered their favorite resorts. These were the peaks of rocky cliffs; the clefts of craggy mounts. Water-falls were thought to be their sporting scenes.

The sky was the home of the god who held a watchful care over every star. They heard him whisper in the gentle breeze, or howl in the tempest. He had dominion over all the heavens, and sometimes amused himself by hurling stars from their stations and causing them on their passage to the earth to change into demons to wrong and perplex the people who inhabited the place of their destination.

The constellations of stars were council gatherings of the gods. The brightest were ruling spirits, appointed by the Great Spirit as guardians of the lesser ones. Clusters of stars were the populous cities of the celestials.

In the stories of the wigwam, mention is made of some of these high born personages coming to earth to dwell among the people; also of men going up and becoming inhabitants of the skies. They say animals have received wings; and some of them from heaven.

Were all the stories that are related of the skies written, it would be found that each star has connected with it some strange event. The history of the tradition of the stars, according to Indian tradition, would be a history indeed, and would rank among the "curiosities of literature."

The earth teemed with all sorts of spirits, good and bad; those of the forest clothed themselves with moss. During a shower of rain, thousands of them are sheltered in a flower.

The Ojibway, as he reclines beneath the shade of his forest trees, imagines these gods to be about him. He detects their tiny voices in the insect's hum. With half closed eyes he beholds them sporting by thousands on a sunray.

They have a special god presiding over the most noted herbs of the earth. These are subject to this being who is called the god of Medicine. Men or women are deemed capable of learning the virtues of roots from him, and often fast in order to gain his favor. In time of war they carry certain roots with them, which according to their idea, prevent the balls of an enemy from striking them.

SACRED SONG TO THE MORNING STAR

TAHIRUSSAWICHI—CHAUI-PAWNEE

I

Oh Morning Star, for thee we watch!
Dimly comes thy light from distant skies;
We see thee, then lost art thou.
Morning Star, thou bringest life to us.

We sing this song slowly with reverent feeling, for we are singing of very sacred things.

BEARCLAW NECKLACE
George Catlin
ca. 1830–40

From Catlin Sketchbook
Courtesy of Gilcrease Institute

The Morning Star is one of the lesser powers. Life and strength and fruitfulness are with the Morning Star. We are reverent toward it. Our fathers performed sacred ceremonies in its honor.

The Morning Star is like a man; he is painted red all over; that is the color of life. He is clad in leggings and a robe is wrapped about him. On his head is a soft downy eagle's feather, painted red. This feather represents the soft, light cloud that is high in the heavens, and the red is the touch of a ray of the coming sun. The soft, downy feather is the symbol of breath and life.

The star comes from a great distance, too far away for us to see the place where it starts. At first we can hardly see it; we lose sight of it, it is so far off; then we see it again, for it is coming steadily toward us all the time. We watch it approach; it comes nearer and nearer; its light grows brighter and brighter.

This is the meaning of this stanza, and the star comes as we sing it four times.

II

Oh Morning Star, thy form we see!
Clad in shining garments dost thou come,
Thy plume touched with rosy light.
Morning Star, thou now art vanishing.

As we sing this stanza the Morning Star comes still nearer and now we see him standing there in the heavens, a strong man shining brighter and brighter. The soft plume in his hair moves with the breath of the new day, and the ray of the sun touches it with color. As he stands there so bright, he is bringing us strength and new life.

As we look upon him he grows less bright, he is receding, going back to his dwelling place whence he came. We watch him vanishing, passing out of our sight. He has left with us the gift of life which Tira'wa atius [the Great Spirit] sent him to bestow.

We sing this stanza four times.

III

Oh youthful Dawn, for thee we watch!
Dimly comes thy light from distant skies;
We see thee, then lost art thou.
Youthful Dawn, thou bringest life to us.

As we sing this stanza we are still standing at the west of the lodge, looking through the long passageway toward the east. Now in the distance we see the Dawn approaching; it is coming, coming along the path of the Morning Star. It is a long path and as the Dawn advances along this path sometimes we catch sight of it and then again we lose it, but all the time it is coming nearer.

The Dawn is new born, its breath has sent new life everywhere, all things stir with the life Tira'wa atius has given this child, his child, whose mother is the Night.

We sing this stanza four times.

IV

Oh youthful Dawn, we see thee come!
Brighter grows thy glowing light
As near, nearer thou dost come.
Youthful Dawn, thou now art vanishing.

As we stand, looking through the long passageway of the lodge, watching and singing, we see the Dawn come nearer and nearer; its brightness fills the sky, the shadowy forms on the earth are becoming visible. As we watch, the Dawn, like the Morning Star, recedes. It is following the star, going back to the place whence it came, to its birthplace.

The day is close behind, advancing along the path of the Morning Star and the Dawn, and, as we watch, the Dawn vanishes from our sight.

We sing this song four times.

Among the Skidi-Pawnee, the ceremony of the morning star was a weird and barbarous rite in which a young girl was sacrificed. They believed that the morning star had great power over their crops, and in certain years, at planting time, they selected a beautiful captive to be offered as a bride to the morning star. She was kept in ignorance of her fate and was treated with great kindness. On the morning of the sacrifice day she was led through the village, begging for wood, unaware that the wood was to be used in burning her. In the afternoon, she was undressed. The right half of her body was painted red and the left half black.

In the final act of the sacrifice the girl was lashed to a scaffold, and a slow fire built under her body just as the morning star was rising.

Armed with small bows, the men and boys of the tribe fired arrows of joint grass into her breast. As the shafts penetrated her skin, oily substances oozed out and the arrows took fire, flaming like tiny torches. The girl was then killed, and her heart cut out and burned. The smoke from the burning heart was believed to possess magical powers, and weapons and tools were passed through it to insure success in their use.

In 1818 the Skidi-Pawnee were holding the morning star sacrifice when a young Pawnee chief named Petalesharro, who had concealed two horses nearby, dashed forward, cut the girl loose, and galloped away with her. When they were safe from pursuit, he gave the girl the horse she was riding, a supply of food, and sent her home to her people.

Petalesharro became a hero when news of his deed reached Washington. The young ladies of Miss White's Seminary presented him with a silver medal and this admonition: "Accept this token of our esteem—always wear it for our sakes, and when again you have the power to save a poor woman from death and torture, think of this and of us, and fly to her relief and her rescue."

Holding the medal in his hand, the handsome warrior replied: "This brings rest to my heart. I feel like the leaf after a storm, and when the wind is still. I listen to you. I am glad. I love the pale faces more than I ever did, and will open my ears wider when they speak. I am glad you heard of what I did. I did not know the act was so good. It came from my heart. I was ignorant of its value. I now know how good it was. You make me know this by giving me this medal."

THE SUN DANCE

CHIEF BUFFALO CHILD LONG LANCE—CROATAN

About half an hour before noon we would hear a big commotion, and then we would see twelve young warriors racing into the camp on horseback, dragging behind them the freshly cut evergreens which would be thrown over the skeleton of the Sun Dance lodge at a given signal from the medicine man. And a little later two men, dressed in special regalia, would come galloping into camp with an eagle's nest [representing the thunderbird's nest], which would be placed at the top of the Sun Dance pole.

At high noon, just as the sun arrived directly overhead, the medicine-man would give the signal for the erection of the lodge.

That was the signal for the cut-loose. Never has one heard such a noise as that which prevails for the next fifteen minutes until the lodge is completed. As fifty men work frantically on the big evergreen enclosure, a hundred warriors come galloping into the campus, shooting, yelling, and racing madly around and around the lodge, while many hundreds of others join in the din with rattles, bells, whistles, and shouting and singing. Children run here and there to dodge the heels of the flying horses. Our parents have forgotten us completely; they have been lost in the excitement of the one big moment of the year. The smell of powder smoke and sweating horses fairly sting our nostrils.

Midst this uproar the Sun Dance woman, who has been fasting in a special teepee for five days, comes out and takes her seat beside the medicine-man just behind the big lodge, which is now going up with startling speed. Before this woman all of the young braves who are to go through the tortures of the Sun Dance come and bow down to be anointed with black paint on their faces and around their wrists.

Then, suddenly, the medicine-man gets up and runs inside the lodge and grabs the eagle's nest. He goes to the foot of the Sun Dance pole, which is still lying on the ground beside a deep hole, and paints a series of black rings around it with the palm of his hand. When he gets up to the top of the pole he draws his blanket completely over him in a squatting position, and thus hidden from view, fastens the nest at the top of the pole. Then comes the final part of building the lodge: five braves rush up and grab the big pole, with the medicine-man still clinging to the top, and set it up in the hole. The medicine-man is now about fifteen feet above the ground, and if he should fall, that would be a sign that the sun did not look favorably upon the dance, and all proceedings would be stopped at once. But we never saw that happen.

Now comes the interesting part of the Sun Dance. All the young men who are to be made "braves" come walking into the lodge, stripped down to their breech-cloths. The medicine-man drops from his precarious perch at the top of the pole and goes to his medicine paraphernalia and takes out a long, sharp knife and several hundred feet of rawhide thong. He takes up a position beside the small medicine fire, and one by one the young men come before him and kneel.

The medicine-man runs the sharp knife into the left breast of the man in front of him and makes a long, deep gash. Then he pulls it out and makes a similar gash about an inch and a half from the first one. Now he runs the knife under the flesh between these two gashes, and while he holds his finger in the connecting hole, he reaches down with the other hand and picks up a stout rawhide thong about three feet long and draws it through the hole. He then ties the flesh up tightly and with his knife repeats the operation on the right breast, using the other end of the thong to tie it up with. When this is done the young man, who has not yet uttered a sound, has one rawhide thong "sewed" into his chest at both ends. The medicine-man now takes a heavier thong, many feet long, and ties one end to the thong in the young man's chest and the other end to the Sun Dance pole.

And it is now that the young aspiring brave begins his dance. He gets up and starts his dance while the next man comes and kneels before the medicine-man. As the drums boom to the singing of the Sun Dance song, the young man dances and jerks upon the long thong, trying to pull out the flesh which it holds and free himself. He dances on and on, jerking with all his might.

Sometimes they danced many hours without being able to free themselves. If the young man lasted all this time without fainting, the medicine-man would order a warrior to come into the lodge on a pony, and he would untie the thong from the pole and fasten it to the horse. The warrior would then race around and around the lodge, dragging the young man behind him in an effort to release the flesh. We children would run in and jump on and off the young man's back as he was dragged around, to increase the weight. If this did not free him, the warrior would back his horse up several feet and then send it forward with a sudden rush—and "swish"—a sickly sound of rending flesh, and the young man would get up, if he could, with his chest hanging with blood and torn muscles. The medicine-man would "doctor" him for a moment with native herbs, and then the young man went his way—now a brave. He had proved his salt, and the tribe would now allow him to go out on the war-path as a full-fledged warrior. Indians would not permit a young man to go on the war-path against an enemy until he had gone through this ordeal, lest he should disgrace the tribe by showing cowardice. Any man who failed to go through the dance until he pulled the flesh loose or fainted in the attempt was never allowed to rank as a brave, nor to fight as a warrior.

*Not since 1853 when the Oneida chief, Eleazar Williams, pretended to be the "Lost Dauphin" has so strange a personality as Chief Buffalo Child Long Lance appeared among the Indians. Long Lance claimed to be a Blackfoot chief and published an autobiography in 1928. His book was widely accepted as one of the best descriptions of a vanished era, and Long Lance was invited to star in a motion picture on the Indians—*The Silent Enemy. *Soon afterward, at the height of his success as an actor, author, and lecturer, he committed suicide. Investigation disclosed that Long Lance was not a Blackfoot, but a mixed-blood of Croatan Indian and Negro descent. He was born in North Carolina about 1893, and his real name was Sylvester Long.*

Although Long Lance obtained his information at second hand, his book is an accurate, vivid, and sympathetic depiction of Indian life.

GETTING IN TOUCH WITH THE SPIRITS

CHIEF BUFFALO CHILD LONG LANCE—CROATAN

The most weird and interesting part of the medicine-man's practices was the sensational rites which he would carry out when "getting in touch with the spirits." Whenever he wanted to get a forecast of the future, get the outcome of some future event or cure some sick person who was lying at the point of death, he would hold this rite in the big medicine-teepee, and the entire tribe would be allowed to witness it. I often watched this as a youngster, and to this day I am puzzled over what I saw. I have never seen any old Indian who could explain it.

An hour or so preceding one of these medicine lodges the camp crier would go through the camp crying out the news that the medicine-man was "preparing to talk with the spirits." This caused great excitement in camp. The entire tribe would go early to the medicine lodge in order to get seats; for only about one hundred could get inside of the lodge, and the rest had to stay outside and listen to the uncanny ceremony. Our mother would take us children with her and bundle us close to her on the woman's side of the lodge.

As we sat and looked on with eyes agape, the medicine-man's assistant would erect four poles in the center of the big lodge and tie them together at the top in tripod fashion. Under these poles there was an area about twelve feet across. In this area the assistant, with the help of four men, would drive into the ground a series of sharp pegs, placing them at intervals of about an inch until the entire area was covered. These pegs were so sharp at the top that they would go through a man's foot if stepped upon. In the center of the twelve-foot area a little square was left clear, a place just large enough for a man to stand in. The only way one could reach this area over the sharp pegs was to jump into it, and that seemingly would mean serious injury or death.

The medicine-man would now enter with four men. These men would undress him, leaving only his breech-cloth on his body, and then lay him down on his back. They would place his two hands together, palm to palm, and with a strong rawhide thong they would bind his two thumbs together so tightly that they would sometimes bleed. They would place each pair of fingers together and bind them together in the same way. Then they would go down to his feet and tie his two big toes together, pulling with all their strength to bind them as tightly as they could.

Now they would take a hide about the size of a blanket and roll it tightly around him from head to foot, like a cigar wrapper. Around this wrapper they would twine him up from neck to ankles with a stout rawhide thong, winding it tightly around and around his body at intervals of every inch down the length of his form until he was securely bound. And still another hide was wrapped around him, and another rawhide thong was wound tightly around his motionless form. Now, as he lay helpless on the ground, he resembled a long brown cigar. Literally, he could not move a finger.

The assistants would now raise the medicine-man to a standing position and carefully balance him on the soles of his bare feet. He would stand there for a while like a post. Then gradually he would begin slightly to bend his knees and draw them up again, and after a while each bend of the knees would take the form of a short jump. These jumps would keep increasing in length until finally he would be leaping around and around the four poles with startling speed, resembling some ghostly post bobbing up and down through the air so fast that the eye could hardly follow him.

Then, suddenly, with a huge leap, so quickly executed that no one could see how he made it, he would dart through space and land with a thud in the one-foot clearing in the center of the area of sharp pegs. He had leaped six feet over these dangerous spikes and landed safely in the little clearing, which was just big enough to hold his two feet—truly a remarkable exploit in itself.

But he has not yet started the real thrilling part of the ceremony.

As he stands there in the center under the poles, still bound securely, he commences to sing his medicine song, accompanied by the boom of the big medicine-drum in the hands of his assistant.

What I am going to describe now may seem strange; it is strange, but it is precisely what happens. How and why, no one knows.

Presently, as the medicine-man stands there singing his weird chant to the spirits, voices from above are heard; voices which seem to emanate from the opening away up at the top of the big medicine-teepee. As everyone can see, there is nothing up there but the night air and the stars above. Where these voices come from no Indian has ever been able to explain. But, according to the medicine-man, they are the voices of the spirits—the spirits with whom he is trying to get in touch. The mystery of it is that no one has ever been able to prove that they were anything else.

These voices speak in a language which we cannot understand. Even the medicine-man cannot understand most of them. All he can say is that they are speaking in foreign tongues, and that they are not the spirits that he wants. There were only four spirits whom our medicine-man, White Dog, could understand. I remember the name of only one of them, and that was "First White Man." And that name had been with our medicine-men for years before our tribe knew that there was a white man in existence.

As these voices keep moaning down into the lodge, the medicine-man rejects them one by one, and continues to ask for one of the four spirits whom he can understand. Sometimes it takes him many minutes to do this. I can remember one or two times when he could not get hold of one of them at all, and he had to end the ceremony without accomplishing his aim.

But when he did get hold of the spirit whom he was seeking he would become excited and talk away so fast that we could hardly hear what he was saying. It seemed that he had to hurry to get in what he wanted to say before the spirit departed. If it was a cure he was after, the dying patient lying there in the medicine lodge would also become excited; and we have seen such get up and walk. If it was information the medicine-man was seeking, he would make his inquiries in short parables of his own, and he would be answered by the spirits in these same unintelligible parables, which later had to be explained to us. It was our language, but it was phrased in a way that we could not understand. And, furthermore, it was the ancient method of speaking our language—the way it was spoken a long time ago—and only our oldest men could understand some of the phraseology and old words.

But the part of the ceremony which made us youngsters afraid came at the conclusion of the medicine-man's interview with the spirits.

These interviews ended in many exciting ways, but always the final scene was accompanied by a howling wind, which would start to roar across the top of the lodge as the spirits ceased talking. The big medicine-teepee would rock and quiver under the strain of this wind, as it screeched through the poles at the top of the teepee and caused us to shake with fright. It was a startling climax. A chaotic medley of noise would come down to us from above—from the round opening at the top of the lodge where the teepee poles jutted out into the night air. Strange voices shrieking in weird pandemonium above the wailing of the winds; the clanking and jingling of unknown objects, and then a sudden jerk of the entire lodge, a flicker of the flames, a terrifying yell from the medicine-man, and then—

He would disappear right in front of our eyes. But in that same instant we would hear him yelling for help. And looking up in the direction of his voice, we would see him hanging precariously by one foot at the top of the Lodge, stripped as naked as the day he was born. The only thing that held him from falling and breaking his neck was his foot, which seemed to be caught in between the skin covering of the teepee and one of the slanting poles which supported it.

"*Kokenaytukishpewow!*—Hurry!" he would yell frantically.

And the men would rush for long poles with which to remove him from his dangerous, dangling perch at the roof of the lodge, lest he should fall and break his neck.

How he got there, no one knows; but he said that the spirits left him there on their way out. But the greatest puzzle to us youngsters was how he got stripped of all those stout bindings!

CURING A WOUNDED WARRIOR

CHIEF PLENTY-COUPS—CROW

In a skirmish with four Pecunie [Blackfeet] scouts, all of whom were slain, a Crow warrior named The-wolf was shot in the chest. Although his wound was apparently fatal, he was cured by Takes-plenty, a Crow medicine man. In explaining this miraculous cure, Chief Plenty-coups said: "Such things were done long ago by good men who were wise. Nobody now understands what our Wise Ones [medicine men] knew before the white man came to change this world."

The fighting was finished, but The-wolf, a good man, was lying on the snow in a circle of blood, and our hearts were beside him.

We raised him up and got the blood out of his mouth. "Try to save him," said Gros Ventres-horse to my uncle, Takes-plenty, one of our Wise Ones, as he untied a fine necklace from his own neck and put it around mine. [It was not customary to offer reward directly to a medicine-man for his services. To show earnestness the necklace was given to Plenty-coups, who was related to the medicine man.]

"I will try. We must not leave his body in the Pecunie country," said Takes-plenty, removing a little buckskin pouch from his shirt.

The-wolf's mind was yet sound, but he was nearly gone. The bullet hole was in his breast, and blood was coming from his mouth and nose, when Takes-plenty opened his pouch and took out a pinch of The-flower-the-buffalo-will-not-eat [?] and a little of another kind of flower I did not know. He chewed them in his mouth, and, stepping to windward, blew them upon The-wolf's breast. He then walked one-quarter round him and did the same thing, then half round, then three-quarters, each time chewing a portion of the two flowers and blowing them upon The-wolf, who lay upon his back with his eyes open. I knew he understood what was going on, and hoped with all my heart he would get well.

Takes-plenty snorted like a buffalo-bull and jumped over The-wolf's body, and I saw the wounded man turn his eyes and try to move his body a little, as though he wished to sit up. But Takes-plenty did not even look at him. He jumped again and again over his body and legs, each time snorting like a buffalo-bull. "Bring me a robe with a tail on it," he said to us, who were watching.

He shook the buffalo's tail before the seeing eyes of The-wolf, snorting and jumping over his body till The-wolf reached out his hand in a weak effort to take hold of the tail. But Takes-plenty did not even look, or did not seem to. I felt like calling out, "Wait! wait!" because he did not see and was now even backing away from The-wolf, who reached farther and farther, at last sitting up.

I stepped out to help him, but Takes-plenty waved me away and kept backing, backing up, his eyes now looking into the dim ones of the wounded man that were growing brighter as he reached out again and again to take hold of the buffalo's tail that fluttered about before them, until he staggered to his feet without help.

They were walking slowly in a circle, when Takes-plenty, without looking our way or stopping the buffalo's tail that kept fluttering before the eyes of The-wolf, said "Open his shirt."

As I did so, I heard his breath whistling through the bullet hole in his breast. I stepped back, and Takes-plenty, standing a little way from him, told The-wolf to stretch himself. When he did, black blood dropped out of the hole to the snow. When red blood came my uncle stopped it with the flowers from his pouch.

The-wolf walked alone among us. "I am all right," he said, and our hearts began to sing.

MARKSMANSHIP OF A MEDICINE MAN

WOODEN LEG—CHEYENNE

Jules Seminole brought a keg of whisky to the camp. He got it at some white man trading post. He was a southern half-breed married to one of our Northern Cheyenne women and accounted as belonging to our tribe. One of our young men solicited him:

"Give me a drink of your whisky."

"No, but I'll bet a drink that I can beat you at shooting," Seminole proposed. "What have you to bet?"

The young man feared defeat. But he went canvassing here and there in an effort to find someone who would take up Seminole's challenge. One after another declined to contest. Finally, in jest rather than in earnest, he put the case before an old medicine man who was totally blind in one eye and partly blind in the other.

"I'll bet a good buffalo robe against the whole keg of whisky that I can beat you at shooting," the old man declared to Seminole.

Seminole evidently suspected some kind of trick. He hesitated, but the urgings of the gathered crowd carried him into acceptance of this counter proposition.

A tree was barked and a black circle target drawn upon this clean surface. Seminole shot first. He had a cartridge rifle. The bullet imbedded itself an inch or so below the black circle.

"Get me a pin," the old medicine man requested of his young helper.

The pin was brought. The aged Cheyenne placed it point forward upon his right palm. He held this palm upward in front of his eyes. His squint wrinkles deepened and his lips formed themselves into a pucker. A sudden puff of his breath caused the pin to vanish. Nobody knew what had become of it.

"Examine the target," the performer told them.

There it was, buried to its head just outside the circle. The people all wondered. The keg of whisky was conceded to its new owner.

"I'll bet a horse against the whisky that you can't do anything like that again," Seminole dared him.

"How," came instantly a responsive agreement.

The target was placed more distant, this at the request of Seminole and by assent of his competitor. Onlookers became involved in the betting. The medicine man found many backers of his mysterious powers. The half-breed adjusted his sights. He took an unusually long and careful and steady aim. "Bang!" His bullet struck within an inch of the circle's center. His betting supporters were gleeful, the opposition were in doubt. They awaited anxiously the next move of their champion.

"Bring me a claw of a redbird," he calmly ordered.

A dozen young men put themselves into his service. They wanted to help him in drinking the whisky. Within a minute he had the required object.

The redbird claw was placed upon the same upturned palm where had been the pin. "The target is too far," came a complaint. Then: "Yes, I can see it now." Puff! The claw was gone. Where? Right into the central black spot of the black circle target!

All comers had a drink of the whisky. A tin cup was brought and the old medicine man dipped in and passed out hot liquid mouthfuls to hundreds of Cheyennes.

WITCHCRAFT

CHIEF KAHKEWAQUONABY—OJIBWAY

Witches and wizards are persons supposed to possess the agency of familiar spirits, from whom they receive power to inflict diseases on their enemies, prevent the good luck of the hunter, and the success of the warrior. They are believed to fly invisibly at pleasure from place to place; to turn themselves into bears, wolves, foxes, owls, bats, and snakes. Such metamorphoses they pretend to accomplish by putting on the skins of these animals, at the same time crying and howling in imitation of the creature they wish to represent. Several of our people have informed me that they have seen and heard witches in the shape of these animals, especially the bear and the fox. They say that when a witch in the shape of a bear is being chased, all at once she will run round a tree or a hill, so as to be lost sight of for a time by her pursuers; and then, instead of seeing a bear, they behold an old woman walking quietly along, or digging up roots, and looking as innocent as a lamb. The fox witches are known by the flame of fire which proceeds out of their mouths every time they bark.

Many receive the name of witches without making any pretensions to the art, merely because they are deformed or ill-looking. Persons esteemed witches or wizards are generally eccentric characters, remarkably wicked, of a ragged appearance and forbidding countenance. The way in which they are made is either by direct communication with the familiar spirit during the days of their fasting, or by being instructed by those skilled in the art. The method they take to bewitch those who have offended them is this: —The necromancer in the first place provides himself with a little wooden image, representing an Indian with a bow and arrow. Setting this figure up at a short distance before him, he will name it after the person whom he wishes to injure; he then takes the bow and arrow and shoots at the image, and wherever the arrow strikes, at that instant, they say, the person is seized with violent pain in the same part.

The causes that urge them to take revenge by witchcraft often arise from quarrels, or from supposed injuries done to them, and not infrequently has it led to murder. A relative of the person thought to be bewitched will go secretly and put the necromancer to death. Many instances, which have come under my own observation, have arisen out of disappointments in marriage. If the witch or wizard is denied the object of his or her desire, then the poor creature in request is immediately threatened with some severe disease, and from fear of being bewitched they are often induced to give their consent to marry. In this way it is that many of the old noted conjurors obtain more than one wife. Frequently, when I have enquired the cause of a disease, the reply has been that it originated in offence given to some witch or wizard.

I have been informed that formerly, when any notorious necromancer was suspected of having bewitched any one, they were often condemned by the councils of the different tribes to execution; but this was always done with great caution, lest the conjuror should get the advantage over them, and thus bewitch the whole assembly.

I have sometimes been inclined to think that, if witchcraft still exists in the world, it is to be found among the aborigines of America. They seem to possess a power which, it would appear, may be fairly imputed to the agency of an evil spirit.

The belief in witches continued even after the Indians were exposed to white skepticism. The Cherokees, among the earliest to take the "white man's road," passed a law to prevent the killing of alleged witches. The Cherokee council first received testimonies on the power of witches to pass into the bodies of animals. Then, without denying the popular belief in witches, they ingeniously decreed that it should be lawful to kill the animal harboring the witch's spirit, but it should not be lawful to kill a witch in human form.

CANNIBALISM AMONG MEDICINE MEN

WILLIAM WARREN—OJIBWAY

The dispersion of the Ojibways from the island of their refuge [La Pointe, Lake Superior] was sudden and entire. The Evil Spirit had found a strong foothold amongst them, during the latter years of their residence on this island. Evil practices became in vogue. Horrid feasts on human flesh became a custom. It is said by my informants, that the medicine men of this period had come to a knowledge of the most subtle poisons, and they revenged the least affront with certain death. When the dead body of a victim had been interred, the murderer proceeded at night to the grave, disinterred it, and taking it to his lodge he made a feast of it, to the relatives, which was eaten during the darkness of midnight, and if any of the invited guests became aware of the nature of the feast, and refused to eat, he was sure to fall under the ill-will of the feaster, and become the next victim. It is said that if a young woman refused the addresses of one of these medicine men, she fell a victim to his poison, and her body being disinterred, her relatives were feasted on it by the horrid murderer.

Such a taste did they at last acquire for human flesh, that parents dared not refuse their children if demanded by the fearful medicine man for sacrifice. And numerous anecdotes are related of circumstances happening during this horrid period, which all tend to illustrate the above assertions, but which the writer has not deemed proper to introduce, on account of the bloody and unnatural scenes which they depict. The Ojibways, at this period, fell entirely under the power of their Satanic medicine men, and priesthood, who even for some time caused themselves to be believed invulnerable to death. This, however, was finally tested one night, by a parent whose beloved and only child had just fallen a victim to the insatiable longing for human flesh, of one of these poisoners. After interring his child, he returned at night with his bow and arrow and watched near the grave. At midnight he saw what appeared to be the form of a black bear, approach and commence digging into the grave. It was also believed that these medicine men possessed the power of transforming themselves into the shapes of animals.

But the determined father, overcoming his fear, launched his barbed arrow into the body of the bear, and without waiting to see the consequence of his shot, he fled to his wigwam. The next morning, the body of one of the most malignant and fearful poisoners was found clothed in a bearskin, weltering in his blood, on the grave of the old man's child, whom he had made a victim.

Whether or not these evil practices were at this particular period caused by dire necessity, either through a failure of their crops, or by being entirely hemmed in by their enemies, as to be prevented from hunting on the main shore, the writer is not enabled to state, though he should be but too happy to give this as a palliating excuse for the horrid custom he is obliged to relate.

It is further stated that these evil practices were carried on to such an extent, that the Che-bi-ug, or "souls of the victims," were at last heard nightly traversing the village, weeping and wailing. On this the inhabitants became panic stricken, and the consequence was that a general and complete desertion of the island of their refuge took place, which left their town and fields entirely desolate, and from that time, they have become overgrown with trees and bushes.

THE PEYOTE CULT

JOHN RAVE—WINNEBAGO

Peyote is the dried fruit of a small cactus that grows in the Southwest and in northern Mexico. A mild narcotic, it stimulates the optic nerve and creates wonderful visions in color. Indians claim that the visions not only improve their morals and bring them into the presence of God, but even cure diseases. Although not officially recognized as a religion, peyote eating is actually a backdoor entrance into Christianity and has converted many Indians who were indifferent to the efforts of missionaries.

During 1893-94 I was in Oklahoma with peyote eaters.

In the middle of the night we were to eat peyote. We ate it and I also did. It was the middle of the night when I got frightened, for a live thing seemed to have entered me. "Why did I do it?" I thought to myself. "I should not have done it, for right at the beginning I have harmed myself. Indeed I should not have done it. I am sure it will injure me. The best thing will be for me to vomit it up. Well, now, I will try it." After a few attempts I gave up. I thought to myself, "Well, now you have done it. You have been going around trying everything and now you have done something that has harmed you. What is it? It seems to be alive and moving around in my stomach. If only some of my own people were here! That would have been better. Now no one will know what has happened to me. I have killed myself."

Just then the object was about to come out. It seemed almost out and I put out my hand to feel it, but then it went back again. "O, my, I should never have done it from the beginning. Never again will I do it. I am surely going to die."

As we continued it became day and we laughed. Before that I had been unable to laugh.

The following night we were to eat peyote again. I thought to myself, "Last night it almost harmed me." "Well, let us do it again," they said. "All right, I'll do it." So there we ate seven peyote apiece.

Suddenly I saw a big snake. I was very much frightened. Then another one came crawling over me. "My God! where are these coming from?" There at my back there seemed to be something. So I looked around and I saw a snake about to swallow me entirely. It had legs and arms and a long tail. The end of this tail was like a spear. "O, my God! I am surely going to die now," I thought. Then I looked again in another direction and I saw a man with horns and long claws and with a spear in his hand. He jumped for me and I threw myself on the ground. He missed me. Then I looked back and this time he started back, but it seemed to me that he was directing his spear at me. Again I threw myself on the ground and he missed me. There seemed to be no possible escape for me. Then suddenly it occurred to me, "Perhaps it is this peyote that is doing this thing to me? Help me, O medicine, help me! It is you who are doing this and you are holy! It is not these frightful visions that are causing this. I should have known that you were doing it. Help me!" Then my suffering stopped. "As long as the earth shall last, that long will I make use of you, O medicine!"

This lasted a night and a day. For a whole night I had not slept at all.

Then we breakfasted. Then I said, when we were through, "Let us eat peyote again to-night." That evening I ate eight peyote.

In the middle of the night I saw God. To God living up above, our Father, I prayed. "Have mercy upon me! Give me knowledge that I may not say and do evil things. To you, O God, I am trying to pray. Do thou, O Son of God, help me, too. This religion, let me know. Help me, O medicine, grandfather, help me! Let me know this religion!" Thus I spoke and sat very quiet. And then I beheld the morning star and it was good to look upon. The light was good to look upon. I had been frightened during the night but now I was happy. Now as the light appeared, it seemed to me that nothing would be invisible to me. I seemed to see everything clearly.

Many years ago I had been sick and it looked as if this illness were going to kill me. I tried all the Indian doctors and then I tried all of the white man's medicines, but they were of no avail. "I am doomed. I wonder whether I will be alive next year." Such were the thoughts that came to me. As soon as I ate the peyote, however, I got over my sickness.

Black Water-spirit at about that time was having a hemorrhage and I wanted him to eat the peyote. "Well, I am not going to live anyhow," he said. "Well, eat this medicine soon then and you will get cured." Consumptives never were cured before this and now for the first time one was cured. Black Water-spirit is living today and is very well.

There was a man named Walking-Priest and he was very fond of whisky; he chewed and he smoked and he gambled. He was very fond of women. He did everything that was bad. Then I gave him some of the peyote and he ate it and he gave up all the bad things he was doing. He had had a very dangerous disease and had even had murder in his heart. But today he is living a good life. That is his desire.

Whoever has any bad thoughts, if he will eat this peyote he will abandon all his bad habits. It is a cure for everything bad.

BURIAL CUSTOMS

CHIEF KAHKEWAQUONABY—OJIBWAY

As soon as an Indian dies his friends proceed to lay him out *on the ground*, putting his best clothes on him, and wrapping his body in skins or blankets. Formerly, coffins were not known, or not used among them. After digging about three feet deep, generally in the course of twelve hours they inter him, with his head towards the west. They then place by the side of the corpse all his former hunting and war implements; such as his bow and arrow, tomahawk, gun, pipe and tobacco, knife, pouch, flint and steel, medicine-bag, kettle, trinkets, and other articles which he carried with him when going on a long journey. The grave is then covered, and on the top of it poles or sticks are placed lengthways, to the height of about two feet, over which birch bark or mats form a covering to secure the body from the rain. The relations or friends of the deceased then sit on the ground in a circle round the head of the grave, when the usual offering to the dead—consisting of meat, soup, or the fire-waters—is made. This is handed to the people present in bowls, a certain quantity being kept back for a burnt offering. While this is preparing at the head of the grave, the old man, or speaker for the occasion, makes a prayer to the soul of the departed, enumerating his good qualities, imploring the blessing of the dead that his Spirit may intercede for them, that they may have plenty of game; he also exhorts his spirit to depart quietly from them. They believe that the soul partakes of a portion of the feast, and especially that which is consumed by fire. If the deceased was a husband, it is often the custom for the widow, after the burial is over, to spring or leap over the grave, and then run zig-zag behind the trees, as if she were fleeing from some one. This is called running away from the spirit of her husband, that it may not haunt her. In the evening of the day on which the burial has taken place, when it begins to grow dark, the men fire off their guns through the hole left at the top of the wigwam. As soon as this firing ceases, the old women commence knocking and making such a rattling at the door as would frighten away any spirit that would dare to hover near. The next ceremony is, to cut into narrow strips, like ribbon, thin birch bark. These they fold into shapes, and hang round inside the wigwam, so that the least puff of wind will move them. With such scarecrows as these, what spirit would venture to disturb their slumbers? Lest this should not prove effectual, they will also frequently take a deer's tail, and after burning or singeing off all the hair, will rub the necks or faces of the children before they lie down to sleep, thinking that the offensive smell will be another preventive to the spirit's entrance. I well remember when I used to be daubed over with this disagreeable fumigation, and had great faith in it all.

I was present at the burial of an old pagan chief by the name of Odahmekoo, of Muncey Town. We had a coffin made for him, which was presented to his relatives; but before they placed the body in it, they bored several holes at the head, in order, as they supposed, to enable the soul to go in and out at pleasure.

During the winter season, when the ground is frozen as hard as a rock, two or three feet deep; finding it almost impossible to penetrate through the frost, having no suitable tools, they are obliged to wind up the corpse in skins and the bark of trees, and then hang it in the fork of a large tree, high enough to be beyond the reach of wolves, foxes, and dogs, that would soon devour it. Thus the body hangs till decomposition takes place, and the bones, falling to the ground, are afterwards gathered up and buried.

THE HAPPY HUNTING GROUNDS

WILLIAM WARREN—OJIBWAY

When an Ojibway dies, his body is placed in a grave, generally in a sitting posture, facing the west. With the body are buried all the articles needed in life for a journey. If a man, his gun, blanket, kettle, fire steel, flint and moccasins; if a woman, her moccasins, axe, portage collar, blanket and kettle. The soul is supposed to start immediately after the death of the body, on a deep beaten path, which leads westward; the first object he comes to, in following this path, is the great Oda-e-min (Heart berry), or strawberry, which stands on the roadside like a huge rock, and from which he takes a handful and eats on his way. He travels on till he reaches a deep, rapid stream of water, over which lies the much dreaded Ko-go-gaup-o-gun or rolling and sinking bridge; once safely over this as the traveller looks back it assumes the shape of a huge serpent swimming, twisting and untwisting its folds across the stream.

After camping out four nights, and travelling each day through a prairie country, the soul arrives in the land of spirits, where he finds his relatives accumulated since mankind was first created; all is rejoicing, singing and dancing; they live in a beautiful country interspersed with clear lakes and streams, forests and prairies, and abounding in fruit and game to repletion—in a word, abounding in all that the red man most covets in this life, and which conduces most to his happiness. It is that kind of paradise which he only by his manner of life on this earth, is fitted to enjoy.

V: ON THE WARPATH

The Indian warrior had no equal as a fighter. He was physically alert, hard, and powerful. With a knowledge of frontier fighting he combined courage and boldness tempered by animal caution.

The warrior of the old frontier—the Iroquois, Ojibway, Shawnee, Wyandott—was at his best in forest fighting. Appearing from nowhere, he would strike suddenly at his enemy and then dissolve into the forest leaving no trail. The Plains Indian—the Sioux, Cheyenne, Crow, Blackfoot—was a master of horseback fighting. At a full gallop, he could swing down and shoot from under his horse's neck without exposing himself to the enemy's fire.

Only in tactics was the Indian deficient, for he seldom planned a campaign in advance or fought in an organized body. After the first shot of battle was fired the chiefs had little authority, and the outcome depended largely upon individual bravery and skill.

Unique among the American Indians was the custom of the death song, by which the warrior expressed his contempt for death. Namebines, an Ojibway chief who had been fatally wounded in a skirmish with the Sioux, sang this song:

The odor of death,
I discern the odor of death
In front of my body.

As he finished singing he turned to his surviving comrades and said: "When you reach home sing this song for the women to dance by and tell them how I died."

V: ON THE WARPATH

BOYHOOD PREPARATION FOR THE WARPATH

OHIYESA—SIOUX

All boys were expected to endure hardship without complaint. In savage warfare, a young man must, of course, be an athlete and used to undergoing all sorts of privations. He must be able to go without food and water for two or three days without displaying any weakness, or to run for a day and a night without any rest. He must be able to traverse a pathless and wild country without losing his way either in the day or night time. He cannot refuse to do any of these things if he aspires to be a warrior.

Sometimes my uncle would waken me very early in the morning and challenge me to fast with him all day. I had to accept the challenge. We blackened our faces with charcoal, so that every boy in the village would know that I was fasting for the day. Then the little tempters would make my life a misery until the merciful sun hid behind the western hills.

I can scarcely recall the time when my stern teacher began to give sudden war-whoops over my head in the morning while I was sound asleep. He expected me to leap up with perfect presence of mind, always ready to grasp a weapon of some sort and to give a shrill whoop in reply. If I was sleepy or startled and hardly knew what I was about, he would ridicule me and say that I need never expect to sell my scalp dear. Often he would vary these tactics by shooting off his gun just outside of the lodge while I was yet asleep, at the same time giving blood-curdling yells. After a time I became used to this.

When Indians went upon the war-path, it was their custom to try the new warriors thoroughly before coming to an engagement. For instance, when they were near a hostile camp, they would select the novices to go after the water and make them do all sorts of things to prove their courage. In accordance with this idea, my uncle used to send me off after water when we camped after dark in a strange place. Perhaps the country was full of wild beasts, and, for aught I knew, there might be scouts from hostile bands of Indians lurking in that very neighborhood.

Yet I never objected, for that would show cowardice. I picked my way through the woods, dipped my pail in the water and hurried back, always careful to make as little noise as a cat. Being only a boy, my heart would leap at every crackling of a dry twig or distant hooting of an owl, until, at last, I reached our teepee. Then my uncle would perhaps say: "Ah, you are a thorough warrior," empty out the precious contents of the pail, and order me to go a second time.

Imagine how I felt! But I wished to be a brave man. Silently I would take the pail and endeavor to retrace my footsteps in the dark.

COUNTING COUP ON A WOUNDED BUFFALO

CHIEF PLENTY-COUPS—CROW

Among the plains tribes, war was a game in which the score was kept by counting coup. Many Indians carried willow wands decorated with feathers and known as "coup sticks." The warrior who touched a living enemy with his hand or coup stick received the highest coup award. Honors of lesser value were awarded for killing or scalping an enemy, or for stealing a horse. The warrior who counted coup was allowed to add a special decoration to his war feathers or to paint his face so that his fellow tribesmen could see his war record at a glance.

Plenty-coups, the famous Crow chief, counted his first coup against a wounded buffalo when he was only nine; but after he reached manhood this deed was dropped from his list of honors because it was not performed against a human enemy.

One day when the chokecherries were black and the plums red on the trees, my grandfather rode through the village, calling twenty of us older boys by name. The buffalo-runners had been out since daybreak, and we guessed what was before us. "Get on your horses and follow me," said my grandfather, riding out on the plains.

We rode fast. Nothing was in sight until Grandfather led us over a hill. There we saw a circle of horsemen about one hundred yards across, and in its center a huge buffalo bull. We knew he had been wounded and tormented until he was very dangerous, and when we saw him there defying the men on horseback we began to dread the ordeal that was at hand.

The circle parted as we rode through it, and the bull, angered by the stir we made, charged and sent us flying. The men were laughing at us when we returned, and this made me feel very small. They had again surrounded the bull, and I now saw an arrow sticking deep in his side. Only its feathers were sticking out of a wound that dripped blood on the ground.

"Get down from your horses, young men," said my grandfather. "A cool head, with quick feet, may strike this bull on the root of his tail with a bow. Be lively, and take care of yourselves. The young man who strikes, and is himself not hurt, may count coup."

I was first off my horse. Watching the bull, I slipped out of shirt and leggings, letting them fall where I stood. Naked, with only my bow in my right hand, I stepped away from my clothes, feeling that I might never see them again. I was not quite nine years old.

The bull saw me, a human being afoot! He seemed to know that now he might kill, and he began to paw the ground and bellow as I walked carefully toward him.

Suddenly he stopped pawing, and his voice was still. He came to meet me, his eyes green with anger and pain. I saw blood dropping from his side, not red blood now, but mixed with yellow.

I stopped walking and stood still. This seemed to puzzle the bull, and he too stopped in his tracks. We looked at each other, the sun hot on my naked back. Heat from the plains danced on the bull's horns and head; his sides were panting, and his mouth was bloody.

I knew that the men were watching me. I could feel their eyes on my back. I must go on. One step, two steps. The grass was soft and thick under my feet. Three steps. "I am a Crow. I have the heart of a grizzly bear," I said to myself. Three more steps. And then he charged!

A cheer went up out of a cloud of dust. I had struck the bull on the root of his tail! But I was in even greater danger than before.

Two other boys were after the bull now, but in spite of them he turned and came at me. To run was foolish. I stood still, waiting. The bull stopped very near me and bellowed, blowing bloody froth from his nose. The other boys, seeing my danger, did not move. The bull was not more than four bows' lengths from me, and I could feel my heart beating like a war-drum.

I stepped to my right. Instantly he charged—but I had dodged back to my left, across his way, and I struck him when he passed. This time I ran among the horsemen, with a lump of bloody froth on my breast. I had had enough.

MAKING A WAR CLUB AND WAR WHISTLE

YELLOW WOLF—NEZ PERCE

The regular war club is generally short handled, about five or six inches aside from the stone at its end. It must be only five or six inches in length for this reason: because in the battles and fights with another tribe, the warriors do not meet face to face and strike at each other. They grab and scuffle. This *kopluts* [war club] hangs on the wrist with a buckskin thong. When the enemy grabs hold of you to throw you down and kill you, if you have a long-handled club to your wrist, he can easily seize it and hold on to it. But if a short handle, you have it well covered with your own hand. You can then club your enemy and you are privileged to break his arm.

I, Yellow Wolf, raised among warriors, made it a study how I should go to war against different tribes and fight from horseback. How I should have the enemy to meet and match when mounted. I would have to strike across from horse to horse, fighting for my life. Trying for the death of my enemy. From all this, I judged I would need a long handle on this club, which you now see as I fashioned it.

At the time I made this *kopluts,* preparing for war, I put this war paint on it which has been there ever since. Not that I did this of myself. It was the belief that I have within me, obtained from the fowls that fly, from the creatures that creep or leap through the wilds, that gave me a Power to be strong in battle, in war, where life is against life. This Power told me to make such a weapon for protecting myself.

It was in this way, by the instructions of this Spirit, that this *kopluts* was made and painted.

I was small, quite young, when I fashioned this *kopluts*. I did not select the stone. Searching around to select, I was given instructions

—directions about the rock to pick from—when and how to make it. This stone I rounded myself. You can select a rock from the river and try breaking this one: *Tock! tock! tock!* [Striking imaginary blows.] The other rock will break. This one is a selected stone for war business.

I was instructed to cover the *kopluts* with elk rawhide, then wrap the handle with the fur of the otter.

I am Heinmot Hihhih [White Thunder, Yellow Wolf's other name]. That thunder, when it rolls and strikes anything, it kills. That thunder gave me its Power to be with this *kopluts,* striking as the lightning strikes. This Spirit guided me in making this weapon.

This war whistle which helped me in dangerous places is made from the wingbone of the crane. Spirits guided me in its making. Guided me from what bird the bone must be taken. It is not to be used in sport and amusement. For war only, I always sounded it in battle. The soldiers then could not hit me. Only in battle or other dangerous places did I sound this whistle. Not at any other time was it to be sounded.

I wore it by the buckskin thong still fast to it. This loop was about my neck and left shoulder. The flute hung under my left arm. There it was away from handling the rifle. These two small eagle-down feathers at the end of the thongs were plucked from over the bird's heart. Their fluttering up in the wind was good. Always moving, you could not see that which does it. There was good prayer in the feather movements.

SCOUTING OUT THE ENEMY

CHIEF STANDING BEAR—SIOUX

One of the most important and indispensable members of Lakota society, and so considered by that society, was one not so often seen or so much talked about—the scout. He was the man who preferred, usually, to work alone, either by night or day, and whose outstanding quality was scrupulous honesty. He ran terrible risks, was not a fighting man, yet knew how to fight when he had to, and was withal the most relied-upon man in the tribe. In him was reposed the utter dependence and faith of a people for their livelihood-food and safety from danger. His training was rigorous, his word was inviolable, and in calling he was bound to serve his tribe. The dangers to which he was exposed demanded of him the keenest development and alertness of senses, particularly observation.

Every natural object was watched for any significance attached to its motion or appearance. No movement was too slight for the scout to ignore, and no sound too meaningless to go unheeded. The soaring maneuvers of buzzard or eagle were to be looked into; the calls of the sand or prairie cranes were announcers of the always important weather changes; a croaking frog proclaimed a tiny marsh or hidden spring, and at once more caution intuitively arose; while a distant smoke column might reveal the advance of an enemy party.

Even the black, horned ground-beetle commonly called tumblebug, once common on the plain, the scout stopped and attentively watched, providing the scout were looking for buffalo. The two horns on the top of the insect's head were movable in all directions, but were invariably pointed and held toward the buffalo herd, probably attracted in that direction by stamping hoofs too distant for even sensitive human ears to detect. Sometimes we called these beetles ballplayers for their habit of rolling up balls, round and perfect as marbles, out of manure of horse or buffalo. A beetle, sometimes two of them, rolled these balls about here and there as if enjoying a game.

It was this ability to discern and observe small things that made the scout's work valuable. Minute details in appearance of objects, and changes in actions and manners of animals were noted; also the condition of man or animal trails he followed—bent twigs, trampled grass, sky and landmarks—things that would fade from a mind equipped with compass and stakes. Not wishing to leave a trail of his own to betray his travels, he built no monuments, however small; but his keen eye registered all, placing them in his memory, there to stay until needed, whether it be a week, a month, or a year.

All the while the scout traveled, he realized that while he watched he was being just as intently watched. Numerous eyes of the animal world were upon him, and human eyes, too. Often he turned quickly to scan the landscape back of him, and if he had reason to suspect the close presence of an enemy scout, he lay in wait for a long while until the enemy watcher was located.

PREPARATION FOR BATTLE

WOODEN LEG—CHEYENNE

All of the best clothing was taken along with him when any warrior set out upon a search for conflict. The articles were put into a special bag—ordinarily a beautifully beaded buckskin pouch, but perhaps a rawhide one—and this was slung at one side of his horse. The bag also contained extra moccasins—beaded moccasins—warbonnet, paints, a mirror, special medicine objects, or anything else of this nature. If a battle seemed about to occur, the warrior's first important preparatory act was to jerk off all his ordinary clothing. He then hurriedly got out his fine garments. If he had time to do so he re-braided his hair, painted his face in his own peculiar way, did everything needful to prepare himself for presenting his most splendid personal appearance. That is, he got himself ready to die.

The idea of full dress in preparation for a battle comes not from a belief that it will add to the fighting ability. The preparation is for death, in case that should be the result of the conflict. Every Indian wants to look his best when he goes to meet the Great Spirit, so the dressing up is done whether the imminent danger is an oncoming battle or a sickness or injury at times of peace. Some Indian tribes did not pay full attention to this matter, some of them seeming not to care whether they took life risks while naked or while only partly clad or shabbily clad. But the Cheyennes and the Sioux were careful in following out the procedure. When any of them got into a fight not expected, with no opportunity to dress properly, they usually ran away and avoided close contact and its consequent risks. Enemy people not understanding their ways might suppose them to be cowards because of such flight. In fact, these same apparent cowards might be the bravest of the brave when they have on their good clothing and feel that they may present a respectable appearance if called from this life to meet the Great Spirit.

The naked fighters, among the Cheyennes and Sioux, were such warriors as specially fortified themselves by prayer and other devotional exercises. They had special instruction from medicine men. Their naked bodies were painted in peculiar ways, each according to the direction of his favorite spiritual guide, and each had his own medicine charms given to him by this guide. A warrior thus made ready for battle was supposed to be proof against the weapons of the enemy. He placed himself in the forefront of the attack or the defense. His thought was: "I am so protected by my medicine that I do not need to dress for death. No bullet nor arrow can harm me now." On the other hand, a warrior not made ready by special religious exercise and appliances had in his heart the thought: "A bullet or an arrow may hit me and kill me. I must dress myself so as to please the Great Spirit if I should go now to Him."

Warbonnets were not worn by all warriors. In fact, there were only a few such distinguished men in each warrior society of our tribe. It was expected that one should be a student of the fighting art for several years, or else that he be an unusually apt learner, before he should put on the crown of eagle feathers. He then did so upon his own initiative, or perhaps because of the commendatory urgings of his seniors. The act meant a profession of fully acquired ability in warfare, a claim of special accomplishment in using cunning and common sense and cool calculation coupled with the bravery attributed to all warriors. The wearer was supposed never to ask mercy in battle. If some immature young man pretended to such high standing before it seemed to his companions that he ought to do so, he was twitted and shamed into awaiting his proper time. I first put on my warbonnet when I was thirty-three years old, fourteen years after I had quit the roaming life. After a man had been accepted as a warbonnet man he remained so throughout his lifetime. War chiefs and tribal chiefs ordinarily were warbonnet men, but this was not a requirement for these positions. Pure modesty might keep the bravest and most capable fighter from making the claim. Also, an admittedly worthy wearer of the warbonnet might not be chosen for or might refuse all official positions. The feathered headpiece, then, was not a sign of public office. It was a token of individual and personal feeling as to his own fighting capabilities.

The warbonnet was made by the man who was to wear it. His wife, mother or sister made only the beaded band for the forehead. The man made also whatever spirit charm objects he might use, or he got a medicine man to make them for him. The women made all of the war shirts, leggings, moccasins and such clothing for the men. They also made all of the common clothing for the men, for themselves, and for all members of the household. The men made their own pipes, weapons, lariat ropes and such other articles as were used by men only.

Our hand mirrors were not used entirely for dressing and painting. We made use of them for signaling. Two persons who understood each other could exchange thoughts in this way over long distances, and even when they could not see each other. Some kinds of such signals were understood by all of our people. The little glass was often useful in approaching a camp when the traveler was in doubt whether it was an assemblage of his own people or of an enemy or unknown people. In such cases, flashes of inquiry and flashes of response, or lack of responses, settled the doubt.

BATTLE TACTICS

CHIEF KAHKEWAQUONABY—OJIBWAY

In war excursions the war chiefs take the lead, and act as captains over their respective warriors. These chiefs direct the order of march and mode of attack, and are men who have distinguished themselves for their bravery, and consequently obtain the confidence of their tribe. The civil chiefs, who in general inherit their chieftainship by descent, are not expected to go to the field of action. They seldom, however, neglect a good opportunity of displaying their wisdom, skill, and bravery, and often accompany their people and engage in the conflict. The more scalps they take, the more they are revered and consulted by their tribe. Their mode of action is entirely different from that of civilized nations. They have no idea of meeting the enemy upon an open plain face to face, to be shot at like dogs, as they say. Their aim is to surprise the enemy by darting upon them in an unexpected moment, or in the dead of night. They always take care, in the first place, to ascertain the position of the enemy. When they find them unprepared or asleep, they creep up slowly and stealthily, like panthers in pursuit of their prey; when sufficiently near, they simultaneously raise the war whoop, and before the enemy awake or have time to defend themselves, the tomahawk is rattling over their heads.

When a village, a wigwam, or a party is thus surprised, there is seldom any mercy shown either to age or sex; all are doomed to feel the weight of the tomahawk and the deep incision of the bloody scalping-knife. When scalping any one, they take hold of the hair of the head, making an incision with the knife round the head to the skull, and then jerk off the scalp. This must be a very painful operation when performed on a living person, yet some have survived. I have seen an Indian woman at Lake Huron, who had been both tomahawked and scalped by the Sioux. She had recovered from her wound when I saw her, but was obliged to wear a wig of cloth. The scalps are stretched on round hoops and carefully dried. They are then painted, and decorated with wampum beads and ribbons.

A HORSE STEALING RAID

CHIEF PLENTY-COUPS—CROW

Stealing horses was an honored occupation among the Plains Indians. Little credit was given to the brave who merely took the horse of a slain opponent; but stealing a mount which was tethered to an enemy tepee required great courage and was attempted only by the boldest warriors. Enemy camps were well guarded by dogs and sentinels, and no mercy was shown to horse thieves.

On Cloud Peak we met the other parties and soon picked up the enemy's trails, one coming in from the Black Hills, and one from the west. The *sign* [trail] was fresh and heavy, as though many lodges were somewhere ahead of us. Near sundown our Wolves [scouts] brought us word that there was a large village on Goose Creek.

And what a village it was! It reached from Goose Creek to Tongue River. Five drums were going at once, and the big flat was covered with horses. I could count more lodges than I had ever seen before at one time. We should stand no chance against such a village, but we could steal some horses. I looked at the sky. The moon was already there waiting for night, and there would be little darkness.

Our leaders were holding a council. By and by they stood up, Bell-rock beckoning me, and Bear-in-the-water calling Covers-his-face. We both went to them to get our orders. We, with several others selected by Half-yellow-face and Fire-wind, were to go into the village and cut as many horses as we could while the rest of the

INDIAN DEERSKIN DRESS, SASH, AND LEGGINGS
George Catlin
ca. 1830–40

From Catlin Sketchbook
Courtesy of Gilcrease Institute

party stood ready to cover our retreat when we should be discovered. My heart sang with pride.

Covers-his-face and I stole together to the edge of the village and waited for darkness. But it did not come. Instead, the moon grew brighter and brighter. But as though to reassure us the five drums kept beating, telling us the enemy was dancing, and that he was too busy with his pleasure to watch his horses. Nights in summer are very short, the light would come soon, and we dared not wait too long. "Let us go in," I whispered finally, and we tied our horses. I hated to leave mine. He was the best I had ever owned, but of course I could not take him with me.

Before I knew it Covers-his-face had disappeared. I was alone among the enemy lodges, and the nearest was a Striped-feathered-arrow [Cheyenne]! No wonder the village was so large. The Sioux were not alone. They had company, and this might make them stupid —sure that no enemy would dare attack them. So many lodges made me feel lonely, and I turned my course to where they were not so close together. My eyes could not look behind, ahead, and on both sides at once. I went away from the thickly pitched lodges until I reached a very tall one that stood a little apart. A fine bay horse was tied there. Immediately I set my heart on owning him. I saw I should have to be careful because the lodge-skin was raised from the ground. And next I made out that the lodge was an Arapahoe! The three worst enemies our people had were combined against us, with the intention, I believed, of making quick war on us. ["Arapahoe" in the Crow tongue means "Tattooed marks, plenty of."]

But my eyes were on the bay horse most of the time now. He was eating grass before the Arapahoe lodge, and the rope around his neck reached into it. Somebody loved him and slept with his hand on the rope. I could not blame him. I thought the bay might be as good as the Deer, my own good war-horse tied at the edge of the village. No Sioux owned a better horse than he. It occurred to me more than once that they might steal him while I was stealing one of their horses.

I crept a little closer. The lodge-skin was lifted in front, the rope going into the blackness inside. I tried to see under the lodge-skin, but the moonlight made a big, bright ring around it that stopped at the lodge-poles as though afraid to go farther. I could see nothing inside and there were no sounds. I would chance it! I was flat on the ground by the bay horse, my knife lifted to cut the rope, when somebody stirred, moved a bit inside the lodge. My hand with the knife came down to my side. The Arapahoe was awake and watching his horse!

The shadow of the bay was on me, and I dared not move. I heard the five drums, one beating in the middle of the village and two at either end, far off. I must not stay there too long. Even if the Arapahoe did not see me, the other Crows might be discovered, and then I should be caught and killed.

I crept out of the bay's shadow like a wolf until I had got his form between me and the eyes I felt sure were watching from the blackness of the Arapahoe lodge. Then I went swiftly until I came to another horse. He was a cream with white mane and tail, a good horse, but not so good as the bay. He was tied to a Sioux lodge that was dark and still. His owner was dancing, and while he enjoyed himself I cut his horse's rope. But I wanted the bay. I could not go away without him. I would have another try anyway.

A cream-colored horse is difficult to see in the night, especially in the moonlight. I would make him help me steal the bay. Leading him, and yet crowding against his body to keep myself hidden from the sharp eyes in the Arapahoe lodge, I managed to reach the bay again, expecting to feel an arrow in my side or see the flash of a gun out of the black hole beneath the lifted lodge-skin. The horses, wondering what was going on, touched their noses together, their warm bodies pressing against my naked sides, while I stared into the black hole. Nothing stirred there. Perhaps the man had gone to sleep. I would find out.

Instead of cutting the bay's rope I tied my own rope around his neck. Dropping the coil at his feet, I kept hold of the other end and slipped away, leading the cream till my rope was stretched. Then the cream and I stood still while I began slowly to pull on my rope. The bay, thinking somebody wanted him, began to come toward me, and as he came I kept coiling my rope, until he stopped short. He had reached the very end of the Arapahoe's rope, you see, and could come no farther. I was very careful now to look and listen. If the Arapahoe pulled in his rope, taking his bay back with it, I would let him have my rope that was tied to his horse's neck and go away from there with the cream. But he did not pull. The bay horse, wondering what somebody was trying to do with him, stood still with two ropes around his neck. The Arapahoe who owned him was asleep!

I led the cream back to the bay and cut the other fellow's rope. I knew it was time I was away from there now, so I hurried with my two horses to the edge of the village where I had left the Deer. But before I was halfway a shot cracked, then another. I sprang upon the bay and, leading the cream, lashed them into a run, wondering what had become of Covers-his-face.

The first Crow I met was Bell-rock. He was leading the Deer. When I raced up to him he tossed me the rope. "Keep him," I called. "Somebody will need him." The big village was aroused. Guns were cracking. There was no time now to stop and change horses, and I tossed the rope of the Deer back to Bell-rock. But he did not catch it. The Deer was left behind; my wonderful war-horse was mine no longer. The Sioux that got him was a lucky man.

I thought that Covers-his-face had been discovered and had started the fight, but instead, those who stampeded the loose horses just outside the village brought on the fighting. I saw that we had a large number of horses, but did not wait to talk to anybody and raced away for the place where we had left our clothes with two men to watch them. It was on the right of Tongue River, just at the canyon. We called it The-place-where-the-cranes-rest. The bay horse was fast, and I reached the place first. "Get ready!" I cried, springing from the bay and getting into my leggings and shirt, "our party is coming."

I could hear the pounding hoofs, even when my shirt was over my head. Before my clothes were decently on me I had seen the pointers [men in the lead to guide the running horses] and close behind them many frightened horses. The enemy was after them too. Guns flashed as our men turned on their horses to shoot back in the gray light of breaking day. There were four Crows in the lead, and they were riding like the wind toward a steep-cut bank, a regular canyon! Did they not know it was there? It seemed to jump up before my eyes and to run to meet my friends. What would they do?

Not knowing yet how I could help them I dashed for the river. I dared not call out or wave my arms to warn them, for fear I might turn the whole band and cause a stampede that would lose what we had gained. I stopped still, my breath nearly choking me, when the first horse went over the brink. They all went over—horses, riders, like a swirl of dry leaves in a gale of wind. And before I could take ten steps they were coming out—alive! I could not believe my eyes! Only one man was hurt. His face was smashed and his horse killed under him. I was happy again.

We soon reached the timber where we had the best of it and drove the enemy back easily. Three days later we rode into our village singing of victory, and our chiefs, Sits-in-the-middle-of-the-land and Iron-bull, came out to meet us, singing Praise Songs. My heart rejoiced when I heard them speak my own name. The village was on Arrow Creek, near the Gap, and was getting ready to move. But Iron-bull stopped all preparation until he could give us hot coffee to drink. It was the first I had ever tasted, and I shall never forget it, or how happy I felt because I had counted my first coup.

This is all of the story; but I left out something I ought to tell you. When we were in the timber where we drove back the enemy, Covers-his-face found that the animal he had stolen in the village was a mare. He felt disgusted and declared he would go back and steal a horse. We tried to talk him out of his plan, but he was determined. "I will wait here for you," said Bear-in-the-water, who had given his horse to the man whose face had been smashed, and so was himself afoot.

"All right," said Bear-rears-up, "if Bear-in-the-water waits here I will wait with him." So we left them to do as they pleased and for ten days heard nothing more of them. We had begun to believe they had been killed, when one day the three came in, each riding a good horse that Covers-his-face had stolen from the Sioux. He told us he had found the lodge of a young man who was so jealous of his wife that he camped far from the nearest lodges of his friends. He had three very good horses tied to his tepee, just one apiece for Covers-his-face and his two friends waiting in the timber. This is what a man gets for being so jealous of a woman that he cannot be sociable with other men.

BURNING AT THE STAKE

WILLIAM WARREN—OJIBWAY

Historians have often stressed the cruelty of the Indians in torturing prisoners; but, compared with their contemporaries in Europe, the Indians were amateurs in the art of torture. The Tuscarora chief Elias Johnson wrote: "It is said the Indian inflicted unspeakable torture upon his enemy taken in battle. But from what we know of them, it is not to be inferred that Indian Chiefs were ever guilty of filling dungeons with innocent victims, or slaughtering hundreds and thousands of their own people, whose only sin was a quiet dissent from some religious dogma. Towards their enemies they were often relentless. They slew them in battle, plotted against them secretly, and in a few instances comparatively, subjected individuals to torture, burned them at the stake, and, perhaps, flayed them alive. At the very time that the Indians were using the tomahawk and scalping knife to avenge their wrongs, peaceful citizens in every country of Europe were incarcerated for no crime whatever, and such refinement of torture invented and practiced, as never entered in the heart of the fiercest Indian warrior that roamed the wilderness."

The origin of burning at the stake is not known. In this selection, William Warren tells the traditional story of how the custom began among the Ojibways.

A noted warrior of the Ojibways was once taken prisoner by his own nephew, who was a young warrior of the Foxes, son of his own sister, who had been captured when young, adopted and married in this tribe. This young man, to show to the Foxes his utter contempt of any ties of blood existing between him and his Ojibway uncle, planted two stakes strongly in the ground, and taking his uncle by the arm, he remarked to him that he "wished to warm him before a good fire." He then deliberately tied his arms and legs to the two stakes, as wide apart as they could be stretched, and the unnatural nephew built a huge fire in front of his uncle. When he had burnt his naked body to a blister on this side, he turned him with his back toward the fire, and when this had also been cruelly burned, he untied him, and turning him loose, he bade him to "return home and tell the Ojibways how the Foxes treated their uncles."

The uncle recovered from his fire wounds, and in a subsequent war excursion, he succeeded in capturing his cruel nephew. He took him to the village of the Ojibways, where he tied him to a stake, and taking a fresh elk skin, on which a layer of fat had purposely been left, he placed it over a fire till it became ablaze; then throwing it over the naked shoulders of his nephew, he remarked. "Nephew, when you took me to visit the village of your people, you warmed me before a good fire. I now in return give you a warm mantle for your back."

The elk skin, covered with thick fat, burned furiously, and "puckering," it tightened around the naked body of his nephew—a dreadful "mantle" which soon consumed him. This act was again retaliated by the Foxes, and death by fire applied in various ways, soon became the fate of all unfortunate captives.

It is not unnatural to suppose that the tale of this occurrence being spread amongst the surrounding tribes, gave the name of Ojibway—"to roast till puckered up," to this tribe.

STRATAGEM OF A WYANDOTT CHIEF

PETER D. CLARKE—WYANDOTT

News came to their old Chief that a war party of Senecas were on their way to his village, they having learnt that his warriors were absent.

The old Wyandott Chief conceived the plan of baffling the enemy's contemplated assault on his village, by having an effigy made representing himself in a sitting posture in his wigwam, and during the night in which he expected the attack, he ordered all the old and young people to be secreted with him outside the village, and the moment he ascertained that the enemy had crossed the stream, he sent some of the boys and women to secrete their canoes. After midnight, or before the dawn of day, the Senecas entered the deserted village and surrounded the old Chief's residence. The leader of the invading party perceiving him through a hole over his door, quietly sitting, as he thought, by his fire which afforded but a dim flickering light, smoking his pipe, his grey head represented with a wig made of the skin of some white-haired animal, "Wauh!" exclaimed the leader of the Senecas, as he broke in, followed by his men upon the old Chief, and with uplifted tomahawk accosted *His Majesty* thus, "a

Wyandott at one time killed a War Chief of our tribe, and the time to have our revenge by slaying you has at last come!" uttering a savage yell as his descending tomahawk came in contact with the *wooden head* of the Wyandott—diff!—"Whoo!" exclaimed the Seneca "what does this mean?" a roar of laughter succeeded the savage yells of the whole party on perceiving the stratagem, and commenced dancing around the fire, yelling and singing their savage war songs, knocking the effigy of the old King about his wigwam with their tomahawks and war clubs.

But their boisterous conviviality was instantly hushed by the distant whoop and yell of Indians. Thinking that it might be a party of Wyandott warriors hurrying home to save their people from being massacred, the Senecas made a hasty retreat, and not finding their canoes where they had landed, they rushed into the stream to swim across.

Owing to the darkness of the night they did not discern a gang of women and boys standing in the water who attacked them with clubs. These, on perceiving that the enemies were not of a large party, gave the signal to the Wyandott boys and women at the opposite side of the stream to attack the refugees. Several of the latter were slain.

The distant yell that started the Senecas from the village was uttered by some of the older boys then about home, as they were ordered by the old Chief.

CHIVALRY OF THE IOWAYS

BLACK HAWK—SAUK

My nation had now some difficulty with the Ioways, with whom we wished to be at peace. Our young men had repeatedly killed some of the Ioways; and these breaches had always been made up by giving presents to the relations of those killed. But the last council we had with them, we promised that, in case any more of their people were killed by ours, instead of presents, we would give up the person, or persons, that had done the injury. We made this determination known to our people; but, notwithstanding, one of our young men killed an Ioway the following winter.

A party of our people were about starting for the Ioway village to give the young man up. I agreed to accompany them. When we were ready to start, I called at the lodge for the young man to go with us. He was sick, but willing to go. His brother, however, prevented him, and insisted on going to die in his place, as he was unable to travel. We started, and on the seventh day arrived in sight of the Ioway village, and when within a short distance of it, halted and dismounted. We all bid farewell to our young brave, who entered the village alone, singing his death-song, and sat down in the square in the middle of the village. One of the Ioway chiefs came out to us. We told him that we had fulfilled our promise—that we had brought the brother of the young man who had killed one of their people—that he had volunteered to come in his place, in consequence of his brother being unable to travel from sickness. We had no further conversation, but mounted our horses and rode off. As we started, I cast my eye towards the village, and observed the Ioways coming out of their lodges with spears and war clubs. We took our trail back, and travelled until dark—then encamped and made a fire. We had not been here long, before we heard the sound of horses coming towards us. We seized our arms; but instead of an enemy, it was our young brave with two horses. He told me that after we had left him, they menaced him with death for some time—then gave him something to eat—smoked the pipe with him—and made him a present of the two horses and some goods, and started him after us. When we arrived at our village, our people were much pleased; and for the noble and generous conduct of the Ioways, on this occasion, not one of their people has been killed since by any of our nation.

THE COURAGE OF AN OLD WARRIOR

WILLIAM WARREN—OJIBWAY

Early one morning the camp was attacked by a large war-party of Foxes, and the men, women and children all murdered, with the exception of a lad and an old man, who, running into a swamp, and becoming fastened in the bog and mire, were captured and taken in triumph by the Foxes to their village, there to suffer death with all the barbarous tortures which a savage could invent.

Bi-aus-wah [the Ojibway chief], at the time of the attack, was away on a hunt, and he did not return till towards evening. His feelings on finding his wigwams in ashes, and the lifeless, scalpless remains of his beloved family and relatives strewed about on the blood-stained ground, can only be imagined. He had lost all that bound him to life, and perfectly reckless he followed the return trail of the Foxes determined to die, if necessary, in revenging the grievous wrong which they had inflicted on him. He arrived at the village of his enemies, a day after their successful war-party had returned, and he heard men, women, and children screaming and yelling with delight, as they danced around the scalps which their warriors had taken.

Secreting himself on the outskirts of the village, the Ojibway chieftain waited for an opportunity to imbrue his hands in the blood of an enemy who might come within reach of his tomahawk. He had not remained long in his ambush, when the Foxes collected a short distance from the village, for the purpose of torturing and burning their two captives. The old man was first produced, and his body being wrapped in folds of the combustible birch bark, the Foxes set fire to it and caused him to run the gauntlet amid their hellish whoops and screams; covered with a perfect blaze of fire, and receiving withal a shower of blows, the old man soon expired.

The young and tender lad was then brought forward, and his doom was to run backwards and forwards on a long pile of burning fagots, till consumed to death. None but a parent can fully imagine the feelings which wrung the heart of the ambushed Ojibway chieftain, as he now recognized his only surviving child in the young captive who was about to undergo these torments. His single arm could not rescue him, but the brave father determined to die for or with his only son, and as the cruel Foxes were on the point of setting fire to the heap of dry fagots on which the lad had been placed, they were surprised to see the Ojibway chief step proudly and boldly into their midst and address them as follows:—

"My little son, whom you are about to burn with fire, has seen but a few winters; his tender feet have never trodden the war path—he has never injured you! But the hairs of my head are white with many winters, and over the graves of my relatives I have hung many scalps which I have taken from the heads of the Foxes; my death is worth something to you, let me therefore take the place of my child that he may return to his people."

Taken totally by surprise, the Foxes silently listened to the chief's proposal, and ever having coveted his death, and now fearing the consequence of his despairing efforts, they accepted his offer, and releasing the son, they bade him to depart, and burnt the brave father in his stead. The young man returned safely to his people.

ORIGIN OF THE FIVE NATIONS

CHIEF ELIAS JOHNSON—TUSCARORA

Even before the arrival of the white man, the intertribal wars of the Indians were frequent. In the New York area, the Iroquois were constantly under attack from powerful enemy nations. To protect themselves, they formed a defensive confederation which brought together at one council fire the five most powerful tribes in the New York region. Representatives of the Five Nations met to make laws and decide upon peace or war. So effective was this wilderness democracy that Benjamin Franklin recommended that the United States model its government after the League of the Iroquois.

The League was organized about 1570. One of the founders was probably Hiawatha, an alert and progressive Mohawk statesman. After his death, the historic Hiawatha was gradually transformed into a legendary figure with the wisdom and power of a god.

In Hiawatha, *Longfellow's hero was an Ojibway. Perhaps his model was tall, handsome, muscular Chief Kah-ge-ga-gah-bowh (George Copway). A close personal friend of Longfellow, Chief Kah-ge-ga-gah-bowh was famed among the Ojibways for his great physical strength and hunting skill.*

There were thus three *Hiawathas: the historic Hiawatha, associated with the founding of the Iroquois League; the legendary Mohawk, Hiawatha, described in this selection by Chief Elias Johnson; and Longfellow's Hiawatha, an Ojibway hero related only in name to the other Hiawathas.*

The council met. Hiawatha entered the assembly with even more than ordinary attention, and every eye was fixed upon him, when he began to address the council in the following words:

"Friends and Brothers:—You being members of many tribes, you have come from a great distance; the voice of war has aroused you up; you are afraid of your homes, your wives and your children; you trembled for your safety. Believe me, I am with you. My heart beats with your hearts. We are one. We have one common object. We come to promote our common interest, and to determine how this can be best done.

"To oppose those hordes of northern tribes, singly and alone, would prove certain destruction. We can make no progress in that way. We must unite ourselves into one common band of brothers. We must have but one voice. Many voices makes confusion. We must have one fire, one pipe and one war club. This will give us strength. If our warriors are united they can defeat the enemy and drive them from our land; if we do this, we are safe.

"Onondaga, you are the people sitting under the shadow of the *Great Tree*, whose branches spread far and wide, and whose roots sink deep into the earth. You shall be the first nation, because you are warlike and mighty.

"Oneida, and you, the people who recline your bodies against the *Everlasting Stone*, that cannot be moved, shall be the second nation, because you always give good counsel.

"Seneca, and you, the people who have your habitation at the foot of the *Great Mountain*, and are overshadowed by its crags, shall be the third nation, because you are all greatly gifted in speech.

"Cayuga, you, whose dwelling is in the *Dark Forest*, and whose home is everywhere, shall be the fourth nation, because of your superior cunning in hunting.

"Mohawk, and you, the people who live in the open country, and possess much wisdom, shall be the fifth nation, because you understand better the art of raising corn and beans and making cabins.

"You five great and powerful nations, with your tribes, must unite and have one common interest, and no foe shall disturb or subdue you.

"And you of the different nations of the south, and you of the west, may place yourselves under our protection, and we will protect you. We earnestly desire the alliance and friendship of you all.

"If we unite in one band the Great Spirit will smile upon us, and we shall be free, prosperous and happy; but if we shall remain as we are we shall incur his displeasure. We shall be enslaved, and perhaps annihilated forever.

"Brothers, these are the words of Hiawatha. Let them sink deep into your hearts. I have done."

A deep and impressive silence followed the delivery of this speech.

On the following day the council again assembled to act on it. High wisdom recommended this deliberation.

The union of the tribes into one confederacy was discussed and unanimously adopted. To denote the character and intimacy of the union they employed the figure of a single council-house, or lodge, whose boundaries be co-extensive with their territories.

Hiawatha, the guardian and founder of the league, having now accomplished the will of the Great Spirit, immediately prepared to make his final departure. Before the great council, which had adopted his advice just before dispersing, he arose, with a dignified air, and addressed them in the following manner:

"Friends and Brothers:—I have now fulfilled my mission here below; I have furnished you seeds and grains for your gardens; I have removed obstructions from your waters, and made the forest habitable by teaching you how to expel its monsters; I have given you fishing places and hunting grounds; I have instructed you in the making and using of war implements; I have taught you how to cultivate corn, and many other arts and gifts. I have been allowed by the Great Spirit to communicate to you. Last of all, I have aided you to form a league of friendship and union. If you preserve this, and admit no foreign element of power by the admission of other nations, you will always be free, numerous and happy. If other tribes and nations are admitted to your councils, they will sow the seed of jealousy and discord, and you will become few, feeble and enslaved.

"Friends and brothers, these are the last words you will hear from the lips of Hiawatha. The Great Creator of our bodies calls me to go; I have patiently awaited his summons; I am ready to go. Farewell."

As the voice of the wise man ceased, sweet strains of music from the air burst on the ears of the multitude. The whole sky appeared to be filled with melody; and while all eyes were directed to catch glimpses of the sights, and enjoy strains of the celestial music that filled the sky, Hiawatha was seen, seated in his snow-white canoe, amid the air, *rising, rising* with every choral chant that burst out. As he rose the sound of the music became more soft and faint, until he vanished amid the summer clouds, and the melody ceased.

VI: WAR BELTS ON THE OLD FRONTIER

In 1492 Columbus, looking for a shorter route to India, landed on one of the Bahamas. Believing he had reached India, he called the natives Indians. Later explorers named them "redskins" because they painted their faces with red ocher.

Columbus was followed by explorers and conquistadors who probed the new continent for gold. Then came the colonists, bringing guns and whisky and strange diseases with which to conquer the Indians. Gradually they pushed the Indians back, and within two hundred years the entire eastern seaboard of the United States was in the hands of the white invaders.

VI: WAR BELTS ON THE OLD FRONTIER

THE WARNING OF THE BEES

PETER D. CLARKE—WYANDOTT

According to legend, the ancient medicine men had prophesied that a white race would some day come from across the great waters and destroy the Indians. They had predicted that the honeybee, seldom found in a wild country, would give warning of the white man's arrival.

One summer day, whilst a party of children of nature were sitting and lying around under shady trees on a bank of the stream, one of their old men suddenly exclaimed, "Hun-haw!" (expressive of regret) "Look here!" said he pointing toward a strange looking insect that was buzzing around some wild flowers near them, "the white man," he continued, "is not very far off, and this strange thing you see flying about here was brought over to this country by the white man from the other side of the 'big waters,' and who, before very long, will come and take the whole country from the red man. Like the white man, this strange thing represents the rapidly increasing and ever busy tribe it belongs to." The insect that attracted their attention was the honeybee. "Thus you see," resumed the Wyandott, "that what has been foretold by our fathers is now coming to pass." Presently the bee came buzzing around them, then darted into the forest.

ARRIVAL OF THE WHITE MEN

JOSEPH NICOLAR—PENOBSCOT

There is no Indian eyewitness account of the landing of Columbus or any other early explorer. Joseph Nicolar, writing in 1893, described the Penobscot tradition of an early landing. The French colonized Neutral Island on the St. Croix River in 1604, and this may be the landing to which Nicolar referred.

Just at this time an exciting news was brought from the extreme north to the effect, that the white man's big canoe had come, and had landed its people who are still remaining on the land on the north shore of the "Ma-quozz-bem-to-cook, Lake River," and have planted some heavy blocks of wood in the form of a cross. These people are white and the lower part of the faces of the elder ones are covered with hair, and the hair is in different colors, and the eyes are not alike, some have dark while others have light colored eyes, some have eyes the color of the blue sky. They have shown nothing only friendship, they take the red man's hands in their own and bow their heads down and make signs in the direction of the stars; and their big canoe is filled with food which they eat and also give some to those that come to them and made signs of friendship. When this news spread, the people took it so quietly and talked about it in such a way, there was no excitement, but everybody took it as though it was an old affair, yet it had such effect upon them, that it was evident the general desire was, that the habits of the strange people must be well learned, and all agree to wait and see what kind of a treatment they will extend to the red people. If the treatment they have already extended be continued, it was thought will be the means of bringing happiness to both races.

CAPTAIN JOHN SMITH AND POWHATAN

CHIEF FLYING HAWK—SIOUX

Not until 1607 did the English plant their first permanent colony in the New World, Jamestown. The colonists were led by hard, shrewd Captain John Smith, who in his books, written many years later, boasted of how he saved the colony by outwitting the Indians. Here is an Indian impression of Smith by Chief Flying Hawk (1852-1931). A nephew of Sitting Bull, Chief Flying Hawk fought in the Custer battle in 1876. Later he joined Buffalo Bill's Wild West Show, and only when he was too old to travel did he retire to his cabin in the Bad Lands. In 1929, the chief dictated his impressions of American history to his friend, M. I. McCreight.

That Virginia venture was a gold-hunting expedition like when Cortez went to steal from Montezuma the Indians' gold and silver and land. They were a lot of fellows out of a job who wanted to live without work by cheating and robbing the native people who did not have guns.

Powhatan was kind to them when they came. He gave them food and helped them to make houses to live in. They stayed a long time and did not work and raise food but got it from the Indians. Then when the corn was not plenty for all, Smith told Powhatan that they had been wrecked and soon ships would come from England and take them back home. Ships came and put more English people on the land but did not bring food for them. They were hungry and asked for more corn from the Indians, but there was not enough for all, and so Powhatan told them he had food only for his own people. The white men had guns and swords and told Powhatan he must give them the corn or they would kill his people. Then there was trouble. They took the food from the Indians and the Indians killed some of them and then they became enemies.

It was when they had stolen a lot of food from the Indians and were in camp to eat it that Smith said Pocahontas came to them through the path in the woods and told them the Indians were coming to kill them, and she put her arms around Smith's neck and cried. It was a good white man's story, but Indians do not believe it. Smith did not tell this story until long after he went back to England to put it in his book. Pocahontas was a girl only twelve or thirteen years old and Smith was a hard man more than forty or fifty winters. Rolfe took her to England but she did not live very long there so far away from her people.

THE PILGRIM INVASION

WILLIAM APES—PEQUOD

The story of the Pilgrims really began in 1606 with the founding of the Plymouth Company, chartered for the purpose of trading in the New World and backed by wealthy Londoners. After several unsuccessful efforts to found a colony in New England, the company hit upon the idea of using as colonists a group of people who opposed the Church of England and were eager to found a religious community built entirely upon their own beliefs.

In the summer of 1620, 102 immigrants were jammed into the Mayflower. *Only a third of the passengers were Pilgrims. The others were adventurers or settlers who had been picked up in London by the Plymouth Company.*

William Apes, a descendant of the Wampanoag sachem King Philip, wrote this critical account of the Pilgrims in 1836.

December, 1620, the Pilgrims landed at Plymouth, and without asking liberty from any one, they possessed themselves of a portion of the country, and built themselves houses, and then made a treaty, and commanded them [the Indians] to accede to it. This, if now done, would be called an insult, and every white man would be called to go out and act the part of a patriot, to defend their country's rights; and if every intruder were butchered, it would be sung upon every hill-top in the Union, that victory and patriotism was the order of the day. And yet the Indians, though many were dissatisfied, without the shedding of blood, or imprisoning any one, bore it. And yet for their kindness and resignation towards the whites, they were called savages, and made by God on purpose for them to destroy. It appears that a treaty was made by the Pilgrims and the Indians, which treaty was kept during forty years; the young chiefs during this time, was showing the Pilgrims how to live in their country, and find support for their wives and little ones; and for all this, they were receiving the applauses of being savages. The two gentlemen chiefs were Squanto and Samoset, that were so good to the Pilgrims.

The next we present before you are things very appalling. We turn our attention to dates, 1623, January and March, when Mr. Weston['s] Colony, came very near starving to death; some of them were obliged to hire themselves to the Indians, to become their servants, in order that they might live. Their principal work was to bring wood and water; but not being contented with this, many of the whites sought to steal the Indian's corn; and because the Indians complained of it, and through their complaint, some one of their number being punished, as they say, to appease the savages. Now let us see who the greatest savages were; the person that stole the corn was a stout athletic man, and because of this, they wished to spare him, and take an old man who was lame and sickly, and that used to get his living by weaving, and because they thought he would not be of so much use to them, he was, although innocent of any crime, hung in his stead. Oh, savage, where art thou, to weep over the Christian's crimes.

Another act of humanity for Christians, as they call themselves, that one Capt. Standish, gathering some fruit and provisions, goes forward with a black and hypocritical heart, and pretends to prepare a feast for the Indians; and when they sit down to eat, they seize the Indian's knives hanging about their necks, and stab them to the heart. The white people call this stabbing, feasting the savages. We suppose it might well mean themselves, their conduct being more like savages than Christians. They took one Wittumumet, the Chief's head, and put it upon a pole in their fort; and for aught we know, gave praise to God for success in murdering a poor Indian; for we know it was their usual course to give praise to God for this kind of victory, believing it was God's will and command, for them to do so.

But we have more to present; and that is, the violation of a treaty that the Pilgrims proposed for the Indians to subscribe to, and they the first to break it. The Pilgrims promised to deliver up every transgressor of the Indian treaty, to them, to be punished according to their laws, and the Indians were to do likewise. Now it appears that an Indian had committed treason, by conspiring against the king's life, which is punishable with death, and Massasoit makes demand for the transgressor, and the Pilgrims refuse to give him up, although by their oath of alliance they had promised to do so. Their reasons were, he was beneficial to them. This shows how grateful they were to their former safeguard, and ancient protector. Now, who would have blamed this venerable old chief if he had declared war at once, and swept the whole colonies away? It was certainly in his power to do it, if he pleased; but no, he forbore, and forgave the whites. But where is there a people, called civilized, that would do it? we presume, none; and we doubt not but the Pilgrims would have exerted all their powers to be avenged, and to appease their ungodly passions. But it will be seen that this good old chief exercised more Christian forbearance than any of the governors of that age, or since. It might well be said he was a pattern for the Christians themselves; but by the Pilgrims he is denounced, as being a savage.

In this history of Massasoit we find that his own head men were not satisfied with the Pilgrims; that they looked upon them to be intruders, and had a wish to expel those intruders out of their coast. A false report was made respecting one Tisquantum, that he was murdered by an Indian, one of Coubantant's men. Upon this news, one Standish, a vile and malicious fellow, took fourteen of his lewd

Pilgrims with him, and at midnight, when a deathless silence reigned throughout the wilderness. At that late hour of the night, meeting a house in the wilderness, whose inmates heard—Move not, upon the peril of your life. At the same time some of the females were so frightened, that some of them undertook to make their escape, upon which they were fired upon. Now it is doubtless the case that these females never saw a white man before, or ever heard a gun fired. It must have sounded to them like the rumbling of thunder, and terror must certainly have filled all their hearts. And can it be supposed that these innocent Indians could have looked up them as good and trusty men? Do you look upon the midnight robber and assassin as being a Christian, and trusty man? These Indians had not done one single wrong act to the whites, but were as innocent of any crime, as any beings in the world. But if the real sufferers say one word, they are denounced, as being wild and savage beasts.

The history of New England writers say, that our tribes were large and respectable. How then, could it be otherwise, but their safety rested in the hands of friendly Indians. In 1647, the Pilgrims speak of large and respectable tribes. But let us trace them for a few moments. How have they been destroyed, is it by fair means? No. How then? By hypocritical proceedings, by being duped and flattered; flattered by informing the Indians that their God was a going to speak to them, and then place them before the cannon's mouth in a line, and then putting the match to it and kill thousands of them. We might suppose that meek Christians had better gods and weapons than cannon. But let us again review their weapons to civilize the nations of this soil. What were they: rum and powder, and ball, together with all the diseases, such as the small pox, and every other disease imaginable; and in this way sweep off thousands and tens of thousands.

KING PHILIP'S WAR

WILLIAM APES—PEQUOD

Within fifty years after the Pilgrims landed, the New England coast was dotted with towns. Each year a stream of immigrants poured into the New World, and each year the colonists demanded and got more land from the Indians.

When the Indians signed away their hunting grounds, they be-

lieved they were only lending *the land to the colonists. The earth, they said, was the mother of all life and could not be bought or sold. Fences that set off the land and plows that defaced it were against the laws of nature.*

The colonists did not understand or pretended not to understand the Indian beliefs. So they went on "buying" land.

This difference of ideas on landownership led to conflicts. The first major clash came in 1637, after the murder of a white trader touched off the Pequod War. The colonists surrounded and set fire to the Pequod stronghold near the Mystic River. In a terrible slaughter, more than 400 Pequod men, women, and children were burned to death or put to the sword. A few less fortunate Pequods were captured. The Pilgrims sent the men and boys to Bermuda to be sold into slavery and gave the women and girls to any Pilgrim who wanted them.

For nearly forty years there was peace—a shaky, uncertain peace. Then, in 1675, came the second great struggle between the colonists and the Indians. Under the brilliant leadership of King Philip, the New England Indians formed a confederation to resist the Pilgrims. The fighting began when the whites, in violation of an old treaty, executed three Indians for murder. In a series of raids, Philip's warriors struck at the heart of New England. Of ninety towns, fifty-two were attacked and twelve were completely destroyed. The struggle ended when Philip was betrayed by his allies, and his forces were surrounded and cut to pieces in a Rhode Island swamp.

William Apes (1798- ?) was ordained a Methodist preacher in 1829. At the Odeon on Federal Street in Boston he delivered in 1836 a stirring eulogy on King Philip. The eulogy was a thinly veiled attack on bigotry and intolerance. Soon after making his speech on King Philip, from which the following selection is taken, Apes disappeared mysteriously. Where or how he died is not known.

At council it appears that Philip made the following speech to his chiefs, counsellors and warriors.

Brothers,—You see this vast country before us, which the Great Spirit gave to our fathers and us; you see the buffalo and deer that now are our support.—Brothers, you see these little ones, our wives and children, who are looking to us for food and raiment; and you now see the foe before you, that they have grown insolent and bold;

that all our ancient customs are disregarded; the treaties made by our fathers and us are broken, and all of us insulted; our council fires disregarded, and all the ancient customs of our fathers; our brothers murdered before our eyes, and their spirits cry to us for revenge. Brothers, these people from the unknown world will cut down our groves, spoil our hunting and planting grounds, and drive us and our children from the graves of our fathers, and our council fires, and enslave our women and children.

This famous speech of Philip was calculated to arouse them to arms, to do the best they could in protecting and defending their rights. Philip's young men were eager to do exploits, and to lead captive their haughty lords. It does appear that every Indian heart had been lighted up at the council fires, at Philip's speech, and that the forest was literally alive with this injured race. And now town after town fell before them. The Pilgrims with their forces were ever marching in one direction, while Philip and his forces were marching in another, burning all before them, until Middleborough, Taunton and Dartmouth were laid in ruins, and forsaken by its inhabitants.

At the great fight at Pocasset, Philip commanded in person, where he also was discovered with his host in a dismal swamp. He had retired here with his army to secure a safe retreat from the Pilgrims, who were in close pursuit of him, and their numbers were so powerful they thought the fate of Philip was sealed. They surrounded the swamp, in hopes to destroy him and his army. At the edge of the swamp Philip had secreted a few of his men to draw them into ambush, upon which the Pilgrims showed fight; Philip's men retreating and the whites pursuing them till they were surrounded by Philip, and nearly all cut off. This was a sorry time to them; the Pilgrims, however, reinforced, but ordered a retreat, supposing it impossible for Philip to escape, and knowing his forces to be great, it was conjectured by some to build a fort to starve him out, as he had lost but few men in the fight. The situation of Philip was rather peculiar, as there was but one outlet to the swamp, and a river before him nearly seven miles to descend. The Pilgrims placed a guard around the swamp for 13 days, which gave Philip and his men time to prepare canoes to make good his retreat; in which he did, to the Connecticut river, and in his retreat lost but fourteen men. We may look upon this move of Philip's to be equal, if not superior to that of Washington crossing the Delaware. For while Washington was assisted by all the knowledge that art and science could give, together with the instruments of defence, and edged tools to prepare rafts, and the like helps for safety across the river, Philip was naked as to any of these things; and yet makes his escape with equal praise.

Philip having now taken possession of the back settlements of Massachusetts, one town after another was swept off. A garrison being established at Northfield by the Pilgrims, and while endeavoring to reinforce it with thirty-six armed, twenty out of their number was killed, and one taken prisoner. At the same time Philip so managed it as to cut off their retreat, and take their ammunition from them.

About the month of August, they [the Indians] took a young lad about fourteen years of age, whom they intended to make merry with the next day; but the Pilgrims said God touched the Indians' heart, and they let him go. About the same time, the whites took an old man of Philip's, whom they found alone; and because he would not turn traitor, and inform them where Philip was, they pronounced him worthy of death; and by them was executed, cutting off first his arms and then his head. We wonder why God did not touch the Pilgrims' heart, and save them from cruelty, as well as the Indians.

But we have another dark and corrupt deed for the sons of the Pilgrims to look at, and that is the fight and capture of Philip's son and wife, and many of his warriors, in which Philip lost about 130 men killed and wounded; this was in August 1676. But the most horrid act was in taking Philip's son, about ten years of age, and selling him to be a slave away from his father and mother. While I am writing, I can hardly restrain my feelings, to think a people calling themselves Christians, should conduct so scandalous, so outrageous, making themselves appear so despicable in the eyes of the Indians; and even now I doubt not but there is men honorable enough to despise the conduct of these pretended Christians. And surely none but such as believe they did right, will ever go and undertake to celebrate that day of their landing, the 22d of December.

Philip's forces had now become very small, so many having been duped away by the whites, and killed, that it was now easy surrounding him. Therefore, upon the 12th of August, Captain Church surrounded the swamp where Philip and his men had encamped, early in the morning, before they had risen, doubtless led on by an Indian who was either compelled or hired to turn traitor. Church had now placed his guard so that it was impossible for Philip to escape without being shot. It is doubtful, however, whether they would have taken him if he had not been surprised. Suffice it to say, however, this was the case. A sorrowful morning to the poor Indians, to lose such a valuable man. When coming out of the swamp, he was fired upon by an Indian, and killed dead upon the spot.

I rejoice that it was even so, that the Pilgrims did not have the pleasure of tormenting him. The white man's gun missing fire lost the honor of killing the truly great man, Philip. The place where Philip fell was very muddy. Upon this news, the Pilgrims gave three cheers; then Church ordering his body to be pulled out of the mud, while one of those tender-hearted Christians exclaims, what a dirty creature he looks like. And we have also Church's speech upon that subject, as follows: For as much as he has caused many a Pilgrim to lie above ground unburied, to rot, not one of his bones shall be buried.

Captain Church now orders him to be cut up. Accordingly, he was quartered and hung up upon four trees; his head and one hand given to the Indian who shot him, to carry about to show. At which sight it so overjoyed the Pilgrims, that they would give him money for it; and in this way obtained a considerable sum. After which, his head was sent to Plymouth, and exposed upon a gibbet for twenty years; and his hand to Boston, where it was exhibited in savage triumph; and his mangled body denied a resting place in the tomb.

I think that as a matter of honor, that I can rejoice that no such evil conduct is recorded of the Indians; that they never hung up any of the white warriors, who were head men. And we add the famous speech of Dr. Increase Mather; he says, during the bloody contest, the pious fathers wrestled hard and long with their God, in prayer, that he would prosper their arms, and deliver their enemies into their hands. The Doctor closes thus: Nor could they, the Pilgrims, cease crying to the Lord against Philip, until they had prayed the bullet through his heart. If this is the way they pray, that is bullets through people's hearts, I hope they will not pray for me; I should rather be excused.

GERM WARFARE AGAINST THE INDIANS

CHIEF ANDREW J. BLACKBIRD—OTTAWA

Many of the tribes that welcomed the Pilgrims to Plymouth—the Pequods, Naticks, Narragansets—were virtually exterminated by the end of the seventeenth century. In other northern colonies the match for empire between France and England was getting under way, with the Indians as pawns. The French pitted the Hurons and Ottawas against the British and their Iroquois allies.

After a long series of clashes the military genius of the Iroquois swung the balance in favor of Britain, and on September 18, 1759, the French stronghold of Quebec fell to the forces of General Wolfe. The capture of Quebec ended French hopes for empire in America.

The most formidable enemies of the British were now the Ottawas and Ojibways (Chippewas) who held most of the Great Lakes region. Many historians claim that the British resorted to germ warfare in order to destroy these hostile tribes, for nearly 2,000 Ottawa and neighboring Indians were struck down by smallpox.

Germ warfare was not an entirely new idea. In 1752 General Jeffrey Amherst recommended the use of smallpox to his subordinates. "You will be well advised," wrote His Excellency, "to infect the Indians with sheets upon which small pox patients have been lying or by any other means which may serve to exterminate this accursed race. I should be very glad if your plan of hunting them down with dogs were to prove practicable."

Chief Andrew J. Blackbird, Ottawa historian, wrote this indictment of the British in 1887.

The Ottawas were greatly reduced in numbers on account of the small-pox which they brought from Montreal during the French war with Great Britain. This small-pox was sold to them shut up in a tin box, with the strict injunction not to open their box on their way homeward, but only when they should reach their country; and that this box contained something that would do them great good, and their people! The foolish people believed really there was something in the box supernatural, that would do them great good. Accordingly, after they reached home they opened the box; but behold there was another tin box inside, smaller. They took it out and opened the second box, and behold, still there was another box inside the second box, smaller yet. So they kept on this way till they came to a very small box, which was not more than an inch long; and when they opened the last one they found nothing but mouldy particles in this last little box! They wondered very much what it was, and a great many closely inspected to try to find out what it meant. But alas, alas! pretty soon burst out a terrible sickness among them. The great Indian doctors themselves were taken sick and died. The tradition says it was indeed awful and terrible. Every one taken with it was sure to die. Lodge after lodge was totally vacated—nothing but the dead bodies lying here and there in their lodges—entire families being swept off with the ravages of this terrible disease. The whole coast of Arbor Croche, or Waw-gaw-naw-ke-zee, where their principal village was situated, on the west shore of the peninsula near the Straits, which is said to have been a continuous village some fifteen or sixteen miles long and extending from what is now called Cross Village to Seven-Mile Point (that is, seven miles from Little Traverse, now Harbor Springs), was entirely depopulated and laid waste. It is generally believed among the Indians of Arbor Croche that this wholesale murder of the Ottawas by this terrible disease sent by the British people, was actuated through hatred, and expressly to kill off the Ottawas and Chippewas because they were friends of the French Government or French King, whom they called "Their Great Father." The reason that today we see no full-grown trees standing along the coast of Arbor Croche, a mile or more in width along the shore, is because the trees were entirely cleared away for this famous long village, which existed before the small-pox raged among the Ottawas.

THE CAPTURE OF FORT MICHILIMACKINAC

WILLIAM WARREN—OJIBWAY

In the spring of 1763 the Indians under Pontiac (1720?-1769) launched an all-out attack against the British on the northwest frontier. Of twelve fortified posts attacked, eight were taken.

Pontiac, an Ottawa chief, was one of the greatest of Indian leaders and like King Philip formed a confederacy of tribes to drive the English from his country. He personally led the siege of Detroit, and at a powwow called upon the French to join him. Hurling a war belt into their midst he said: "My Brothers! I did not wish to ask you to fight with us against the English, and I did not believe you would take part with them. You will say you are not with them. I know it, but your conduct amounts to the same thing. You will tell them all we do and say. You carry our counsels and plans to them. Now take your choice. You must be entirely French, like ourselves, or entirely English. If you are French, take this belt for yourselves and your young men, and join us. If you are English, we declare war against you!"

Despite Pontiac's shrewdness the French refused to take part in the war. Several attempts to seize Detroit by stratagem failed, and on the Pennsylvania frontier the Indians were defeated and routed. At last, on August 17, 1765, Pontiac reluctantly signed a treaty of peace.

The most spectacular victory scored by the Indians during the Pontiac War was the capture of Fort Michilimackinac (Mackinaw). This description of the capture, written in 1852, was based upon details furnished by old men of the Ojibway tribe.

For upwards of four years after the French had ceded the country to the British, the allied Algic tribes, after a short lull of quiet and comparative peace, under the masterly guidance of Pontiac, maintained the war against what they considered as the usurpation, by the British, of the hunting grounds which the Great Spirit had given to their ancestors.

Such was the force and accuracy of the organization which this celebrated leader had effected among the northern tribes of his fellow red men, that, on the same day, which was the 4th of June, 1763, and the anniversary of the king's birth (which the Indians knew was a day set apart by the English as one of amusement and celebration), they attacked and besieged twelve of the wide-spread western stockaded forts, and succeeded in taking possession of nine [?]. In this alliance, the Ojibways of Lakes Huron and Michigan were most active parties, and into their hands was entrusted by their common leader, the capture of the British fort at Mackinaw [city]. "That fort," according to the description of an eminent writer, "standing on the south side of the strait between lakes Huron and Michigan, was one of the most important positions on the frontiers. It was the place of deposit, and point of departure between the upper and lower countries; the traders always assembled there, on their voyages to and from Montreal. Connected with it, was an area of two acres, inclosed with cedar wood pickets, and extending on one side so near to the water's edge, that a western wind always drew the waves against the foot of the stockade. There were about thirty houses within the limits, inhabited by about the same number of families. The only ordinance on the bastions were two small brass pieces. The garrison numbered between ninety and one hundred."

The important enterprise of the capture of this important and indispensable post, was entrusted into the hands of Mih-neh-weh-na, the great war chieftain of the Ojibways of Mackinaw, and by the manner in which he superintended and managed the affair, to a complete and successful issue, he approved himself a worthy lieutenant of the great head and leader of the war, the Ottawa chieftain Pontiac.

The Ottawas of Lake Michigan being more friendly disposed to the British, were not called on by the politic Ojibway chieftain for help in this enterprise, and a knowledge of the secret plan of attack was carefully kept from them, for fear that they would inform their English friends, and place them on their guard. In fact, every person of his own tribe whom he suspected of secret good-will towards any of the new British traders, Min-neh-weh-na sent away from the scene of the intended attack, with the admonition that death would be their sure fate, should the British be informed of the plan which had been formed to take possession of the fort.

In this manner did he guard with equal foresight and greater success than Pontiac himself, against a premature development of their plans. Had not the loving Indian girl informed the young officer at Fort Detroit of Pontiac's secret plan [to seize Detroit], that important post, and its inmates, would have shared the same fate as befell the fort at Mackinaw.

Of all the northern tribes who occupied the great lakes, the Ojibways allowed only the Osaugees to participate with them in their secret councils, in which was developed the plan of taking the fort, and these two tribes only were actively engaged in this enterprise.

The fighting men of the Ojibways and Osaugees gradually collected in the vicinity of the fort as the day appointed for the attack approached. They numbered between four and six hundred. An active trade was in the mean time carried on with the British traders, and every means resorted to for the purpose of totally blinding the suspicions which the more humane class of the French population found means to impart to the officers of the fort, respecting the secret animosity of the Indians. These hints were entirely disregarded by Major Etherington, the commandant of the fort, and he even threatened to confine any person who would have the future audacity to whisper these tales of danger into his ears. Everything, therefore, favored the scheme which the Ojibway chieftain had laid to ensnare his confident enemies. On the eve of the great English king's birthday, he informed the British commandant that as the morrow was to be a day of rejoicing, his young men would play the game of ball, or Baug-ah-ud-o-way [lacrosse], for the amusement of the whites, in front of the gate of the fort. In this game the young men of the Osaugee tribe would play against the Ojibways for a large stake. The commandant expressed his pleasure and willingness to the crafty chieftain's proposal, little dreaming that this was to lead to a game of blood, in which those under his charge were to be the victims.

During the whole night the Ojibways were silently busy in making preparations for the morrow's work. They sharpened their knives and tomahawks, and filed short off their guns. In the morning these weapons were entrusted to the care of their women, who, hiding them under the folds of their blankets, were ordered to stand as near as possible to the gate of the fort, as if to witness the game which the men were about to play. Over a hundred on each side of the Ojibways and Osaugees, all chosen men, now sallied forth from their wigwams, painted and ornamented for the occasion, and proceeding to the open green which lay in front of the fort, they made up the stakes for which they were apparently about to play, and planted the posts toward which each party was to strive to take the ball.

This game of Baug-ah-ud-o-way is played with a bat and wooden ball. The bat is about four feet long, terminating at one end into a circular curve, which is netted with leather strings, and forms a cavity where the ball is caught, carried, and if necessary thrown with great force, to treble the distance that it can be thrown by hand. Two posts are planted at the distance of about half a mile. Each party has its particular post, and the game consists in carrying or throwing the ball in the bat to the post of the adversary. At the commencement of the game, the two parties collect midway between the two posts; the ball is thrown up into the air, and the competition for its possession commences in earnest. It is the wildest game extant among the Indians, and is generally played in full feathers and ornaments, and with the greatest excitement and vehemence. The great object is to obtain possession of the ball; and, during the heat of the excitement, no obstacle is allowed to stand in the way of getting at it. Let it fall far out into the deep water, numbers rush madly in and swim for it, each party impeding the efforts of the other in every manner possible. Let it fall into a high inclosure, it is surmounted, or torn down in a moment, and the ball recovered; and were it to fall into the chimney of a house, a jump through the window, or a smash of the door, would be considered of no moment; and the most violent hurts and bruises are incident to the headlong, mad manner in which it is played. It will be seen by this hurried description, that the game was very well adapted to carry out the scheme of the Indians.

On the morning of the 4th of June, after the cannon of the fort had been discharged in commemoration of the king's natal day, the ominous ball was thrown up a short distance in front of the gate of Fort Mackinaw, and the exciting game commenced. The two hundred players, their painted persons streaming with feathers, ribbons, fox and wolf tails, swayed to and fro as the ball was carried backwards and forwards by either party, who for the moment had possession of it. Occasionally a swift and agile runner would catch it in his bat, and making tremendous leaps hither and thither to avoid the attempts of his opponents to knock it out of his bat, or force him to throw it, he would make a sudden dodge past them, and choosing a clear track, run swiftly, urged on by the deafening shouts of his party and the by-standers, towards the stake of his adversaries, till his onward course was stopped by a swifter runner, or an advanced guard of the opposite party.

The game, played as it was, by the young men of two different tribes, became exciting, and the commandant of the fort even took his stand outside his open gates, to view its progress. His soldiers stood carelessly unarmed, here and there, intermingling with the Indian women, who gradually huddled near the gateway, carrying under their blankets the weapons which were to be used in the approaching work of death.

In the struggle for its possession, the ball at last was gradually carried towards the open gates, and all at once, after having reached a proper distance, an athletic arm caught it up in his bat, and as if by accident threw it within the precincts of the fort. With one deafening yell and impulse, the players rushed forward in a body, as if to regain it, but as they reached their women and entered the gateway, they threw down their wooden bats and grasping the shortened guns, tomahawks, and knives, the massacre commenced, and the bodies of the unsuspecting British soldiers soon lay strewn about, lifeless, horribly mangled, and scalpless. The careless commander was taken captive without a struggle, as he stood outside the fort, viewing the game, which the Ojibway chieftain had got up for his amusement.

Not a hair on the head of the many Frenchmen who witnessed this scene was hurt by the infuriated savages, and there stands not on record a stronger proof of the love borne them by the tribe engaged in this business than this very fact, for the passions of an Indian warrior, once aroused by a scene of this nature, are not easily appeased, and generally everything kindred in any manner to his foe, falls a victim to satiate his blood-thirsty propensities.

LOGAN DEFENDS HIS CONDUCT

CHIEF JAMES LOGAN—CAYUGA

The most famous of Indian orators, Chief James Logan (1725?-1780) was widely known on the Ohio and Pennsylvania frontiers for his pleasant personality, handsome features, and friendship for the white men.

In the spring of 1774, a gang of white settlers attacked and massacred a settlement of peaceful Indians at the mouth of Yellow Creek, Ohio. Among the murdered were members of Logan's family. He and other Indians took up the tomahawk and avenged the Yellow Creek massacre in a series of barbarous attacks on settlers and their families.

The Indian uprising was suppressed, but Logan refused to attend a peace conference. Instead, he sent by the interpreter a defense of his conduct of which Thomas Jefferson said: "I may challenge the whole orations of Demosthenes and Cicero, and of any more eminent orator, if Europe has furnished more eminent, to produce a single passage, superior to the speech of Logan."

I appeal to any white man to say, if he ever entered Logan's cabin hungry, and he gave him not meat; if he ever came cold and naked, and he clothed him not. During the course of the last long and bloody war, Logan remained idle in his cabin, an advocate for peace. Such was my love for the whites, that my countrymen pointed as they passed, and said, "Logan is the friend of white men." I had even thought to have lived with you, but for the injuries of one man. Colonel Cresap, the last spring, in cold blood, and unprovoked, murdered all the relations of Logan, not sparing even my women and children. There runs not a drop of my blood in the veins of any living creature.

This called on me for revenge. I have sought it: I have killed many: I have fully glutted my vengeance. For my country, I rejoice at the beams of peace. But do not harbor a thought that mine is the joy of fear. Logan never felt fear. He will not turn on his heel to save his life.

Who is there to mourn for Logan?—Not one.

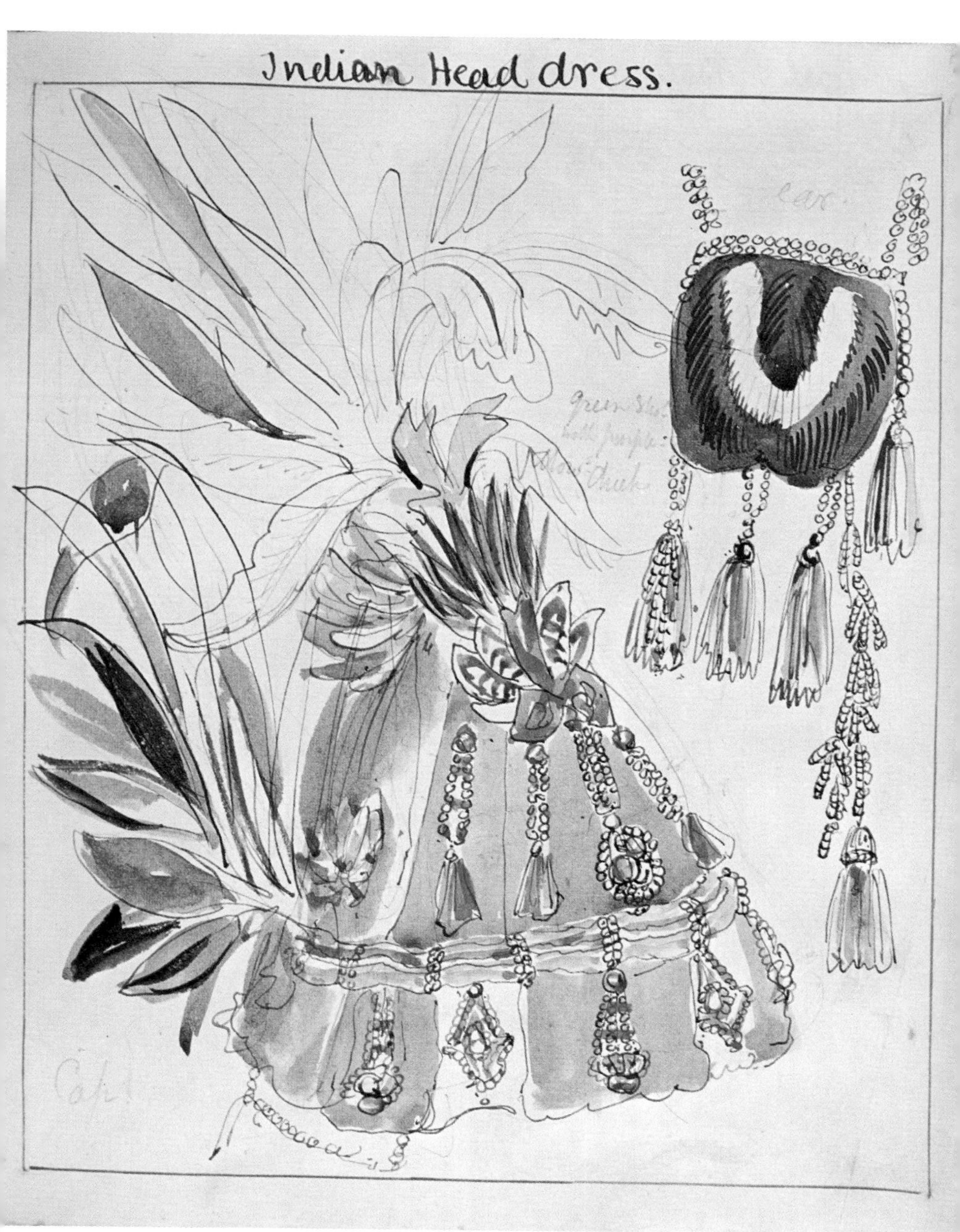

From Catlin Sketchbook
Courtesy of Gilcrease Institute

INDIAN HEADDRESS
George Catlin
ca. 1830–40

VII: FIGHTING THE LONG KNIVES

The Revolutionary War (1775-1783) was the first conflict on American soil in which the Indians did not play a decisive role. At the outbreak of war, the British turned to the Indians for help. The Americans urged the Indians to keep out of the struggle but the British promised bigger hunting grounds. Most of the Indians threw in their lot with the British. The famous Delaware chief, Buckongehelas, described the Indian view of the war: "You see a great and powerful nation divided! You see the father fighting against the son, and the son against the father! The father has called on his Indian children, to assist him in punishing his children, the Americans, who have become refractory! I took time to consider what I should do—whether or not I should receive the hatchet of my father, to assist him! At first I looked upon it as a family quarrel, in which I was not interested. However, at length it appeared to me, that the father was in the right; and his children deserved to be punished a little! That this must be the case, I concluded from the many cruel acts his offspring had committed from time to time on his Indian children; in encroaching on their land, stealing their property, shooting at, and murdering without cause, men, women and children."

A few Indians joined the American army as scouts, but most of the powerful tribes—the Delawares, Shawnees, Mohawks, Senecas, and Cherokees—aided the English by terrorizing American border towns. Thayendanegea, or Joseph Brant (1742-1807) headed the Mohawks in the famous Cherry Valley Massacre. Young King (1760?-1835), Seneca sachem, ravaged the frontiers and was probably the leader of the Senecas in the terrible massacre at Wyoming, Pennsylvania (1778).

In August, 1779, a punitive army under Major General John Sullivan invaded the country of the Six Nations. Sullivan drove back the Indians and British under Thayendanegea, destroyed forty towns, cut down 1,500 peach trees, burned 150,000 bushels of wheat. The destruction was so complete that the Indians never fully recovered.

During the Revolution, the Americans were called "Long Knives" by the Indians because they so often fought with sabers and dirks.

VII: FIGHTING THE LONG KNIVES

WITH THE BRITISH IN THE REVOLUTION

CHIEF HOPOCAN—DELAWARE

Among the Indians who joined the British was the Delaware, Chief Hopocan (Captain Pipe), who led his warriors in forays against the American outposts in the Northwest. During a council at Detroit in 1781, he presented the British commandant with a long stick strung with American scalps. Chief Hopocan began his presentation speech by uttering the word "Father" in a contemptuous tone.

Father! Some time ago you put a war-hatchet into my hands, saying, "Take this weapon and try it on the heads of my enemies, the Long Knives, and let me know afterwards if it was sharp and good."

Father! At the time you gave me this weapon, I had neither cause nor wish to go to war against a foe who had done me no injury. But you say you are my father—and call me your child—and in obedience to you I received the hatchet. I knew that if I did not obey you, you would withhold from me the necessaries of life, which I could procure nowhere but here.

Father! You may perhaps think me a fool, for risking my life at your bidding—and that in a cause in which I have no prospect of gaining any thing. For it is your cause, and not mine—you have raised a quarrel among yourselves—and you ought to fight it out. It is *your* concern to fight the Long Knives. You should not compel your children, the Indians, to expose themselves to danger for your sake.

Father! Many lives have already been lost on *your account*. The tribes have suffered, and been weakened. Children have lost parents and brothers. Wives have lost husbands. It is not known how many more may perish before *your war* will be at an end.

Father! I have said, you may perhaps think me a fool, for thus thoughtlessly rushing on your enemy! Do not believe this, Father: Think not that I want sense to convince me, that although you now pretend to keep up a perpetual enmity to the Long Knives, you may, before long, conclude a peace with them.

Father! You say you love your children, the Indians. This you have often told them; and indeed it is your interest to say so to them; that you may have them at your service.

But, Father! Who of us can believe that you can love a people of a different color from your own; better than those who have a white skin, like yourselves?

Father! Pay attention to what I am going to say. While you, Father, are setting me on your enemy, much in the same manner as a hunter sets his dog on the game; and while I am in the act of rushing on that enemy of yours, with the bloody destructive weapon you gave me, I may, perchance, happen to look back at the place from whence you started me, and what shall I see? Perhaps, I may see my father shaking hands with the Long Knives; yes, with those very people he now calls his enemies. I may *then* see him laugh at my folly for having obeyed his orders; and yet I am now risking my life at his command! Father! Keep what I have said in remembrance.

Now, Father! Here is what has been done with the hatchet you gave me [handing the commandant the stick with the scalps on it]. I have done with the hatchet what you ordered me to do, and found it sharp. Nevertheless, I did not do all that I might have done. No, I did not. My heart failed within me. I felt compassion for your enemy. Innocence had no part in your quarrels; therefore I distinguished—I spared. I took some live flesh [prisoners], which, while I was bringing to you, I spied one of your large canoes, on which I put it for you. In a few days you will receive this flesh, and find that the skin is of the same color with your own.

Father! I hope you will not destroy what I have saved. You, Father, have the means of preserving that which would perish with us from want.

The warrior is poor, and his cabin is always empty; but your house, Father, is always full.

COLONEL CRAWFORD BURNED AT THE STAKE

PETER D. CLARKE—WYANDOTT

As the Revolutionary War drew to a close, a new western horizon was visible to eager settlers. Especially tempting were the rich lands of the Ohio Valley in which the Wyandotts and Delawares had their hunting grounds. To wrest this wilderness from the Indians required force and cunning.

The task of outwitting the Indians was given to Colonel William Crawford, one of the most noted frontiersmen of his day. He had fought the Indians with Washington and Braddock, campaigned against Pontiac in 1763, and was a favorite officer of Washington in the Revolutionary War.

In May, 1782, at Washington's request, he led an expedition against the Wyandott and Delaware Indians on the Sandusky River in Ohio. Only a short time before, a community of Moravian Indians, many of whom were Delawares, had been attacked and destroyed by the whites. The Indians believed that Colonel Crawford was responsible for the Moravian massacre.

This story of how he met his death was written in 1870.

Between 1780 and 1791, the band of Delawares inhabiting the banks of the Muskingum, in south-eastern Ohio, were accused by the whites of supplying the savages of the West with provisions, whilst on their way to the frontier settlements, thereby encouraging them to carry on their warfare against the frontier settlers. These Delawares thus accused were a Christian people, of the Moravian persuasion, and had a Missionary Church and School established among them. They knew enough not to expose themselves to the vengeance of the whites situated as they were, by harbouring and encouraging the western savages, as they were accused of.

Here was a sample of vengeance wreaked upon an innocent and harmless people for the crime of others. Colonel Crawford never received any orders from the United States Government to destroy this Christian community with fire or sword. One Sunday morning they were visited by a military force led by the Colonel.

Slowly, and somewhat hesitatingly, as the metallic sound of the church bell was ringing in the ears of this community, people were seen wending their way toward their place of worship, viewing the military with distrust. Crawford told the Delawares that he was in pursuit of some savages who had lately been attacking some of the frontier settlers, and they must not think that he had any hostile intentions against them (the Delawares), and not to feel any way alarmed whilst attending their Church. But some of the keen-eyed Delawares who thought they saw evil lurking in the eye of Crawford kept outside.

To keep from being suspected, Crawford went inside of the Church, followed by some of his men. A large number of the Moravians, men, women and children were in meeting, and whilst attentively listening to the word of God, spoken to them by their missionary, through an interpreter, Crawford, at a given signal, rushed out with his men and fastened the doors of the Church. What became of the missionary preacher American historians give no account, much less this treachery.

What next? one might ask, whilst the cries of the imprisoned congregation were heard imploring the "savage" white man to be let out. What next? after the Christian Indians were shut up in their house of worship, the windows guarded with bristling bayonets. What next? The house of God was set on fire, and the wailings of the imprisoned Christians regaled the ears of Crawford (until their voice was hushed by the stifling smoke), who, but a moment before, had told them not to feel alarmed whilst attending Church; and where the Christians were just heard singing praises to God, was now heard the roar and crackling sound of the consuming element!

Those of this Delaware band who kept away from the Church on that fatal Sunday, betook themselves to flight, and went to Detroit, thence to the River Thames, in Upper Canada, where a tract of land was assigned to them by the British Government for their homes; and the place where they built their town on the banks of the Thames, still bears its first name, "Moravian Town."

Thus were a community of Christians destroyed for the crime of selling corn to some strange Indians whilst passing through their village, on the Muskingum river. They were accused of keeping a "half-way place" of entertainment for hostile Indians, between the border settlements and the interior of Ohio.

Truly, the Aborigines of America are a doomed race! But this belongs to the future; we will now return to Colonel Crawford, [who] again started off with a military force for the purpose of "chastising the hostile Indians" in Ohio. This Colonel's known rule of warfare was an undistinguished destruction of sexes, whether Christians or heathens. About three miles north of upper Sandusky, in an oak timber grove, Crawford found the Indians, who had been retreating before him for several days, northward. He made a desperate effort to drive the Indians from this grove, at the point of the bayonet, when seeing the greater portion of his men killed and wounded in the conflict; but he was defeated and taken prisoner by the Delawares, who took vengeance on him for destroying some of their people with "fire," some years before, on the Muskingum. He was taken to where they encamped, on the banks of a tributary of the Sandusky river, called "Ty-o-mauh-te" (a Wyandott name, signifying a stream around a prairie, or partly bounded by the stream) some distance from the battle ground. His trial spun out through the night, and next morning's sun saw him led to the stake by his executioners, with blackened faces.

A Delaware Chief addressed the assembled Indians of the different tribes at the execution, telling them how Crawford once burnt a Church and congregation of Delawares on the Muskingum river, thus:—"With forked tongue he diverted suspicion from their minds his intention to destroy them; and he turned a deaf ear to their cries whilst declaring their innocence of the crime which he accused them of, when they saw he was going to destroy them. They begged for mercy, but that mercy was denied them at his hands, which he now begs of us to extend toward him. I, myself," continued the Chief, "was among those at the door of our church who had some misgivings as to the truth of his words when telling us not to think that he came with any hostile intention toward us; and we who kept outside of the church, were powerless to avert the impending doom over our people when we saw them surrounded, and the doors closed and fastened by this white man," pointing toward Crawford, "and his soldiers." "Ka-ha-lauh!" (yes) exclaimed the Delawares, and cried out, "Burn him, burn him!" A white man was present (whom the Americans called a traitor to the Government, the Republic), who interceded for Crawford; but the Delawares were not to be moved by his entreaties; they said he must die. The doomed man, as his last resort, requested his intercessor, Simon Girty (who could speak the Delaware tongue) to tell them that if they would spare his life, now in their hands, he would give them one thousand dollars in money. "Mut-taw-cooh!" (no) was their answer to this offer.

Nevertheless Girty continued to plead for him; but when his ears were suddenly cut off by his executioners, he told Girty not to plead for him any more, his fate was sealed. He was tied to a stake in the midst of a bed of glowing coals of quick, consuming fire, made of dry oak bark; and Colonel Crawford was burnt.

Nine years after Colonel Crawford's death, the Indians of the Old Northwest scored their greatest victory. About 1,200 warriors led by the Miami chief, Little Turtle, ambushed and routed an army of 1,400 soldiers under General Arthur St. Clair. An Indian historian wrote in 1870 of this battle: "It has been remarked by Indian scouts who watched the movements of this army, that it appeared to them more like an emigration party escorted by a military force, than a regular army or military campaign, and that during the night, until they were attacked, some of St. Clair's men who were sitting around their camp fires, appeared sad and ill at ease, while others hung their heads, apparently brooding over the uncertainty of their situation. The whole encampment was inclosed with brush piles, and in the center of which was St. Clair's quarters, and all their flour, in bags, was extemporized for breastworks during the deadly conflict. The yells of a thousand Indians broke the ominous silence of the night, just before the dawn of day, and the battle of the forest commenced. All now was confusion in the camp. The bags of flour used for breastworks were soon riddled by bullets, scattering the flour over the encampment as if whitened with snow." St. Clair later reported that his retreat "was a precipitate one, in fact a flight."

Finally in 1794, at the Battle of Fallen Timbers, the Indians were routed by "Mad Anthony" Wayne; and on August 3, 1795, they gathered at Greenville, Ohio, and signed a treaty of peace which stripped them of their hunting grounds west of the Ohio.

AN ATTACK ON A FLATBOAT

PETER D. CLARKE—WYANDOTT

Before the close of the 18th century, some of the whites had commenced migrating from the then Western States to the south-western regions, by way of the Ohio and Mississippi, in flatboats, built square at each end, and 35 or 40 feet in length, ten or twelve feet in breadth, and the deck barricaded with thick planks about six feet in height, leaving a narrow gangway outside and over the gunwales. A sort of rudely constructed floating fort to protect the emigrants from the attacks of hostile Indians when brought in close proximity, occasionally, with the shore, as the craft followed the main channel of the river. One day a party of Potawatamie Indian scouts led by their war Chief, named Wauh-bun-se, was watching a craft of this description from their covert on the north bank of the Ohio, between, now, the States of Ohio and Illinois; and as the boat reached about opposite to them, they started for another point down the river to attack the floating fort when brought ashore.

"What is the reason," repeatedly exclaimed the pilot at the bow of the boat, "that you can't keep off from shore?" at the same time motioning with his hand to the man at the helm, signifying keep off from land. "I am trying my best I tell you," gruffly replied the steersman, but in spite of his redoubled efforts, the boat continued to be mysteriously going towards land. The pilot now began to examine the side of the boat next to land, closely into the water. To his great surprise he discovered an Indian, in a state of nudity, swimming under water like an otter, and tugging away landward with all his might, and holding one end of a rope with his teeth, the other end being fastened to the boat. It was the Potawatamie war Chief himself thus towing the floating fort toward land; and, to get breath, he occasionally emerged his head at the side of the boat to avoid detection. The pilot silently left the gangway unobserved by the Indian, and quietly returned with fixed bayonet, and as the latter came up along side to get breath again, "chug!" went the bayonet into his back! Down sank the Indian out of sight, who swam and reached shore, scarcely alive from fatigue and loss of blood; but the water washed the blood from his wound whilst making for land, and with some powerful medicinal roots, used by Indians, the leader of the scouts recovered from his terrible bayonet wound.

THE BRITISH CAMPAIGN IN THE NORTHWEST

BLACK HAWK—SAUK

The War of 1812 got under way with an American attempt to invade Canada through Detroit, in the Old Northwest. Control of this passage was vital to the success of American arms.

The Northwest bristled with powerful tribes of Indians who now held the balance of power. Most of them tried to remain neutral, but the gauche diplomacy of the American frontier agents forced Black Hawk, Tecumseh, and other Indian leaders to enter the struggle on the side of the British.

In his autobiography, dictated at Rock River in 1833, Black Hawk described the role played by the Sauk and Fox Indians in the Northwest campaign.

News reached us that a war was going to take place between the British and the Americans. Runners continued to arrive from different tribes, all confirming the report of the expected war. The British agent, Colonel Dixon, was holding talks with, and making presents to, the different tribes. I had not made up my mind whether to join the British or remain neutral. I had not discovered one good trait in the character of the Americans that had come to the country! They made fair promises, but never fulfilled them! Whilst the British made but few—but we could always rely upon their word!

Several of our chiefs and head men were called upon to go to Washington, to see their Great Father. Soon our friends returned from their visit to our Great Father. Their Great Father (they said) wished us, in the event of war taking place with England, not to interfere on either side—but to remain neutral. He did not want our help—but wished us to hunt and support our families, and live in peace. He said that British traders would not be permitted to come on the Mississippi, to furnish us with goods—but we would be well supplied by an American trader. Our chiefs then told him that the British traders always gave us credits in the fall, for guns, powder and goods, to enable us to hunt, and clothe our families. He replied that the trader at Fort Madison would have plenty of goods—that we should go there in the fall, and he would supply us on credit, as the British traders had done.

This information pleased us all very much. In a short time we were ready to start to Fort Madison, to get our supply of goods, that we might proceed to our hunting grounds. We passed merrily down the river—all in high spirits. We arrived at the fort, and made our encampment. Myself and principal men paid a visit to the war chief at the fort. He received us kindly, and gave us some tobacco, pipes and provision. The trader came in, and we all rose and shook hands with him—for on him all our dependence was placed, to enable us to hunt, and thereby support our families. We waited a long time, expecting the trader would tell us that he had orders from our Great Father to supply us with goods—but he said nothing on the subject. I got up, and told him, in a short speech, what we had come for—and hoped he had plenty of goods to supply us—and told him that he should be well paid in the spring—and concluded, by informing him, that we had determined to follow our Great Father's advice, and not go to war.

He said that he was happy to hear that we intended to remain at peace. That he had a large quantity of goods; and that, if we made a good hunt, we would be well supplied: but remarked, that he had received no instructions to furnish us any thing on credit!—nor could he give us any without receiving the pay for them on the spot!

We informed him what our Great Father had told our chiefs at Washington—and contended that he could supply us if he would—believing that our Great Father always spoke the truth! But the war chief said that the trader could not furnish us on credit—and that he had received no instructions from our Great Father at Washington! We left the fort dissatisfied and went to our camp. What was now to be done, we knew not. We questioned the party that brought us the news from our Great Father, that we would get credit for our winter's supplies, at this place. They still told the same story, and insisted upon its truth. Few of us slept that night—all was gloom and discontent!

In the morning, a canoe was seen descending the river—it soon arrived, bearing an express, who brought intelligence that La Gutrie, a British trader, had landed at Rock Island, with two boats loaded with goods—and requested us to come up immediately—because he had good news for us, and a variety of presents. The express presented us with tobacco, pipes and wampum.

The news run through our camp like fire in the prairie. Our lodges were soon taken down, and all started for Rock Island. Here ended all hopes of our remaining at peace—having been forced into war by being deceived!

Our party were not long in getting to Rock Island. When we came in sight, and saw tents pitched, we yelled, fired our guns, and commenced beating our drums. Guns were immediately fired at the island, returning our salute, and a British flag hoisted! We landed, and were cordially received by La Gutrie—and then smoked the pipe with him! After which he made a speech to us, that had been sent by Colonel Dixon, and gave us a number of handsome presents—a large silk flag, and a keg of rum, and told us to retire—take some refreshments and rest ourselves, as he would have more to say to us on the next day.

We, accordingly, retired to our lodges (which had been put up in the mean time), and spent the night. The next morning we called upon him, and told him that we wanted his two boats' load of goods to divide among our people—for which he should be well paid in the spring with furs and peltries. He consented—told us to take them—and do as we pleased with them. Whilst our people were dividing the goods, he took me aside, and informed me that Colonel Dixon was at Green Bay, with twelve boats, loaded with goods, guns, and ammunition—and wished me to raise a party immediately and go to him. A party of two hundred warriors were soon collected and ready to depart.

I started with my party to Green Bay. On our arrival there, we found a large encampment, and were well received by Dixon, and the war chiefs that were with him. He gave us plenty of provisions, tobacco and pipes, and said he would hold a council with us the next day.

In the encampment, I found a large number of Pottowatomies, Kickapoos, Ottawas and Winnebagoes. I visited all their camps, and found them in high spirits. They had all received new guns, ammunition, and a variety of clothing. In the evening a messenger came to me to visit Colonel Dixon. I went to his tent, in which were two other war chiefs, and an interpreter. He received me with a hearty shake of the hand, and presented me to the other chiefs, who shook my hand cordially, and seemed much pleased to see me. After I was seated, Colonel Dixon said: "General Black Hawk, I sent for you, to explain to you what we are going to do, and the reasons that have brought us here. Our friend, La Gutrie, informs us in the letter you brought from him, what has lately taken place. You will now have to hold us fast by the hand. Your English father has found out that the Americans want to take your country from you—and has sent me and his braves to drive them back to their own country. He has, likewise, sent a large quantity of arms and ammunition—and we want all your warriors to join us."

He then placed a medal round my neck, and gave me a paper, which I lost in the late war [Black Hawk War], and a silk flag, saying—"You are to command all the braves that will leave here the day after to-morrow, to join our braves near Detroit."

I told him that I was very much disappointed—as I wanted to descend the Mississippi, and make war upon the settlements. He said he had been "ordered to lay the country waste around St. Louis—that he had been a trader on the Mississippi many years—had always been kindly treated, and could not consent to send brave men to murder women and children! That there were no soldiers there to fight; but where he was going to send us, there were a number of soldiers: and, if we defeated them, the Mississippi country should be ours!" I was pleased with this speech; it was spoken by a brave!

The next day, arms and ammunition, tomahawks, knives, and clothing, were given to my band. We had a great feast in the evening; and the morning following, I started with about five hundred braves, to join the British army. The British war chief accompanied us. We passed Chicago. The fort had been evacuated by the American soldiers, who had marched for Fort Wayne. They were attacked a short distance from that fort, and defeated! They had a considerable quantity of powder in the fort at Chicago, which they had promised to the Indians; but the night before they marched, they destroyed it. I think it was thrown into the well! If they had fulfilled their word to the Indians, I think they would have gone safe.

On our arrival, I found that the Indians had several prisoners. I advised them to treat them well. We continued our march, and joined the British army below Detroit; and soon after had a fight! The

Americans fought well, and drove us with considerable loss! I was surprised at this, as I had been told that the Americans could not fight!

Our next movement was against a fortified place. I was stationed, with my braves, to prevent any person going to, or coming from the fort. I found two men taking care of cattle, and took them prisoners. I would not kill them, but delivered them to the British war chief. Soon after, several boats came down the river, full of American soldiers. They landed on the opposite side, took the British batteries, and pursued the soldiers that had left them. They went too far, without knowing the forces of the British, and were defeated! I hurried across the river, anxious for an opportunity to show the courage of my braves; but before we reached the ground, all was over! The British had taken many prisoners, and the Indians were killing them! I immediately put a stop to it, as I never thought it brave, but cowardly, to kill an unarmed and helpless enemy!

We remained here some time. I cannot detail what took place, as I was stationed, with my braves, in the woods. It appeared, however, that the British could not take this fort—for we were marched to another some distance off. When we approached it, I found it a small stockade, and concluded that there were not many men in it. The British war chief sent a flag—Colonel Dixon carried it, and returned. He said a young war chief commanded, and would not give up without fighting! Dixon came to me and said, "You will see, tomorrow, how easily we will take that fort." I was of opinion that they would take it; but when the morning came, I was disappointed. The British advanced—commenced an attack, and fought like braves; but by braves in the fort, were defeated, and a great number killed! The British army were making preparations to retreat. I was now tired of being with them—our success being bad, and having got no plunder. I determined on leaving them and returning to Rock River, to see what had become of my wife and children, as I had not heard from them since I started. That night, I took about twenty of my braves, and left the British camp for home.

THE INVASION OF CANADA

WILLIAM APES—PEQUOD

Not all Indians fought with the British. A few Iroquois and New England Indians joined the American forces and took part in the farcical invasion of Canada.

William Apes enlisted in the army at the age of fourteen and participated in the ill-fated invasions led by Generals Dearborn (1812) and Wilkinson (1813).

Wandering about, I fell in company with a sergeant and a file of men who were enlisting soldiers for the United States army. They thought I would answer their purpose, but how to get me was the thing. Now they began to talk to me, then treated me to some spirits and when that began to operate they told me all about the war, and what a fine thing it was to be a soldier. I was pleased with the idea of being a soldier, took some more liquor and some money, had a cockade fastened on my hat, and was off in high spirits for my uniform. Now my enlistment was against the law, but I did not know it; I could not think why I should risk my life and limbs in fighting for the white man, who had cheated my forefathers out of their land. By this time I had acquired many bad practices. In a little time I became almost as bad as any of them; could drink rum, play cards, and act as wickedly as any.

Shortly after this we were ordered to Staten Island, where we remained about two months. Then we were ordered to join the army destined to conquer Canada. As the soldiers were tired of the island, this news animated them very much. They thought it a great thing to march through the country and assist in taking the enemy's land.

In the meantime I had been transferred to the ranks. This I did not like; to carry a musket was too fatiguing, and I had a positive objection to being placed on the guard, especially at night. As I had only enlisted for a drummer, I thought that this change by the officer was contrary to law, and as the bond was broken, liberty was granted me; therefore being heartily tired of a soldier's life, and having a desire to see my father once more, I went off very deliberately; I had no idea that they had a lawful claim on me, and was greatly surprised as well as alarmed, when arrested as a deserter from the army. Well, I was taken up and carried back to the camp, where the officers put me under guard. We shortly after marched for Canada, and during this dreary march the officers tormented me by telling me that it was their intention to make a fire in the woods, stick my skin full of pine splinters, and after having an Indian pow-wow over me burn me to death. Thus they tormented me day after day.

We went into winter quarters at Plattsburgh. Another change now took place,—we had several pieces of heavy artillery with us, and of course horses were necessary to drag them, and I was taken from the ranks and ordered to take charge of one team. This made my situation rather better. I now had the privilege of riding. The soldiers were badly off, as the officers were very cruel to them, and for every little offence they would have them flogged. One day the officer of our company got angry at me, and pricked my ear with the point of his sword.

We soon joined the main army, and pitched our tents with them. It was now very cold, and we had nothing but straw to lay on. There was also a scarcity of provisions, and we were not allowed to draw our full rations. The people generally, have no idea of the extreme sufferings of the soldiers on the frontiers during the last war; they were indescribable, the soldiers eat with the utmost greediness raw corn and every thing eatable that fell in their way. In the midst of our afflictions, our valiant general [Dearborn] ordered us to march forward to subdue the country in a trice.

After we had proceeded about thirty miles, we fell in with a body of Canadians and Indians—the woods fairly resounded with their yells. Our "brave and chivalrous" general ordered a picked troop to disperse them; we fired but one cannon and a retreat was sounded to the great mortification of the soldiers who were ready and willing to fight. But as our general did not fancy the smell of gunpowder, he thought it best to close the campaign, by retreating with seven thousand men, before a "host" of seven hundred. Thus were many a poor fellow's hopes of conquest and glory blasted by the timidity of one man. This little brush with an enemy that we could have crushed in a single moment cost us several men in killed and wounded. The army now fell back on Plattsburgh, where we remained during the winter.

When the spring opened, we were employed in building forts. We soon received orders to march, and joined the army under Gen. Wilkinson, to reduce Montreal. We marched to Odletown in great splendour, "Heads up and eyes right," with a noble commander at our head, and the splendid city of Montreal in our view. The city no doubt presented a scene of the wildest uproar and confusion; the people were greatly alarmed as we moved on with all the pomp and glory of an army flushed with many victories. But when we reached Odletown, John Bull met us with a picked troop. They soon retreated, and some took refuge in an old fortified mill, which we pelted with a goodly number of cannon balls. It appeared as if we were determined to sweep every thing before us. It was really amusing to see our feminine general with his night-cap on his head, and a dishcloth tied round his precious body, crying out to his men "Come on, my brave boys, we will give John Bull a bloody nose." We did not succeed in taking the mill, and the British kept up an incessant cannonade from the fort. Some of the balls cut down the trees, so that we had frequently to spring out of their way when falling. I thought it was a hard time, and I had reason too, as I was in the front of the battle, assisting in working a twelve pounder, and the British aimed directly at us. Their balls whistled around us, and hurried a good many of the soldiers into the eternal world, while others were most horribly mangled. Indeed they were so hot upon us, that we had not time to remove the dead as they fell. The horribly disfigured bodies of the dead—the piercing groans of the wounded and the dying—the cries for help and succour from those who could not help themselves—were most appalling. I can never forget it. We continued fighting till near sundown, when a retreat was sounded along our line, and instead of marching forward to Montreal, we wheeled about, and having once set our faces towards Plattsburgh, and turned our backs ingloriously on the enemy, we hurried off with all possible speed. We carried our dead and wounded with us. Oh, it was a dreadful sight to behold so many brave men sacrificed in this manner.

In this way our campaign closed. During the whole of this time the Lord was merciful to me, as I was not suffered to be hurt.

THE OJIBWAYS REMAIN NEUTRAL

WILLIAM WARREN—OJIBWAY

We-esh-coob, the war-chief of the Pillagers [a band of Ojibways], with a party of his people from Leech Lake, happened to be present at the island of Michilimacinac. He was vainly urged by the British agents to join their arms with his band of warriors, who were noted as being the bravest of the Ojibway tribe. At a council held within the fort, this chief was asked, for the last time, by the British commandant, to array himself under their flag. We-esh-coob, in more decided terms than ever, refused, and his words so exasperated the commandant, that he rose from his seat, and forgot himself so far as to say to the Pillagers:—

"I thought you were men, but I see that you are but women, not fit even to wear the breech-cloth. Go back to your homes. I do not wish the assistance of women. Go, put on the clothing which more befits you, and remain quiet in your villages."

As he delivered this violent speech, he was proceeding to leave the council room, when We-esh-coob, having quietly listened to the interpretation thereof, rose to his feet, and approaching the angry Englishman, he put his hand on his epaulette and gently held him back. "Wait," said he, "you have spoken; now let me speak. You say that we should not wear the breech-cloth, but the dress of women." Then pointing to the opposite shore of the lake, towards the site of the old English fort which the Ojibways had taken in 1763, We-esh-coob exclaimed:—

"Englishman! have you already forgotten that we once made you cry like children? yonder! who was the woman then?

"Englishman! you have said that we are women. If you doubt our manhood, you have young men here in your strong house. I have also young men. You must come out on some open place, and we will fight. You will better know, whether we are fit, or not, to wear the breech-cloth.

"Englishman! you have said words which the ears of We-esh-coob have never before heard," and throwing down his blanket in great excitement, he pointed to different scars on his naked body, and exclaimed: "I thought I carried about me the marks which proved my manhood."

The English officer whose irritation had somewhat abated during the delivery of this answer, grasped the unusually excited Indian by the hand, and requested the interpreter to beg him to forget his hasty words. Peace and good-will were thus restored, but this bitter taunt tended greatly to strengthen the minds of the Ojibways against the agents who were continually engaged amongst them, to draw them into the war.

"WE ARE DETERMINED TO DEFEND OUR LANDS"

TECUMSEH—SHAWNEE

Tecumseh (1768?-1813) was perhaps the greatest of all Indian leaders. Brilliant, capable, and honest, he held fast to the principle that the Indians must never yield an inch of land to the Americans. "No difficulties deter him," wrote his enemy, General William H. Harrison. "If it were not for the vicinity of the United States, he would, perhaps, be the founder of an Empire that would rival in glory Mexico or Peru."

Like King Philip and Pontiac before him, Tecumseh attempted to unite the Indians in a defensive confederation. His brother, Tenskwatawa the prophet, preached a return to the native virtues of the Indians, and together they won the allegiance of the Shawnees and neighboring tribes. They established a large settlement at the junction of Tippecanoe Creek and the Wabash River. By 1811 the settlement was strong enough to present a threat to American security.

Tecumseh and Harrison met several times in an effort to avoid a war that seemed inevitable. Tecumseh spoke bitterly of broken promises and illegal treaties. He pointed out that Harrison had assembled a few Indians, filled them with firewater, and then bought from them the hunting lands which were a common possession that could not be ceded by or purchased from individual tribes.

During the last conference with Tecumseh, Harrison ordered that a chair be pulled up for the famous chief. "Your Father," said the interpreter, "requests you to take a chair." "My Father!" replied Tecumseh scornfully. "The sun is my father, and the earth is my mother. I will repose upon her bosom." And he seated himself Indian-fashion on the ground.

Shortly after this interview, while Tecumseh was away enlisting the aid of the Creeks, Harrison moved swiftly against the Indians at Tippecanoe. His plan was to strike before Tecumseh could return. Tenskwatawa, in command during Tecumseh's absence, accepted the challenge. After a bitter struggle the Indians were driven back, and Harrison burned their village. Tecumseh's hopes for a united Indian nation were shattered, and Harrison had won the popularity which later put him into the White House.

During the War of 1812 Tecumseh joined the British in Canada with the rank of brigadier general. In September, 1813, General Proctor, commander of the British garrison at Malden, Canada, quietly began preparations to withdraw before the advancing army of General Harrison. Tecumseh got wind of the plans. In this brilliant speech he hurled an accusation of cowardice at Proctor.

Father! Listen to your children! You have them now all before you.

The war before this [Revolutionary War], our British father gave the hatchet to his red children, when our old chiefs were alive. They are now dead. In that war our father was thrown flat on his back by the Americans, and our father took them by the hand without our knowledge. We are afraid that our father will do so again this time.

The summer before last, when I came forward with my red brethren, and was ready to take up the hatchet in favor of our British father, we were told not to be in a hurry—that he had not yet determined to fight the Americans.

Listen! When war was declared, our father stood up and gave us the tomahawk, and told us that he was then ready to strike the Americans—that he wanted our assistance—and that he would certainly get us our lands back, which the Americans had taken from us.

Listen! You told us, at that time, to bring forward our families to this place, and we did so. You also promised to take care of them—they should want for nothing, while the men would go and fight the enemy—that we need not trouble ourselves about the enemy's garrison—that we knew nothing about them—and that our father would attend to that part of the business. You also told your red children that you would take good care of your garrison here, which made our hearts glad.

Father, listen! Our fleet has gone out. We know they have fought.

We have heard the great guns. But we know nothing of what has happened [Perry had defeated the British on Lake Erie, September 10]. Our ships have gone one way, and we are much astonished to see our father tying up everything and preparing to run away the other, without letting his red children know what his intentions are. You always told us to remain here, and take care of our lands. It made our hearts glad to hear that was your wish. Our great father, the king, is the head, and you represent him. You always told us that you would never draw your foot off British ground. But now, father, we see you are drawing back, and we are sorry to see our father doing so without seeing the enemy. We must compare our father's conduct to a fat dog, that carries its tail upon its back, but when affrighted, it drops it between its legs and runs off.

Father, listen! The Americans have not yet defeated us by land. Neither are we sure that they have done so by water. We therefore wish to remain here, and fight our enemy, should they make their appearance. If they defeat us, we will then retreat with our father.

At the battle of the rapids, last war, the Americans certainly defeated us. And when we returned to our father's fort, at that place the gates were shut against us. We were afraid that it would now be the case; but instead of that, we now see our British father preparing to march out of his garrison.

Father! You have got the arms and ammunition which our great father sent for his red children. If you have an idea of going away, give them to us, and you may go and welcome for us. Our lives are in the hands of the Great Spirit. We are determined to defend our lands, and if it be his will, we wish to leave our bones upon them.

Tecumseh's last words were prophetic. Proctor accepted his challenge to stand against the enemy, and on October 5, 1813, at the Battle of the Thames, the great Shawnee warrior fought his last fight. After posting his braves Tecumseh called his chiefs around him and said: "Brother warriors, we are now about to enter into an engagement from which I shall never come out—my body will remain on the field of battle." He unbuckled his sword and handed it to one of the chiefs, saying, "When my son becomes a noted warrior and able to wield a sword, give this to him."

Tecumseh discarded his British uniform and put on the plain deerskin of a Shawnee warrior.

The Americans claimed that Tecumseh was killed by Colonel Richard Johnson during a cavalry charge. But the Wyandott historian Peter D. Clarke wrote, after talking with Indians who had fought in the battle: "Among the retreating Indians was a Potawatamie brave, who, on perceiving an American officer (supposed to be Colonel Johnson) on horse, close upon him, turned to tomahawk his pursuer, but was shot down by him with his pistol. The fallen Potawatamie brave was probably taken for Tecumseh by some of Harrison's infantry, and mutilated soon after the battle. Several of Harrison's army claimed to have killed Tecumseh. 'I killed Tecumseh; I have some of his beard,' one would say; 'I killed Tecumseh,' another would clamour; 'I have a piece of his skin to make me a razor strop!' None of these braggadocios were in the last battle, in which the brave chief received his mortal wound."

THE SURRENDER OF WILLIAM WEATHERFORD

WILLIAM WEATHERFORD—CREEK

The Creeks made a bid for independence in 1813-1814, under the leadership of William Weatherford (1780-1824). Driven back by General Andrew Jackson, he finally gambled his army in a desperate clash at the Great Horseshoe bend of the Tallapoosa and was defeated. To save further bloodshed, Weatherford gave himself up to General Jackson. His surrender speech is a famous example of Indian eloquence.

I am in your power: do with me what you please. I am a soldier. I have done the white people all the harm I could. I have fought them, and fought them bravely. If I had an army, I would yet fight, and contend to the last. But I have done—my people are all gone—I can do no more than weep over the misfortunes of my nation. Once I could animate my warriors to battle: but I cannot animate the dead. My warriors can no longer hear my voice—their bones are at Talladega, Tallaschatchee, Emuckfaw, and Tohopeka. I have not surrendered myself thoughtlessly. Whilst there were chances of success, I never left my post, nor supplicated peace. But my people are gone, and now I ask it for my nation, and for myself.

On the miseries and misfortunes brought upon my country, I look back with the deepest sorrow, and wish to avert still greater calamities. If I had been left to contend with the Georgian army [militia of Georgia], I would have raised my corn on one bank of the river, and have fought them on the other. But your people have destroyed my nation. You are a brave man. I rely upon your generosity. You will exact no terms of a conquered people, but such as they should accede to. Whatever they may be, it would now be madness and folly to oppose them. If they are opposed, you shall find me among the sternest enforcers of obedience. Those who would still hold out, can be influenced only by a mean spirit of revenge; and, to this, they must not, and *shall not*, sacrifice the last remnant of their country.

After promising to use his influence to keep peace, Weatherford was set free by Jackson. He kept his promise, and his people remained at peace with the Americans.

THE BLACK HAWK WAR

BLACK HAWK—SAUK

Black Hawk (1767-1838) was a great warrior—fierce, loyal, courageous, dignified. Contemporary portraits show a care-plowed face in which every line expresses intelligence and nobility.

Black Hawk was the most distinguished chief of his tribe. On his blanket was painted a blood-red hand, signifying that he had killed and scalped an enemy when he was only fifteen. By the time he was thirty-five he had counted coup on nearly forty Osage and Cherokee warriors. Once he led a war party into the country of the Osages but found only four enemy warriors, whom he released. "Great as was my hatred for this people," commented the chief, "I could not kill so small a party." During the siege of an American fort, he discovered two white boys hiding in a bush. "I thought of my own children," he said later, "and passed on without noticing them."

National renown came to Black Hawk in 1832, when he was forced into a war with the American troops in northern Illinois. The government in Washington rushed more troops to the frontier. Young Abe Lincoln, then twenty-three, joined a company of volunteers and was elected captain.

The odds were too great against Black Hawk. His braves were pushed north into Wisconsin, and on a little island in the Bad Axe River the old warrior made his last stand. He never learned that his Winnebago guides were in the pay of the whites and had deliberately led him into a trap.

Black Hawk surrendered and was sent to Washington, where he confronted President Andrew Jackson. "I took up the tomahawk," he told Jackson, "to avenge injuries which could no longer be borne. Had I borne them longer, my people would have said: 'Black Hawk is a squaw. He is too old to be a chief.'"

DEDICATION

To Brigadier Gen'l H. Atkinson.

SIR,—The changes of fortune, and vicissitudes of war, made you my conqueror. When my last resources were exhausted, my warriors worn down with long and toilsome marches, we yielded, and I became your prisoner.

The story of my life is told in the following pages. It is intimately connected, and in some measure, identified with a part of the history of your own. I have, therefore, dedicated it to you.

The changes of many summers have brought old age upon me, and I cannot expect to survive many moons. Before I set out on my journey to the land of my fathers, I have determined to give my motives and reasons for my former hostilities to the whites, and to vindicate my character from misrepresentation. The kindness I received from you whilst a prisoner of war, assures me that you will vouch for the facts contained in my narrative, so far as they came under your observation.

I am now an obscure member of a nation that formerly honored and respected my opinions. The path to glory is rough, and many gloomy hours obscure it. May the Great Spirit shed light on yours—and that you may never experience the humility that the power of the American government has reduced me to, is the wish of him, who, in his native forests, was once as proud and bold as yourself.

10th Moon, 1833. BLACK HAWK

The whites were settling the country fast. I was out one day hunting in a bottom, and met three white men. They accused me of killing their hogs. I denied it, but they would not listen to me. One of them took my gun out of my hand and fired it off—then took out the flint, gave back my gun, and commenced beating me with sticks, and ordered me off. I was so much bruised that I could not sleep for several nights.

Some time after this occurrence, one of my camp cut a bee-tree, and carried the honey to his lodge. A party of white men soon followed, and told him that the bee-tree was theirs, and that he had no right to cut it. He pointed to the honey, and told them to take it. They were not satisfied with this, but took all the packs of skins that he had collected during the winter, to pay his trader and clothe his family in the spring, and carried them off!

How could we like such people, who treated us so unjustly? We determined to break up our camp, for fear that they would do worse —and when we joined our people in the spring, a great many of them complained of similar treatment.

This summer our agent came to live at Rock Island. The trader explained to me the terms of the treaty that had been made [a treaty signed in 1804 by four drunken Indians without any authority from their tribe], and said we would be obliged to leave the Illinois side of the Mississippi, and advised us to select a good place for our village and remove to it in the spring.

We started to our hunting grounds, in good hopes that something would be done for us. During the winter, I received information that three families of whites had arrived at our village, and destroyed some of our lodges, and were making fences and dividing our cornfields for their own use—and were quarrelling among themselves about their lines in the division! I immediately started for Rock River, a distance of ten days' travel, and on my arrival, found the report to be true. I went to my lodge, and saw a family occupying it.

What *right* had these people to our village, and our fields, which the Great Spirit had given us to live upon? My reason teaches me that land cannot be sold. The Great Spirit gave it to his children to live upon, and cultivate, as far as is necessary for their subsistence; and so long as they occupy and cultivate it, they have the right to the soil—but if they voluntarily leave it, then any other people have a right to settle upon it. Nothing can be sold but such things as can be carried away.

The white people brought whisky into our village, made our people drunk, and cheated them out of their horses, guns, and traps! Consequently, I visited all the whites and begged them not to sell whisky to my people. One of them continued the practice openly. I took a party of my young men, went to his house, and took out his barrel and broke in the head and turned out the whisky. I did this for fear some of the whites might be killed by my people when drunk.

It was ascertained that a great war chief [General E. P. Gaines], with a large number of soldiers, was on his way to Rock River. The war chief arrived, and convened a council at the agency. He said: "I hope you will consult your own interest and leave the country you are occupying, and go to the other side of the Mississippi."

I replied: "That we had never sold our country. We never received any annuities from our American father! And we are determined to hold on to our village!"

The war chief said: "I came here, neither to beg nor hire you to leave your village. My business is to remove you, peaceably if I can, but forcibly if I must! I will now give you two days to remove in—and if you do not cross the Mississippi within that time, I will adopt measures to force you away!"

The war chief appointed the next day to remove us. We crossed the Mississippi during the night and encamped some distance below Rock Island. The great war chief convened another council, for the purpose of making a treaty with us. In this treaty, he agreed to give us corn in place of that we had left growing in our fields. I touched the goosequill to this treaty, and was determined to live in peace.

The corn that had been given us was soon found to be inadequate to our wants; when loud lamentations were heard in the camp, by our women and children, for their roasting-ears, beans, and squashes. To satisfy them, a small party of braves went over, in the night, to steal corn from their own fields. They were discovered by the whites, and fired upon. Complaints were again made of the depredations committed by some of my people, *on their own corn fields!*

> [Invited by the Winnebagoes to plant corn in their territory, Black Hawk and his people crossed the Mississippi. When warned by General Atkinson that this act was contrary to the treaty, he decided to return.]

I received news that three or four hundred white men, on horseback, had been seen about eight miles off. I immediately started three young men, with a white flag, to meet them and conduct them to our camp, that we might hold a council with them and descend Rock River again. I directed them, in case the whites had encamped, to return, and I would go and see *them.* After this party had started, I sent five young men to see what might take place. The first party went to the encampment of the whites and were taken prisoners. The last party had not proceeded far before they saw about twenty men coming towards them in full gallop! They stopped, and finding that the whites were coming so fast, in warlike attitude, they turned and retreated, but were pursued, and two of them overtaken and killed! The others made their escape. When they came in with the news, I was preparing my flags to meet the war chief. The alarm was given. Nearly all my young men were absent, about ten miles off. I started with what I had left (about forty), and had proceeded but a short distance before we saw a part of the army approaching. I raised a yell, and said to my braves: "Some of our people have been killed!—wantonly and cruelly murdered! We must revenge their death!"

In a little while we discovered the whole army coming towards us in full gallop! We were now confident that our first party had been killed. I immediately placed my men in front of some bushes, that we might have the first fire, when they approached close enough. They made a halt some distance from us. I gave another yell, and ordered my brave warriors to charge upon them—expecting that we would all be killed. They did charge! Every man rushed and fired, and the enemy retreated in the utmost confusion and consternation before my little, but brave band of warriors!

After pursuing the enemy some distance, I found it useless to follow them, as they rode so fast, and returned to my encampment with a few of my braves. I lighted my pipe, and sat down to thank the Great Spirit for what we had done. I had not been long meditating, when two of the three young men I had sent out with the flag to meet the American war chief entered. My astonishment was not greater than my joy to see them living and well.

I had resolved upon giving up the war—and sent a flag of peace to the American war chief, expecting, as a matter of right, reason, and justice that our flag would be respected. Yet instead I was forced into war, with about five hundred warriors, to contend against three or four thousand.

Finding that all was safe, I made a dog feast [a ceremony in which a dog was sacrificed and eaten]. Before my braves commenced feasting, I took my medicine bags, and addressed them in the following language:

"Braves and Warriors: These are the medicine bags of our forefather, Muk-a-ta-quet, who was the father of the Sac nation. They were handed down to the great war chief of our nation, Na-na-makee, who has been at war with all the nations of the lakes and all the nations of the plains, and have never yet been disgraced! I expect you all to protect them!"

Ne-a-pope, with a party of twenty, remained in our rear, to watch for the enemy whilst we were proceeding to the Ouisconsin, with our women and children. We arrived, and had commenced crossing them to an island, when we discovered a large body of the enemy coming towards us. We were now compelled to fight, or sacrifice our wives and children to the fury of the whites. I met them with fifty warriors about a mile from the river, when an attack immediately commenced. I was mounted on a fine horse, and was pleased to see my warriors so brave. I addressed them in a loud voice, telling them to stand their ground, and never yield it to the enemy. At this time I was on the rise of a hill, where I wished to form my warriors that we might have some advantage over the whites. But the enemy succeeded in gaining this point, which compelled us to fall back into a deep ravine, from which we continued firing at them and they at us, until it began to grow dark. My horse having been wounded twice during this engagement, and fearing from his loss of blood that he would soon give out, I ordered my warriors to return.

In this skirmish, with fifty braves, I defended and accomplished my passage over the Ouisconsin, with a loss of only six men, though opposed by a host of mounted militia. I would not have fought there, but to gain time for my women and children to cross to an island. A warrior will duly appreciate the embarrassments I labored under—and whatever may be the sentiments of the white people, in relation to this battle, my nation, though fallen, will award to me the reputation of a great brave in conducting it. We returned to the Ouisconsin, and crossed over to our people. Here some of my people left me, and descended the Ouisconsin, hoping to escape to the west side of the Mississippi, that they might return home. I had no objection to their leaving me, as my people were all in a desperate condition—being worn out with travelling, and starving from hunger.

A party of whites, being in advance of the army, came upon our people, who were attempting to cross the Mississippi. They tried to give themselves up—the whites paid no attention to their entreaties—but commenced *slaughtering* them! In a little while the whole army arrived. Our braves, but few in number, finding that the enemy paid no regard to age or sex, and seeing that they were murdering helpless women and little children, determined to *fight until they were killed.* As many women as could, commenced swimming the Mississippi, with their children on their backs. A number of them were drowned, and some shot, before they could reach the opposite shore.

The massacre, which terminated the war, lasted about two hours. Our loss in killed, was about sixty, besides a number that were drowned. The loss of the enemy could not be ascertained by my braves, exactly; but they think that they killed about sixteen, during the action.

After hearing this sorrowful news, I started, with my little party, to the Winnebago village at Prairie La Cross. On my arrival there, I entered the lodge of one of the chiefs, and told him that I wished him to go with me to his father—that I intended to give myself up to the American war chief, and die, if the Great Spirit saw proper. I then started, with several Winnebagoes, and went to their agent, at Prairie du Chien, and gave myself up.

VIII: COVERED WAGONS AND IRON HORSES

By 1850 the Indians who wanted no part of the white man's civilization, and who refused to be corralled in reservations, were getting ready for what was to be their last fight. In Montana and in the Dakotas, on the great plains and on the deserts of New Mexico and Arizona, they were soon to stake their lives and their hopes against the military power of the United States.

The Indians wanted peace, but immigrants overran their hunting grounds in a rush to reach the California gold fields. As covered wagons creaked west and Indian protests went unheeded, angry bands of warriors attacked the immigrant trains. Soldiers were sent to subdue the Indians, and the great tribes of the plains—the Cheyenne, Sioux, Comanche—fought desperately to preserve their way of life. Ironically, they were defeated not by the American army but by white hunters who ruthlessly slaughtered the buffalo for their hides and left the flesh to rot on the plains. Without their "commissary on the hoof," even the Indians who had vowed to die fighting with bow in hand crept miserably into reservations in order to save their women and children from starvation.

INDIAN COUNCIL
Oil on canvas
George Catlin
1847
(Note "Catlin, 1847" on decorative banding on the second tipi from the right)

Courtesy of Gilcrease Institute

MANDAN CEMETERY
Oil on canvas
George Catlin
Undated

Courtesy of Gilcrease Institute

VIII: COVERED WAGONS AND IRON HORSES

ATTACKING THE UNION PACIFIC

CHIEF STANDING BEAR—SIOUX

Chief Standing Bear was born in the month "when the bark of the trees cracked, in the year of breaking up of camp" (December, 1868). Five months later, on the completion of the first transcontinental railroad, a golden spike was driven into a silver-bound tie at Ogden, Utah.

Soon after I was born, one of our scouts came into camp one day, and very excitedly stated that a big snake was crawling across the prairie. This caused much excitement. Close observation revealed the fact that a stream of smoke was following the supposed snake. It was the first railroad train of the Union Pacific Railroad. To the Indians this was a great curiosity, and they would climb high in the hills to watch the train run along and listen to the funny noises it made. When they saw that the "snake" ran on an iron track and did not leave it, they began to be a little braver, and came in closer to better examine the strange affair.

One day some of a war-party of our tribe were returning home. They were very thirsty, and stopped at the railroad station to get some water. The white man in charge of the station compelled them to leave without giving them any water. He was perhaps afraid of Indians, or possibly had done something to them and thought they had come to punish him. His actions made the Indians very angry. They thought it was strange that the white people would run a railroad train across their land, and now would not even let them have a drink of water.

So the war-party came home and reported the treatment they had received from the white man. A council was called, and it was decided to do something. My mother heard the men talking, and, after leaving me in the care of my grandmother, she took a short-handled axe and followed the men. When they came to the railroad track, it was decided to tear up some of the rails and the pieces of wood to which they were fastened. My mother cut the ties and the men hauled them away, after which the whole band went back a mile or so and waited to see what would happen when the train came along.

When the train crew sighted the Indians in the distance, they began to shoot at them. The Indians then whipped up their ponies and gave chase. The men on the train were so busy jeering at the Indians and making fun of their attempt to catch up with them that they failed to watch the track ahead, not suspecting that the Indians would be smart and cunning enough to lay a trap for them. When the train reached the broken spot, it ran off the track and was badly wrecked.

My mother had hidden near by, and after the train smash-up she ran to it. It happened to be a freight, carrying supplies of all sorts to the distant West, and among the cargo was quite a quantity of maple sugar, gingham, and beads. My mother obtained from this train wreck the first beads ever seen by the Sioux Nation. Prior to that time, all the fancy work on moccasins or clothing was made with porcupine quills, which were dyed. In using these quills, the women would hold them in their mouths until soft, then, when they were used, the quill was flattened with the finger nail.

Being a very smart woman, my mother conceived the idea of using some of these beads in place of the quills, to see what they would look like. She beaded a strip of buffalo skin, using yellow beads for the background, instead of the white ones which are now used so much. This beaded strip she sewed on a buffalo calf skin, which I wore as a blanket. So I was the first Sioux Indian to wear beads around my body on a blanket.

THE WAGON BOX FIGHT

FIRE THUNDER—SIOUX

In 1866 the Bozeman Trail was built to link the gold fields near Virginia City, Montana, with the Union Pacific Railroad. The trail ran through the heart of the Sioux country, and three forts were put up to protect it. The Sioux, led by Red Cloud (1822-1909), laid siege to the forts. So effective was their encirclement that it was almost impossible for the soldiers to relieve or reinforce their garrisons. On December 21, 1866, Captain William J. Fetterman, who had boasted that he could ride through the entire Sioux Nation with eighty men, ventured out from Fort Kearny to attack a war party of Sioux. His command was wiped out.

In 1867 Captain James W. Powell and thirty-two men of Fort Kearny were detailed to guard the woodcutters who went out each day. As only the running gear of the wagons was used to transport cordwood, he took off the wagon boxes. There were fourteen boxes, and he arranged these in a wide circle where the woodcutters were working. He cut loopholes in the sides for use in case of an Indian attack. New Springfield breech-loading rifles had just been issued to his men. These rapid-firing weapons had never been tested in battle, and the Indians were unaware of their existence.

On August 2, 1867, Captain Powell and his detail were attacked by a large party of Sioux under the leadership of Red Cloud. In this and later battles, the new Springfield rifle severely crippled the Indian's power to resist the white invader.

Fire Thunder, who fought in the Wagon Box Fight, reminisced about it many years later.

The following is taken from Black Elk Speaks *by John G. Neihardt.*

There is a wide flat prairie with hills around it, and in the middle of this the Wasichus [whites] had put the boxes of their wagons in a circle, so that they could keep their mules there at night. There were not many Wasichus, but they were lying behind the boxes and they shot faster than they ever shot at us before. We thought it was some new medicine of great power that they had, for they shot so fast that it was like tearing a blanket. Afterwards I learned that it was because they had new guns that they loaded from behind, and this was the first time they used these guns. We came on after sunrise. There were many, many of us, and we meant to ride right over them and rub them out. But our ponies were afraid of the ring of fire the guns of the Wasichus made, and would not go over. Our women were watching us from the hills and we could hear them singing and mourning whenever the shooting stopped. We tried hard, but we could not do it, and there were dead warriors and horses piled all around the boxes and scattered over the plain. Then we left our horses in a gulch and charged on foot, but it was like greengrass withering in a fire. So we picked up our wounded and went away. I do not know how many of our people were killed, but there were very many. It was bad.

FIGHTING THE MEXICANS

GERONIMO—APACHE

The Apache leader Geronimo (1829-1909) was fierce and uncompromising in his hatred of the Mexicans. In his autobiography, dictated in 1906, he told this story of how his mother, wife, and three children were murdered by the Mexicans and how he avenged their deaths.

At the time Geronimo's family was slain, the Mexican government was paying a bounty in gold for Apache scalps—$100 for a warrior's scalp, $50 for a squaw's scalp, and $25 for a child's scalp.

The total profit from Geronimo's family was only $175!

In the summer of 1858, being at peace with the Mexican towns as well as with all the neighboring Indian tribes, we went south into Old Mexico to trade. Our whole tribe went through Sonora toward Casa Grande, our destination, but just before reaching that place we stopped at another Mexican town called by the Indians "Kas-ki-yeh." Here we stayed for several days, camping just outside the city. Every day we would go into town to trade, leaving our camp under the protection of a small guard so that our arms, supplies, and women and children would not be disturbed during our absence.

Late one afternoon when returning from town we were met by a few women and children who told us that Mexican troops from some other town had attacked our camp, killed all the warriors of the guard, captured all our ponies, secured our arms, destroyed our supplies, and killed many of our women and children. Quickly we separated, concealing ourselves as best we could until nightfall, when we assembled at our appointed place of rendezvous—a thicket by the river. Silently we stole in one by one: sentinels were placed, and, when all were counted, I found that my aged mother, my young wife, and my three small children were among the slain. There were no lights in camp, so without being noticed I silently turned away and stood by the river. How long I stood there I do not know, but when I saw the warriors arranging for a council I took my place.

That night I did not give my vote for or against any measure; but it was decided that as there were only eighty warriors left, and as we were without arms or supplies, and were furthermore surrounded by the Mexicans far inside their own territory, we could not hope to fight successfully. So our chief, Mangus-Colorado, gave the order to start at once in perfect silence for our homes in Arizona, leaving the dead upon the field.

I stood until all had passed, hardly knowing what I would do—I had no weapon, nor did I hardly wish to fight, neither did I contemplate recovering the bodies of my loved ones, for that was forbidden. I did not pray, nor did I resolve to do anything in particular, for I had no purpose left. I finally followed the tribe silently, keeping just within hearing distance of the soft noise of the feet of the retreating Apaches. During the march as well as while we were camped I spoke to no one and no one spoke to me—there was nothing to say.

Within a few days we arrived at our own settlement. There were the decorations that Alope [Geronimo's wife] had made—and there were the playthings of our little ones. I burned them all, even our tepee. I also burned my mother's tepee and destroyed all her property. [This was in accordance with Apache custom, which required that the property of deceased relatives be destroyed.]

I was never again contented in our quiet home. I had vowed vengeance upon the Mexican troopers who had wronged me, and whenever I saw anything to remind me of former happy days my heart would ache for revenge upon Mexico.

As soon as we had again collected some arms and supplies Mangus-Colorado, our chief, called a council and found that all our warriors were willing to take the warpath against Mexico. I was appointed to solicit the aid of other tribes in this war.

When I went to the Chiricahua Apaches, Cochise, their chief, called a council at early dawn. Silently the warriors assembled at an open place in a mountain dell and took their seats on the ground, arranged in rows according to their ranks. Silently they sat smoking. At a signal from the chief I arose and presented my cause as follows:

"Kinsmen, you have heard what the Mexicans have recently done without cause. You are my relatives—uncles, cousins, brothers. We are men the same as the Mexicans are—we can do to them what they have done to us. Let us go forward and trail them—I will lead you to their city—we will attack them in their homes. I will fight in front of the battle—I only ask you to follow me to avenge this wrong done by these Mexicans—will you come?

"It is well—you will all come."

I returned to my own settlement, reported this success to my chieftain, and immediately departed to the southward into the land of the Nedni Apaches. Their chief, Whoa, heard me without comment, but he immediately issued orders for a council, and when all were ready gave a sign that I might speak. I addressed them as I had addressed the Chiricahua tribe, and they also promised to help us.

It was in the summer of 1859, almost a year from the date of the massacre of Kaskiyeh, that these three tribes were assembled on the Mexican border to go upon the warpath. Their faces were painted, the war bands fastened upon their brows, their long scalp-locks ready for the hand and knife of the warrior who could overcome them.

When all were ready the chieftains gave command to go forward. None of us were mounted and each warrior wore moccasins and also a cloth wrapped about his loins. This cloth could be spread over him when he slept, and when on the march would be ample protection as clothing. In battle, if the fight was hard, we did not wish much clothing. Each warrior carried three days' rations, but as we often killed game while on the march, we seldom were without food.

I acted as guide into Mexico, and we followed the river courses and mountain ranges because we could better thereby keep our movements concealed. We entered Sonora and went southward past Quitaco, Nacozari, and many smaller settlements.

When we were almost at Arispe we camped, and eight men rode out from the city to parley with us. These we captured, killed, and scalped. This was to draw the troops from the city, and the next day they came. The skirmishing lasted all day without a general engagement, but just at night we captured their supply train, so we had plenty of provisions and some more guns.

That night we posted sentinels and did not move our camp, but rested quietly all night, for we expected heavy work the next day. Early the next morning the warriors were assembled to pray—not for help, but that they might have health and avoid ambush or deceptions by the enemy.

As we had anticipated, about ten o'clock in the morning the whole Mexican force came out. There were two companies of cavalry and two of infantry. I recognized the cavalry as the soldiers who had killed my people at Kaskiyeh. This I told to the chieftains, and they said that I might direct the battle.

I was no chief and never had been, but because I had been more deeply wronged than others, this honor was conferred upon me, and I resolved to prove worthy of the trust. I arranged the Indians in a hollow circle near the river, and the Mexicans drew their infantry up in two lines, with the cavalry in reserve. We were in the timber, and they advanced until within about four hundred yards, when they halted and opened fire. Soon I led a charge against them, at the same time sending some braves to attack their rear. In all the battle I thought of my murdered mother, wife, and babies—of my vow of vengeance, and I fought with fury. Many fell by my hand, and constantly I led the advance. Many braves were killed. The battle lasted about two hours.

At the last four Indians were alone in the center of the field—myself and three other warriors. Our arrows were all gone, our spears broken off in the bodies of dead enemies. We had only our hands and knives with which to fight, but all who had stood against us were dead. Then two armed soldiers came upon us from another part of the field. They shot down two of our men and we, the remaining two, fled toward our own warriors. My companion was struck down by a saber, but I reached our warriors, seized a spear, and turned. The one who pursued me missed his aim and fell by my spear. With his saber I met the trooper who had killed my companion and we grappled and fell. I killed him with my knife and quickly rose over his body, brandishing his saber, seeking for other troopers to kill. There were none. Over the bloody field, covered with the bodies of Mexicans, rang the fierce Apache war-whoop.

Still covered with the blood of my enemies, still holding my conquering weapon, still hot with the joy of battle, victory, and vengeance, I was surrounded by the Apache braves and made war chief of all the Apaches. Then I gave orders for scalping the slain.

I could not call back my loved ones, I could not bring back the dead Apaches, but I could rejoice in this revenge. The Apaches had avenged the massacre of Kaskiyeh.

Geronimo's raids on Sonora were so frequent that in 1876, the Mexicans complained to the American government. After a chase Geronimo was arrested and confined on a reservation at San Carlos, Arizona. In 1884, he left the reservation and with a small band of warriors attacked outposts in New Mexico and Sonora. "We were reckless of our lives," he said later, "because we felt that every man's hand was against us. If we returned to the reservation we would be put in prison and killed; if we stayed in Mexico they would continue to send soldiers to fight us; so we gave no quarter to anyone and asked no favors."

Geronimo's little band was finally surrounded by American troops, and in August, 1886, he surrendered to General Nelson Miles. "The earth, the sun, and the winds all listen to me," said Geronimo. "Yusn [God] listens to me. I do not lie to you. I lay my arms down. I will not ask for mercy. If you wish, line us up and shoot us today or tomorrow. I won't care. I'll take my medicine like a man. So here's my gun."

Geronimo surrendered on condition that he and his men be sent to their families in Florida. Imprisoned instead, they were sent to Alabama and finally to Fort Sill, Oklahoma, where Geronimo died in 1909.

THE RETREAT OF THE NEZ PERCES

CHIEF JOSEPH—NEZ PERCE

The discovery of gold in the Nez Perce country of Oregon in 1860 lured a swarm of diggers, followed by land-hungry squatters. Some of the Nez Perce chieftains signed away their homelands to the white men, but the Wal-lam-wat-kin band, led by Chief Joseph, refused to give up the beautiful Wallowa Valley in eastern Oregon.

When American troops attempted in 1877 to force the "non-

treaty" Wal-lam-wat-kins upon a reservation, Chief Joseph and his people struck their tepees and headed for the Canadian border. The retreat of Chief Joseph is one of the greatest military feats of all time. Surrounded by hostile troops, and moving through an almost impassable wilderness, the Nez Perces traveled nearly twelve hundred miles from the Blue Mountains of Oregon to the Bear Paw Mountains of northern Montana. With fewer than three hundred warriors, and encumbered with women and children, Chief Joseph outmaneuvered and outfought the troops of Generals Howard, Gibbon, and Sturgis in fifteen engagements. Only when he believed himself to be safe across the Canadian border did he pause in his flight.

Joseph had miscalculated. He was still about twenty miles from Canada when General Miles with fresh troops attacked his little force. With the skill of a professional engineer, Joseph entrenched his people; but he surrendered after five days of artillery bombardment.

Two years later, Chief Joseph dictated this story of his retreat.

My friends, I have been asked to show you my heart. I am glad to have a chance to do so. I want the white people to understand my people. Some of you think an Indian is like a wild animal. This is a great mistake. I will tell you all about our people, and then you can judge whether an Indian is a man or not. I believe much trouble and blood would be saved if we opened our hearts more. I will tell you in my way how the Indian sees things. The white man has more words to tell you how they look to him, but it does not require many words to speak the truth. What I have to say will come from my heart, and I will speak with a straight tongue. Ah-cum-kin-i-ma-me-hut [the Great Spirit] is looking at me, and will hear me.

My name is In-mut-too-yah-lat-lat [Thunder-traveling-over-the-mountains]. I am chief of the Wal-lam-wat-kin band of Chute-pa-lu, or Nez Perces [nose-pierced Indians]. I was born in eastern Oregon, thirty-eight winters ago.

Our fathers gave us many laws, which they had learned from their fathers. These laws were good. They told us to treat all men as they treated us; that we should never be the first to break a bargain; that it was a disgrace to tell a lie; that we should speak only the truth; that it was a shame for one man to take from another his wife, or his property without paying for it. We were taught to believe that the Great Spirit sees and hears everything, and that he never forgets; that hereafter he will give every man a spirit-home according to his deserts: if he has been a good man, he will have a good home; if he has been a bad man, he will have a bad home. This I believe, and all my people believe the same.

When my father was a young man there came to our country a white man [Rev. Mr. Spaulding] who talked spirit-law. He won the affections of our people because he spoke good things to them. At first he did not say anything about white men wanting to settle on our lands. Nothing was said about that until about twenty winters ago, when a number of white people came into our country and built houses and made farms. At first our people made no complaint. They thought there was room enough for all to live in peace, and they were learning many things from the white men that seemed to be good. But we soon found that the white men were growing rich very fast, and were greedy to possess everything the Indian had.

> [Here Chief Joseph discusses the councils which his father attended. Many efforts were made to persuade Joseph's father to sell the Wallowa lands, but his father steadfastly refused to sign any treaty with the whites. Finally, the government agent urged Joseph's father to move to the Lapwai Indian reservation.]

Soon after this my father sent for me. I saw he was dying. I took his hand in mine. He said: "My son, my body is returning to my mother earth, and my spirit is going very soon to see the Great Spirit Chief. When I am gone, think of your country. You are the chief of these people. They look to you to guide them. Always remember that your father never sold his country. You must stop your ears whenever you are asked to sign a treaty selling your home. A few years more, and white men will be all around you. They have their eyes on this land. My son, never forget my dying words. This country holds your father's body. Never sell the bones of your father and your mother." I pressed my father's hand and told him I would protect his grave with my life. My father smiled and passed away to the spirit-land.

I buried him in that beautiful valley of winding waters. I love that land more than all the rest of the world. A man who would not love his father's grave is worse than a wild animal.

For a short time we lived quietly. But this could not last. White men had found gold in the mountains around the land of winding water. They stole a great many horses from us, and we could not get them back because we were Indians. The white men told lies for each other. They drove off a great many of our cattle. Some white men branded our young cattle so they could claim them. We had no friend who would plead our cause before the law councils. It seemed to me that some of the white men in Wallowa were doing these things on purpose to get up a war. They knew that we were not strong enough to fight them. I labored hard to avoid trouble and bloodshed. We gave up some of our country to the white men, thinking that then we could have peace. We were mistaken. The white man would not let us alone. We could have avenged our wrongs many times, but we did not. Whenever the Government has asked us to help them against other Indians, we have never refused. When the white men were few and we were strong we could have killed them all off, but the Nez Perces wished to live at peace.

If we have not done so, we have not been to blame. I believe that the old treaty has never been correctly reported. If we ever owned the land we own it still, for we never sold it. In the treaty councils the commissioners have claimed that our country had been sold to the Government. Suppose a white man should come to me and say, "Joseph, I like your horses, and I want to buy them." I say to him, "No, my horses suit me, I will not sell them." Then he goes to my neighbor, and says to him: "Joseph has some good horses. I want to buy them, but he refuses to sell." My neighbor answers, "Pay me the money, and I will sell you Joseph's horses." The white man returns to me, and says, "Joseph, I have bought your horses, and you must let me have them." If we sold our lands to the Government, this is the way they were bought.

On account of the treaty made by the other bands of the Nez Perces, the white men claimed my lands. We were troubled greatly by white men crowding over the line. Some of these were good men, and we lived on peaceful terms with them, but they were not all good.

Nearly every year the agent came over from Lapwai and ordered us on to the reservation. We always replied that we were satisfied to live in Wallowa. We were careful to refuse the presents or annuities which he offered.

Year after year we had been threatened, but no war was made upon my people until General Howard came to our country two years ago and told us that he was the white war-chief of all that country. He said: "I have a great many soldiers at my back. I am going to bring them up here, and then I will talk to you again. I will not let white men laugh at me the next time I come. The country belongs to the Government, and I intend to make you go upon the reservation."

I remonstrated with him against bringing more soldiers to the Nez Perces country. He had one house full of troops all the time at Fort Lapwai.

The next spring the agent at Umatilla agency sent an Indian runner to tell me to meet General Howard at Walla Walla. I could not go myself, but I sent my brother and five other head men to meet him, and they had a long talk.

General Howard said: "You have talked straight, and it is all right. You can stay in Wallowa." He insisted that my brother and his company should go with him to Fort Lapwai. When the party arrived there General Howard sent out runners and called all the Indians in to a grand council. I was in that council. I said to General Howard, "We are ready to listen." He answered that he would not talk then, but would hold a council next day, when he would talk plainly. I said to General Howard: "I am ready to talk to-day. I have been in a great many councils, but I am no wiser. We are all sprung from a woman, although we are unlike in many things. We can not be made over again. You are as you were made, and as you were made you can remain. We are just as we were made by the Great Spirit, and you can not change us; then why should children of one mother and one father quarrel—why should one try to cheat the other? I do not believe that the Great Spirit Chief gave one kind of men the right to tell another kind of men what they must do."

General Howard replied: "You deny my authority, do you? You want to dictate to me, do you?"

Then one of my chiefs—Too-hool-hool-suit—rose in the council and said to General Howard: "The Great Spirit Chief made the world as it is, and as he wanted it, and he made a part of it for us to live upon. I do not see where you get authority to say that we shall not live where he placed us."

General Howard lost his temper and said: "Shut up! I don't want to hear any more of such talk. The law [treaty] says you shall go upon the reservation to live, and I want you to do so, but you persist in disobeying the law. If you do not move, I will take the matter into my own hand, and make you suffer for your disobedience."

Too-hool-hool-suit answered: "Who are you, that you ask us to talk, and then tell me I shan't talk? Are you the Great Spirit? Did you make the world? Did you make the sun? Did you make the rivers to run for us to drink? Did you make the grass to grow? Did you make all these things, that you talk to us as though we were boys? If you did, then you have the right to talk as you do."

General Howard replied, "You are an impudent fellow, and I will put you in the guard-house," and then ordered a soldier to arrest him.

Too-hool-hool-suit made no resistance. He asked General Howard: "Is that your order? I don't care. I have expressed my heart to you. I have nothing to take back. I have spoken for my country. You can arrest me, but you can not change me or make me take back what I have said."

The soldiers came forward and seized my friend and took him to the guard-house. My men whispered among themselves whether they should let this thing be done. I counseled them to submit. I knew if we resisted that all the white men present, including General Howard, would be killed in a moment, and we would be blamed. If I had said nothing, General Howard would never have given another unjust order against my men. I saw the danger, and, while they dragged Too-hool-hool-suit to prison, I arose and said: "*I am going to talk now.* I don't care whether you arrest me or not." I turned to my people and said: "The arrest of Too-hool-hool-suit was wrong, but we will not resent the insult. We were invited to this council to express our hearts, and we have done so." Too-hool-hool-suit was prisoner for five days before he was released.

In the council, next day, General Howard informed me, in a haughty spirit, that he would give my people *thirty days* to go back home, collect all their stock, and move on to the reservation, saying, "If you are not here in that time, I shall consider that you want to fight, and will send my soldiers to drive you on."

I said: "War can be avoided, and it ought to be avoided. I want no war. My people have always been the friends of the white man. Why are you in such a hurry? I can not get ready to move in thirty days. Our stock is scattered, and Snake River is very high. Let us wait until fall, then the river will be low. We want time to hunt up our stock and gather supplies for winter."

General Howard replied, "If you let the time run over one day, the soldiers will be there to drive you on to the reservation, and all your cattle and horses outside of the reservation at that time will fall into the hands of the white men."

I knew I had never sold my country, and that I had no land in Lapwai; but I did not want bloodshed. I did not want my people killed. I did not want anybody killed. Some of my people had been murdered by white men, and the white murderers were never punished for it. I told General Howard about this, and again said I wanted no war. I wanted the people who lived upon the lands I was to occupy at Lapwai to have time to gather their harvest.

I said in my heart that, rather than have war, I would give up my country. I would give up my father's grave. I would give up everything rather than have the blood of white men upon the hands of my people.

General Howard refused to allow me more than thirty days to move my people and their stock. I am sure that he began to prepare for war at once.

When I returned to Wallowa I found my people very much excited upon discovering that the soldiers were already in the Wallowa Valley. We held a council, and decided to move immediately, to avoid bloodshed.

Too-hool-hool-suit, who felt outraged by his imprisonment, talked for war, and made many of my young men willing to fight rather than be driven like dogs from the land where they were born. He declared that blood alone would wash out the disgrace General Howard had put upon him. It required a strong heart to stand up against such talk, but I urged my people to be quiet, and not to begin a war.

Many of the Nez Perces came together in Rocky Cañon to hold a grand council. I went with all my people. This council lasted ten days. There was a great deal of war-talk, and a great deal of excitement.

Again I counseled peace, and I thought the danger was past. We had not complied with General Howard's order because we could not, but we intended to do so as soon as possible. I was leaving the council to kill beef for my family, when news came that the young man whose father had been killed [by a white man five years before] had gone out with several other hot-blooded young braves and killed four white men. He rode up to the council and shouted: "Why do you sit here like women? The war has begun already." I was deeply grieved. All the lodges were moved except my brother's and my own. I saw clearly that war was upon us when I learned that my young men had been secretly buying ammunition. I heard then that Too-hool-hool-suit, who had been imprisoned by General Howard, had succeeded in organizing a war-party.

My friends among white men have blamed me for the war. I am not to blame. When my young men began the killing, my heart was hurt. Although I did not justify them, I remembered all the insults I had endured, and my blood was on fire. Still I would have taken my people to the buffalo country without fighting, if possible.

I could see no other way to avoid a war. We moved over to White Bird Creek, sixteen miles away, and there encamped, intending to collect our stock before leaving; but the soldiers attacked us, and the first battle was fought. We numbered in that battle sixty men, and the soldiers a hundred. The fight lasted but a few minutes, when the soldiers retreated before us for twelve miles. They lost thirty-three killed, and had seven wounded. When an Indian fights, he shoots only to kill; but soldiers shoot at random. None of the soldiers were scalped. We do not believe in scalping, nor in killing wounded men. Soldiers do not kill many Indians unless they are wounded and left upon the battle-field. Then they kill Indians.

Seven days after the first battle, General Howard arrived in the Nez Perces country, bringing seven hundred more soldiers. It was now war in earnest. We crossed over Salmon River, hoping General Howard would follow. We were not disappointed. He did follow us, and we got back between him and his supplies, and cut him off for three days. He sent out two companies to open the way. We attacked them, killing one officer, two guides, and ten men.

We withdrew, hoping the soldiers would follow, but they had got fighting enough for that day. They intrenched themselves, and next day we attacked them again. The battle lasted all day, and was renewed next morning. We killed four and wounded seven or eight.

About this time General Howard found out that we were in his rear. Five days later he attacked us with three hundred and fifty soldiers and settlers. We had two hundred and fifty warriors. The fight lasted twenty-seven hours. We lost four killed and several wounded. General Howard's loss was twenty-nine men killed and sixty wounded.

The following day the soldiers charged upon us, and we retreated with our families and stock a few miles, leaving eighty lodges to fall into General Howard's hands.

Finding that we were outnumbered, we retreated to Bitter Root Valley. Here another body of soldiers came upon us and demanded our surrender. We refused. They said, "You can not get by us." We answered, "We are going by you without fighting if you will let us, but we are going by you anyhow." We then made a treaty with these soldiers. We agreed not to molest anyone, and they agreed that we might pass through the Bitter Root country in peace. We bought provisions and traded stock with white men there.

We understood that there was to be no more war. We intended to go peaceably to the buffalo country, and leave the question of returning to our country to be settled afterward.

With this understanding we traveled on for four days, and, thinking that the trouble was all over, we stopped and prepared tent-poles to take with us. We started again, and at the end of two days we saw three white men passing our camp. Thinking that peace had been made, we did not molest them. We could have killed or taken them prisoners, but we did not suspect them of being spies, which they were.

That night the soldiers surrounded our camp. About daybreak one of my men went out to look after his horses. The soldiers saw him and shot him down like a coyote. I have since learned that these soldiers were not those we had left behind. They had come upon us from another direction. The new white war-chief's name was Gibbon. He charged upon us while some of my people were still asleep. We had a hard fight. Some of my men crept around and attacked the soldiers from the rear. In this battle we lost nearly all our lodges, but we finally drove General Gibbon back.

Finding that he was not able to capture us, he sent to his camp a few miles away for his big guns [cannons], but my men had captured them and all the ammunition. We damaged the big guns all we could, and carried away the powder and lead. In the fight with General Gibbon we lost fifty women and children and thirty fighting men. We remained long enough to bury our dead. The Nez Perces never make war on women and children; we could have killed a great many women and children while the war lasted, but we would feel ashamed to do so cowardly an act.

We never scalp our enemies, but when General Howard came up and joined General Gibbon, their Indian scouts dug up our dead and scalped them. I have been told that General Howard did not order this great shame to be done.

We retreated as rapidly as we could toward the buffalo country. After six days General Howard came close to us, and we went out and attacked him, and captured nearly all his horses and mules [about two hundred and fifty head]. We then marched on to the Yellowstone Basin.

On the way we captured one white man and two white women. We released them at the end of three days. They were treated kindly. The women were not insulted. Can the white soldiers tell me of one time when Indian women were taken prisoners, and held three days and then released without being insulted? Were the Nez Perce women who fell into the hands of General Howard's soldiers treated with as much respect? I deny that a Nez Perce was ever guilty of such a crime.

A few days later we captured two more white men. One of them stole a horse and escaped. We gave the other a poor horse and told him he was free.

Nine days' march brought us to the mouth of Clarke's Fork of the Yellowstone. We did not know what had become of General Howard, but we supposed that he had sent for more horses and mules. He did not come up, but another new war-chief [General Sturgis] attacked us. We held him in check while we moved all our women and children and stock out of danger, leaving a few men to cover our retreat.

Several days passed, and we heard nothing of General Howard, or Gibbon, or Sturgis. We had repulsed each in turn, and began to feel secure, when another army, under General Miles, struck us. This was the fourth army, each of which outnumbered our fighting force, that we had encountered within sixty days.

We had no knowledge of General Miles's army until a short time before he made a charge upon us, cutting our camp in two, and capturing nearly all of our horses. About seventy men, myself among them, were cut off. My little daughter, twelve years of age, was with me. I gave her a rope, and told her to catch a horse and join the others who were cut off from the camp. I have not seen her since, but I have learned that she is alive and well.

I thought of my wife and children, who were now surrounded by soldiers, and I resolved to go to them or die. With a prayer in my mouth to the Great Spirit Chief who rules above, I dashed unarmed through the line of soldiers. It seemed to me that there were guns on every side, before and behind me. My clothes were cut to pieces and my horse was wounded, but I was not hurt. As I reached the door of my lodge, my wife handed me my rifle, saying: "Here's your gun. Fight!"

The soldiers kept up a continuous fire. Six of my men were killed in one spot near me. Ten or twelve soldiers charged into our camp and got possession of two lodges, killing three Nez Perces and losing three of their men, who fell inside our lines. I called my men to drive them back. We fought at close range, not more than twenty steps apart, and drove the soldiers back upon their main line, leaving their dead in our hands. We secured their arms and ammunition. We lost, the first day and night, eighteen men and three women. General Miles lost twenty-six killed and forty wounded. The following day General Miles sent a messenger into my camp under the protection of a white flag. I sent my friend Yellow Bull to meet him.

Yellow Bull understood the messenger to say that General Miles wished me to consider the situation; that he did not want to kill my people unnecessarily. Yellow Bull understood this to be a demand for me to surrender and save blood. Upon reporting this message to me, Yellow Bull said he wondered whether General Miles was in earnest. I sent him back with my answer, that I had not made up my mind, but would think about it and send word soon. A little later he sent some Cheyenne scouts with another message. I went out to meet them. They said they believed that General Miles was sincere and really wanted peace. I walked on to General Miles's tent. He met me and we shook hands. He said, "Come, let us sit down by the fire and talk this matter over." I remained with him all night; next morning Yellow Bull came over to see if I was alive, and why I did not return.

Yellow Bull said to me: "They have got you in their power, and I am afraid they will never let you go again. I have an officer in our camp, and I will hold him until they let you go free."

I said: "I do not know what they mean to do with me, but if they kill me you must not kill the officer. It will do no good to avenge my death by killing him."

Yellow Bull returned to my camp. I did not make any agreement that day with General Miles. The battle was renewed while I was with him. I was very anxious about my people. I knew that we were near Sitting Bull's camp in King George's land, and I thought maybe the Nez Perces who had escaped would return with assistance.

On the following morning I returned to my camp by agreement, meeting the officer who had been held a prisoner in my camp at the flag of truce. My people were divided about surrendering.

THE LAST STAND OF THE NEZ PERCES

YELLOW WOLF—NEZ PERCE

Although the Nez Perces had entrenched themselves for a long siege, their shelter pits were not proof against the artillery of General Miles. Chief Joseph knew that unless help came from Sitting Bull, the fight could not last much longer.

Yellow Wolf (1855-1935) records his emotions on the cold October day in 1877 when defeat came to the Nez Perces.

Evening came, and the battle grew less. Darkness settled and mostly the guns died away. Only occasional shots. I went up toward our camp. I did not hurry. Soldiers guarding, sitting down, two and two. Soldiers all about the camp, so that none could escape from there. A long time I watched. It was snowing. The wind was cold! Stripped for battle, I had no blanket. I lay close to the ground, crawling nearer the guard line.

It was past middle of night when I went between those guards. I was now back within the camp circle. I went first and drank some water. I did not look for food.

On the bluffs Indians with knives were digging rifle pits. Some had those broad-bladed knives [trowel bayonets] taken from soldiers at the Big Hole. Down in the main camp women with camas hooks [a tool used for digging bulbs of the camas plant] were digging shelter pits. All this for tomorrow's coming.

Shelter pits for the old, the women, the children.

Rifle pits for the warriors, the fighters.

You have seen hail, sometimes, leveling the grass. Indians were so leveled by the bullet hail. Most of our few warriors left from the Big Hole had been swept as leaves before the storm. Chief Ollokot, Lone Bird, and Lean Elk were gone.

Outside the camp I had seen men killed. Soldiers ten, Indians ten. That was not so bad. But now, when I saw our remaining warriors gone, my heart grew choked and heavy. Yet the warriors and no-fighting men killed were not all. I looked around.

Some were burying their dead.

A young warrior, wounded, lay on a buffalo robe dying without complaint. Children crying with cold. No fire. There could be no light. Everywhere the crying, the death wail.

My heart became fire. I joined the warriors digging rifle pits. All the rest of night we worked. Just before dawn, I went down among the shelter pits. I looked around. Children no longer crying. In deep shelter pits they were sleeping. Wrapped in a blanket, a still form lay on the buffalo robe. The young warrior was dead. I went back to my rifle pit, my blood hot for war. I felt not the cold.

Morning came, bringing the battle anew. Bullets from everywhere! A big gun throwing bursting shells. From rifle pits, warriors returned shot for shot. Wild and stormy, the cold wind was thick with snow. Air filled with smoke of powder. Flash of guns through it all. As the hidden sun traveled upward, the war did not weaken.

I felt the coming end. All for which we had suffered lost!

Thoughts came of the Wallowa where I grew up. Of my own country when only Indians were there. Of tepees along the bending river. Of the blue, clear lake, wide meadows with horse and cattle herds. From the mountain forests, voices seemed calling. I felt as dreaming. Not my living self.

The war deepened. Grew louder with gun reports. I raised up and looked around. Everything was against us. No hope! Only bondage or death! Something screamed in my ear. A blaze flashed before me. I felt as burning! Then with rifle I stood forth, saying to my heart, "Here I will die, fighting for my people and our homes!"

THE SURRENDER SPEECH OF CHIEF JOSEPH

CHIEF JOSEPH—NEZ PERCE

I am tired of fighting. Our chiefs are killed. Looking Glass is dead. Too-hool-hool-suit is dead. The old men are all dead. It is the young men who say no and yes. He who led the young men is dead. It is cold and we have no blankets. The little children are freezing to death. My people, some of them, have run away to the hills and have no blankets, no food. No one knows where they are—perhaps they are freezing to death. I want to have time to look for my children and see how many of them I can find. Maybe I shall find them among the dead. Hear me, my chiefs, I am tired. My heart is sad and sick. From where the sun now stands I will fight no more forever.

THE COURAGE OF SITTING BULL

OHIYESA—SIOUX

The most controversial personality in the history of the Indian wars was the great Sioux chief and medicine man Sitting Bull (1834?-1890). By all except a few Agency Indians, Sitting Bull was respected and admired. The Cheyenne warrior Wooden Leg said of him: "I have no ears for hearing anybody say he was not a brave man. He had a big brain and a good one, a strong heart and a generous one." But there were other opinions. Major James McLaughlin, Agent at Standing Rock, wrote that Sitting Bull had "an evil face and shifty eyes. Crafty, avaricious, mendacious, and ambitious, even his people knew him as a physical coward." McLaughlin's opinion was probably inspired by personal dislike. More interesting and valuable are the comments of Ohiyesa, an educated Sioux.

Sitting Bull's history has been written many times by newspaper men and army officers, but I find no account of him which is entirely correct. I met him personally in 1884, and since his death I have gone thoroughly into the details of his life with his relatives and contemporaries. It has often been said that he was a physical coward and not a warrior. Judge of this for yourselves from the deed which first gave him fame in his own tribe, when he was about twenty-eight years old.

In an attack upon a band of Crow Indians, one of the enemy took his stand, after the rest had fled, in a deep ditch from which it seemed impossible to dislodge him. The situation had already cost the lives of several warriors, but they could not let him go to repeat such a boast over the Sioux!

"Follow me!" said Sitting Bull, and charged. He raced his horse to the brim of the ditch and struck at the enemy with his coup-staff, thus compelling him to expose himself to the fire of the others while shooting his assailant. But the Crow merely poked his empty gun into his face and dodged back under cover. Then Sitting Bull stopped; he saw that no one had followed him, and he also perceived that the enemy had no more ammunition left. He rode deliberately up to the barrier and threw his loaded gun over it; then he went back to his party and told them what he thought of them.

"Now," said he, "I have armed him, for I will not see a brave man killed unarmed. I will strike him again with my coup-staff to count the first feather; who will count the second?"

Again he led the charge, and this time they all followed him. Sitting Bull was severely wounded by his own gun in the hands of the enemy, who was killed by those that came after him.

SITTING BULL DEFENDS HIS CHARACTER

SITTING BULL—SIOUX

What treaty that the whites have kept has the red man broken? Not one. What treaty that the whites ever made with us red men have they kept? Not one. When I was a boy the Sioux owned the world. The sun rose and set in their lands. They sent 10,000 horsemen to battle. Where are the warriors today? Who slew them? Where are our lands? Who owns them?

What white man can say I ever stole his lands or a penny of his money? Yet they say I am a thief. What white woman, however lonely, was ever when a captive insulted by me? Yet they say I am a bad Indian. What white man has ever seen me drunk? Who has ever come to me hungry and gone unfed? Who has ever seen me beat my wives or abuse my children? What law have I broken? Is it wrong for me to love my own? Is it wicked in me because my skin is red; because I am a Sioux; because I was born where my fathers lived; because I would die for my people and my country?

CUSTER WARNED BY HIS INDIAN SCOUTS

CHIEF PLENTY-COUPS—CROW

By the Laramie Treaty of 1868, the Black Hills of the southern Dakota Territory were guaranteed to the Sioux "for as long as the grass shall grow." But on July 30, 1874, gold was discovered on French Creek in the Black Hills. The government made little effort to keep eager prospectors out of the Indian territory.

It was now clear to the Indians that they would have to fight to hold their land. Under the leadership of Sitting Bull, Crazy Horse, Gall, and other chiefs, the Sioux and Cheyenne united for the struggle.

Sitting Bull and his tribe were ordered to be on government reservations by January 1, 1875. Otherwise, troops would be sent to drive them back. He answered: "When you come for me you need bring no guides. You will easily find me. I shall be right here. I shall not run away."

The army began a three-pronged advance into the hostile country. General Crook and General John Gibbon led two commands. The third command was under the leadership of General George Custer. Riding with him was Mark Kellogg, special correspondent for the Bismarck Tribune *to report Custer's expected victory over Sitting Bull and his braves.*

On June 25 Custer's Crow scouts discovered an enormous Indian encampment on the Little Big Horn in Montana. Despite the fact that he was outnumbered at least three to one, Custer divided his regiment and prepared to attack.

When finally Half-yellow-face came back to us, I learned what he saw on the Little Bighorn. He had at first been with Son-of-the-morning-star [Custer] but at last, when the soldiers divided, he had been sent away with another chief [Major Reno]. He told me that Hairy-moccasin, a Crow Wolf, had first discovered the big enemy village and told Son-of-the-morning-star, and that he, Half-yellow-face, had then tried to stop Son-of-the-morning-star from attacking it. He said that when the soldier-chief gave the order that divided his men, he had spoken to him, through an interpreter, saying, "Do not divide your men. There are too many of the enemy for us, even if we all stay together." He said Son-of-the-morning-star had not liked those words and that he had replied, "You do the scouting, and I will attend to the fighting."

As soon as the soldiers had begun to separate into bands, as they had been ordered, Half-yellow-face had stripped and painted his face. "Why are you doing all this?" Son-of-the-morning-star had asked. "Because you and I are going home today, and by a trail that is strange to us both," Half-yellow-face had answered. It was then that Son-of-the-morning-star sent Half-yellow-face with that other chief [Reno].

THE CUSTER BATTLE

IRON HAWK—SIOUX

The Custer battle on June 25, 1876, is the most disputed battle in history. Although hundreds of accounts have been written, no one knows exactly *what happened to Custer.*

Before attacking the Indians, Custer divided his forces. Major Reno led a battalion of three troops, and Captain Benteen had command of three troops. Five troops—about 213 men—were led by General Custer.

Major Reno was the first to charge the Indian camp but was driven off with heavy losses. His men entrenched themselves on a hilltop and were joined by Captain Benteen's force.

Custer, unaware that Reno had already been defeated, attacked the center or possibly the far end of the village. His battalion was wiped out. Not a single man escaped. Two days after the battle, the remnant of Major Reno's force was rescued by General Gibbon.

Iron Hawk, author of this selection, was fourteen years old at the time of the Custer fight.

The following is taken from Black Elk Speaks *by John G. Neihardt.*

I went into our tepee and got dressed for war as fast as I could; but I could hear bullets whizzing outside, and I was so shaky that it took me a long time to braid an eagle feather into my hair. Also, I had to hold my pony's rope all the time, and he kept jerking me and trying to get away. While I was doing this, crowds of warriors on horses were roaring by up stream, yelling: "Hoka hey!" [Hurry up!] Then I rubbed red paint all over my face and took my bow and arrows and got on my horse. I did not have a gun, only a bow and arrows.

When I was on my horse, the fight up stream seemed to be over, because everybody was starting back downstream and yelling: "It's a good day to die!" Soldiers were coming at the other end of the village, and nobody knew how many there were down there.

A man by the name of Little Bear rode up to me on a pinto horse, and he had a very pretty saddle blanket. He said: "Take courage, boy! The earth is all that lasts!" So I rode fast with him and the others downstream, and many of us Hunkpapas [band of Sioux] gathered on the east side of the river at the foot of a gulch that led back up the hill where the second soldier band [Custer's] was. There was a very brave Shyela [Cheyenne] with us, and I heard someone say: "He is going!" I looked, and it was this Shyela. He had on a spotted war bonnet and a spotted robe made of some animal's skin and this was fastened with a spotted belt. He was going up the hill alone and we all followed part way. There were soldiers along the ridge up there and they were on foot holding their horses. The Shyela rode right close to them in a circle several times and all the soldiers shot at him. Then he rode back to where we had stopped at the head of the gulch. He was saying: "Ah, ah!" Someone said: "Shyela friend, what is the matter?" He began undoing his spotted belt, and when he shook it, bullets dropped out. He was very sacred and the soldiers could not hurt him. He was a fine looking man.

We stayed there awhile waiting for something and there was shooting everywhere. Then I heard a voice crying: "Now they are going, they are going!" We looked up and saw the cavalry horses stampeding. These were all gray horses.

I saw Little Bear's horse rear and race up hill toward the soldiers. When he got close, his horse was shot out from under him, and he got up limping because the bullet went through his leg; and he started hobbling back to us with the soldiers shooting at him. His brother-friend, Elk Nation, went up there on his horse and took Little Bear behind him and rode back safe with bullets striking all around him. It was his duty to go to his brother-friend even if he knew he would be killed.

By now a big cry was going up all around the soldiers up there and the warriors were coming from everywhere and it was getting dark with dust and smoke.

We saw soldiers start running down hill right towards us. Nearly all of them were afoot, and I think they were so scared that they didn't know what they were doing. They were making their arms go as though they were running very fast, but they were only walking. Some of them shot their guns in the air. We all yelled "Hoka hey!" and charged toward them, riding all around them in the twilight that had fallen on us.

I met a soldier on horseback, and I let him have it. The arrow went through from side to side under his ribs and it stuck out on both sides. He screamed and took hold of his saddle horn and hung on, wobbling, with his head hanging down. I kept along beside him, and I took my heavy bow and struck him across the back of the neck. He fell from his saddle, and I got off and beat him to death with my bow. I kept on beating him awhile after he was dead, and every time I hit him I said "Hownh!" I was mad, because I was thinking of the women and little children running down there, all scared and out of breath. These Wasichus wanted it, and they came to get it, and we gave it to them. I did not see much more. I saw Brings Plenty kill a soldier with a war club. I saw Red Horn Buffalo fall. There was a Lakota riding along the edge of the gulch, and he was yelling to look out, that there was a soldier hiding in there. I saw him charge in and kill the soldier and begin slashing him with a knife.

Then we began to go towards the river, and the dust was lifting so that we could see the women and children coming over to us from across the river. The soldiers were all rubbed out there and scattered around.

The women swarmed up the hill and began stripping the soldiers. They were yelling and laughing and singing now. I saw something funny. Two fat old women were stripping a soldier, who was wounded and playing dead. When they had him naked, they began to cut something off that he had, and he jumped up and began fighting with the two fat women. He was swinging one of them around, while the other was trying to stab him with her knife. After awhile, another woman rushed up and shoved her knife into him and he died really dead. It was funny to see the naked Wasichu fighting with the fat women.

By now we saw that our warriors were all charging on some soldiers that had come from the hill up river to help the second band that we had rubbed out. They ran back and we followed, chasing them up on their hill again where they had their pack mules. We could not hurt them much there, because they had been digging to hide themselves and they were lying behind saddles and other things.

I was down by the river and I saw some soldiers come down there with buckets. They had no guns, just buckets. Some boys were down there, and they came out of the brush and threw mud and rocks in the soldiers' faces and chased them into the river. I guess they got enough to drink, for they are drinking yet. We killed them in the water.

Afterwhile it was nearly sundown, and I went home with many others to eat, while some others stayed to watch the soldiers on the hill. I hadn't eaten all day, because the trouble started just when I was beginning to eat my first meal.

LOOTING AFTER THE CUSTER BATTLE

WOODEN LEG—CHEYENNE

After the great throng of Indians had crowded upon the little space where had been the last band of fighting soldiers, a strange incident happened: It appeared that all of the white men were dead. But there was one of them who raised himself to a support on his left elbow. He turned and looked over his left shoulder, and then I got a good view of him. His expression was wild, as if his mind was all tangled up and he was wondering what was going on here. In his right hand he held his six-shooter. Many of the Indians near him were scared by what seemed to have been a return from death to life. But a Sioux warrior jumped forward, grabbed the six-shooter and wrenched it from the soldier's grasp. The gun was turned upon the white man, and he was shot through the head. Other Indians struck him or stabbed him. I think he must have been the last man killed in this great battle where not one of the enemy got away.

This last man had a big and strong body. His cheeks were plump. All over his face was a stubby black beard. His mustache was much longer than his other beard, and it was curled up at the ends. The spot where he was killed is just above the middle of the group of white stone slabs now standing on the slope southwest from the big stone [Custer monument]. I do not know whether he was a soldier chief or an ordinary soldier. I did not notice any metal piece or any special marks on the shoulders of his clothing, but it may be they were there. Some of the Cheyennes say now that he wore two white metal bars. But at that time we knew nothing about such things.

One of the dead soldier bodies attracted special attention. This was one who was said to have been wearing a buckskin suit. I had not seen any such soldier during the fighting. When I saw the body it had been stripped and the head was cut off and gone. Across the breast was some writing made by blue and red coloring into the skin. On each arm was a picture drawn with the same kind of blue and red paint. One of the pictures was of an eagle having its wings spread out. Indians told me that on the left arm had been strapped a leather packet having in it some white paper and a lot of the same kind of green picture-paper found on all of the soldier bodies. Some of the Indians guessed that he must have been the big chief of the soldiers, because of the buckskin clothing and because of the paint markings on his breast and arms. But none of the Indians knew then who had been the big chief. They were only guessing at it.

The sun was just past the middle of the sky. The first soldiers, up the valley, had come about the middle of the forenoon. The earlier part of the fighting against these second soldiers had been slow, all of the Indians staying back and approaching gradually. At each time of charging, though, the mixup lasted only a few minutes.

I took one scalp. As I went walking and leading my horse among the dead I observed one face that interested me. The dead man had a long beard growing from both sides of his face and extending several inches below the chin. He had also a full mustache. All of the beard hair was of a light yellow color, as I now recall it. Most of the soldiers had beard growing, in different lengths, but this was the longest one I saw among them. I think the dead man may have been thirty or more years old. "Here is a new kind of scalp," I said to a companion. I skinned one side of the face and half of the chin, so as to keep the long beard yet on the part removed. I got an arrow shaft and tied the strange scalp to the end of it. This I carried in a hand as I went looking further.

I found a metal bottle, as I was walking among the dead men. It was about half full of some kind of liquid. I opened it and found that the liquid was not water. Soon afterward I got hold of another bottle of the same kind that had in it the same kind of liquid. I showed these to some other Indians. Different ones of them smelled and sniffed. Finally a Sioux said:

"Whisky."

Bottles of this kind were found by several other Indians. Some of them drank the contents. Others tried to drink, but had to spit out their mouthfuls. Bobtail Horse got sick and vomited soon after he had taken a big swallow of it. It became the talk that this whisky explained why the soldiers became crazy and shot each other and themselves instead of shooting us. One old Indian said, though, that there was not enough whisky gone from any of the bottles to make a white man soldier go crazy. We all agreed that the foolish actions of the soldiers must have been caused by the prayers of our medicine men. I believed this was the true explanation. My belief became changed, though, in later years. I think now it was the whisky.

I slept late that next morning after the great battle. The sun had been up an hour before I awoke. I went to the willow lodge of my father and mother. When I had eaten the breakfast given to me by my mother I got myself ready again to risk death in an effort to kill other white men who had come to kill us. I combed and braided my hair. My braids in those days were full and long, reaching down my breast beyond the waist belt. I painted anew the black circle around my face and the red and yellow space enclosed within the circle. I was in doubt about which clothing to wear, but my father said the soldier clothing looked the best, even though the coat sleeves ended far above my wrists and the legs of the breeches left long bare spots between them and the tops of my moccasins. I put on my big white hat captured at the Rosebud fight. My sister Crooked Nose got my horse for me. Soon afterward I was on my way up and across the valley and on through the river to the hill where the first soldiers were staying.

I had both my rifle and six shooter. I still was without my medicine shield and my other medicine protectors that had been lost on Powder River. Most of the other Cheyennes and Sioux had theirs. The shields all were of specially shrunken and toughened buffalo skin covered with buckskin fringed and painted, each with his own choice of designs, for the medicine influence. I went with other young men to the higher hills around the soldiers. I stayed at a distance from them and shot bullets from my new rifle. I did not shoot many times, as it appeared I was too far away, and I did not want to waste any of my cartridges. So I went down and hid in a gulch near the river.

Some soldiers came to get water from the river, just as our old men had said they likely would do. The white men crept down a deep gulch and then ran across an open space to the water. Each one had a bucket, and each would dip his bucket for water and run back into the gulch. I put myself, with others, where we could watch for these men. I shot at one of them just as he straightened up after having dipped his bucket into the water. He pitched forward into the edge of the river. He went wallowing along the stream, trying to swim, but having a hard time at it. I jumped out from my hiding place and ran toward him. Two Sioux warriors got ahead of me. One of them waded after the man and struck him with a rifle barrel. Finally he grabbed the man, hit him again, and then dragged him dead to the shore, quite a distance down the river. I kept after them, following down the east bank. Some other Sioux warriors came. I was the only Cheyenne there. The Sioux agreed that my bullet had been the first blow upon the white soldier, so they allowed me to choose whatever I might want of his belongings.

I searched into the man's pockets. In one I found a folding knife and a plug of chewing tobacco that was soaked and spoiled. In another pocket was a wad of the same kind of green paper taken from the soldiers the day before. It too was wet through. I threw it aside. In this same pocket were four white metal pieces of money. I knew they were of value in trading, but I did not know how much was their value. In later times I have learned they were four silver dollars. A young Cheyenne there said: "Give the money to me." I did not care for it, so I gave it to him. He thanked me and said: "I shall use it to buy for myself a gun." I do not remember now his name, but he was a son of One Horn. A Sioux picked up the wad of green paper I had thrown upon the ground. It was almost falling to pieces, but he began to spread out some of the wet sheets that still held together. Pretty soon he said:

"This is money. This is what white men use to buy things from the traders."

I had seen much other paper like it during the afternoon before. Wolf Medicine had offered to give me a handful of it. But I did not take it. I had already thrown away some of it I had found. But even after I was told it could be used for buying things from the traders, I did not want it. I was thinking then it would be a long time before I should see or care to see any white man trader.

Three different soldiers, among all of the dead in both places of battle, attracted special notice from the Indians. The first was the man wearing the buckskin suit and who had the colored writing and pictures on his breast and arms. Another was the black man killed among the first soldiers on the valley. The third was one having gold among his teeth. We did not understand how this metal got there, nor why it was there.

Paper boxes of ammunition were in the leather bags carried on the saddles of the soldiers. Besides, in all of the belts taken from the dead men there were cartridges. Some belts had only a few left in them. In others the loops still contained many, an occasional one almost full. I did not see or hear of any belt entirely emptied of its cartridges.

All during that forenoon, as well as during the afternoon and night before, both in the camps and on the battle grounds, Indians were saying to each other: "I got some tobacco." "I got coffee." "I got two horses." "I got a soldier saddle." "I got a good gun." Some got things they did not understand.

One young Cheyenne took something from a dead soldier just after all of them had been killed. He was puzzled by it. Some others looked at it. I was with them. It was made of white metal and had glass on one side. On this side were marks of some kind. While the Cheyenne was looking at it he got it up toward his ear. Then he put it up close.

"It is alive!" he said.

Others put it to their ears and listened. I put it up to mine.

"Tick-tick-tick-tick-tick-tick," it was saying.

We talked about its use. We agreed generally it was that soldier's special medicine. Many Indians came and wondered about it. The young man decided to keep it for his own medicine.

When I was getting ready the next morning to go and fight again the soldiers staying on the hilltop, the Cheyenne young man had a crowd around him again examining his strange white man medicine. They were listening, but it made no sound. After different ones had studied it, he finally threw it away as far as he could throw it.

"It is not good medicine for me," he said. "It is dead."

I saw another soldier medicine thing something like this one, but the other one was larger and it did not make the ticking noise. It acted, though, like it was alive. When it was held with the glass side up a little arrow fluttered around. When it was held quiet for a while the arrow gradually stopped fluttering. Every time it stopped the point of the arrow was toward the north, down the valley. There was talk then of other soldiers coming from that direction, so it was decided this medicine object was useful for finding out at any time where might be soldiers. Long Shield had it when I saw it. He gave it to High Walking. Another Cheyenne got a pair of field glasses. We understood them. This was a big pair.

Cleaners for the rifles puzzled us a while. They were in joints and were carried in a long hole in the end of the wooden stock. Pretty soon we learned what was their use. I saw one rifle that had a shell of cartridge in its barrel. A Sioux had it. He could not put into the gun any other cartridge, so he threw it into the river.

Yellow Weasel, a Cheyenne, got a bugle. He tried to make a noise with it, but he could not. Others tried. Different ones puffed and blowed at it. But nobody could make it sound out. After a while we heard a bugle making a big noise somewhere among the Sioux. The Cheyennes said: "The Sioux got a good one. This one Yellow Weasel has is no good. He might as well throw it away." But he kept it, and it was not long before he was making it sound.

WHY THE INDIANS FOUGHT CUSTER

SITTING BULL—SIOUX

Sitting Bull had an adopted son in the battle, and according to Indian custom was supposed to stay out and let his son win combat honors. He said later: "They tell you I murdered Custer. It is a lie. I am not a war chief. I was not in the battle that day. His eyes were blinded that he could not see. He was a fool and he rode to his death. He made the fight, not I. Whoever tells you I killed the Yellow Hair is a liar."

After the battle, Sitting Bull fled to Canada. In 1881 he surrendered at Fort Buford and was confined at Fort Randall until 1883, when he was released and joined Buffalo Bill's Wild West Show. He was a great success. At Bismarck a New York belle paid him a dollar to kiss her. In Philadelphia, where crowds lined up to shake his hand, a man asked him if he did not regret killing Custer and his soldiers. Sitting Bull replied: "I have answered to my people for the Indians slain in that fight. The chief that sent Custer must answer to his people."

During an interview in Canada in 1877, Sitting Bull explained why his people had fought Custer.

The pale-faces had things that we needed in order to hunt. We needed ammunition. Our interests were in peace. I never sold that

DRESS OF CHRISTIANIZED INDIAN
Missisauga Tribe, Upper Canada
George Catlin
ca. 1830–40

From Catlin Sketchbook
Courtesy of Gilcrease Institute

much land. [Here Sitting Bull picked up with his thumb and forefinger a little pulverized dirt, lifted it, and let it fall and blow away.] I never made or sold a treaty with the United States. I came in to claim my rights and the rights of my people. I was driven in force from my land. I never made war on the United States Government. I never stood in the white man's country. I never committed any depredations in the white man's country. I never made the white man's heart bleed. The white man came on my land and followed me. The white man made me fight for my hunting grounds. The white man made me kill him or he would kill my friends, my women, and my children.

We have all fought hard. We did not know Custer. There was not as many Indians as the white man says. There was not more than two thousand. I did not want to kill any more men. I did not like that kind of work. I only defended my camp. When we had killed enough, that was all that was necessary.

THE GHOST DANCE RELIGION

MASSE HADJO—SIOUX

In 1888 a young Paiute medicine man named Wovoka received a revelation from the Great Spirit. Wovoka repeated to his people what the Great Spirit had told him: their dead ancestors would soon come back to earth, the buffalo would run again, and the white invaders would be destroyed. In preparation for the new era, the Indians must practice the ceremonial dances and songs of the new religion.

The Ghost Dance religion spread rapidly among other tribes. It brought new hope to Indians who were dying from hunger and disease on reservations. Wovoka urged the Indians to be patient and tolerant. "You must not hurt anybody or do harm to anyone," he wrote to the Cheyennes. "You must not fight. Do right always."

When the Indians of the Plains gathered for the Ghost Dance, the Americans feared that an outbreak was coming. The editor of the Chicago Tribune *published a harsh criticism of the Ghost Dancers. Masse Hadjo, an educated Sioux, defended the new religion in a letter to the editor.*

You say, "If the United States army would kill a thousand or so of the dancing Indians there would be no more trouble." I judge by the above language you are a "Christian," and are disposed to do all in your power to advance the cause of Christ. You are doubtless a worshiper of the white man's Saviour, but are unwilling that the Indians should have a "Messiah" of their own.

The Indians have never taken kindly to the Christian religion as preached and practiced by the whites. Do you know why this is the case? Because the Good Father of all has given us a better religion—a religion that is all good and no bad, a religion that is adapted to our wants. You say if we are good, obey the Ten Commandments and never sin any more, we may be permitted eventually to sit upon a white rock and sing praises to God forevermore, and look down upon our heathen fathers, mothers, brothers and sisters who are howling in hell.

It won't do. The code of morals as practiced by the white race will not compare with the morals of the Indians. We pay no lawyers or preachers, but we have not one-tenth part of the crime that you do. If our Messiah does come we shall not try to force you into our belief. We will never burn innocent women at the stake or pull men to pieces with horses because they refuse to join in our ghost dances. You white people had a Messiah, and if history is to be believed nearly every nation has had one. You had twelve Apostles; we have only eleven, and some of those are already in the military guard-house. We also had a Virgin Mary and she is in the guard-house. You are anxious to get hold of our Messiah, so you can put him in irons. This you may do—in fact, you may crucify him as you did that other one, but you cannot convert the Indians to the Christian religion until you contaminate them with the blood of the white man. The white man's heaven is repulsive to the Indian nature, and if the white man's hell suits you, why, you keep it. I think there will be white rogues enough to fill it.

THE MASSACRE AT WOUNDED KNEE

TURNING HAWK, AND OTHERS—SIOUX

The American government acted quickly to put down the Ghost Dance "outbreak." Sitting Bull, a leader in the new movement, was murdered "while resisting arrest," and other Indian leaders were seized and put under guard.

On December 29, 1890, a party of about three hundred ghost-dancing Cheyenne men, women, and children under Chief Big Foot approached the Pine Ridge Agency in South Dakota. They were met by troops who ordered them to give up their weapons.

After most of the Indians had been disarmed, someone, probably an Indian, shot off a musket. The American forces opened fire with Hotchkiss guns on the mass of huddled Cheyennes. In the confusion, a few soldiers were caught in the ring of fire and killed by the bullets of their comrades.

Warriors fought desperately with knives and their bare hands. But when the smoke cleared, more than a hundred braves lay dead and the bodies of 120 women and children who had tried to escape were scattered over a distance of two miles from the scene of the fight.

Sioux leaders, who had served as scouts for the American forces, gave this testimony during a government inquiry on February 11, 1891.

Turning Hawk. When we heard that these people were coming toward our agency we also heard this. These people were coming toward Pine Ridge Agency, and when they were almost on the agency they were met by the soldiers and surrounded and finally taken to the Wounded Knee creek, and there at a given time their guns were demanded. When they had delivered them up, the men were separated from their families, from their tipis, and taken to a certain spot. When the guns were thus taken and the men thus separated, there was a crazy man, a young man of very bad influence and in fact a nobody, among that bunch of Indians fired his gun, and of course the firing of a gun must have been the breaking of a military rule of some sort, because immediately the soldiers returned fire and indiscriminate killing followed.

Spotted Horse. This man shot an officer in the army; the first shot killed this officer. I was a voluntary scout at that encounter and I saw exactly what was done, and that was what I noticed; that the first shot killed an officer. As soon as this shot was fired the Indians immediately began drawing their knives, and they were exhorted from all sides to desist, but this was not obeyed. Consequently the firing began immediately on the part of the soldiers.

Turning Hawk. All the men who were in a bunch were killed right there, and those who escaped that first fire got into the ravine, and as they went along up the ravine for a long distance they were pursued on both sides by the soldiers and shot down, as the dead bodies showed afterwards. The women were standing off at a different place from where the men were stationed, and when the firing began, those of the men who escaped the first onslaught went in one direction up the ravine, and then the women, who were bunched together at another place, went entirely in a different direction through an open field, and the women shared the same fate as the men who went up the deep ravine.

American Horse. The men were separated, as has already been said, from the women, and they were surrounded by the soldiers. Then came next the village of the Indians and that was entirely surrounded by the soldiers also. When the firing began, of course the people who were standing immediately around the young man who fired the first shot were killed right together, and then they turned their guns, Hotchkiss guns, etc., upon the women who were in the lodges standing there under a flag of truce, and of course as soon as they were fired upon they fled, the men fleeing in one direction and the women running in two different directions. So that there were three general directions in which they took flight.

There was a woman with an infant in her arms who was killed as she almost touched the flag of truce, and the women and children of course were strewn all along the circular village until they were dispatched. Right near the flag of truce a mother was shot down with her infant; the child not knowing that its mother was dead was still nursing, and that especially was a very sad sight. The women as they were fleeing with their babes were killed together, shot right through, and the women who were very heavy with child were also killed. All the Indians fled in these three directions, and after most all of them had been killed a cry was made that all those who were not killed or wounded should come forth and they would be safe. Little boys who were not wounded came out of their places of refuge, and as soon as they came in sight a number of soldiers surrounded them and butchered them there.

The massacre at Wounded Knee marked the end of Indian resistance to civilization.

The Indians had fought their last fight.

IX: THE WHITE MAN'S ROAD

The Indian was awed by the white man's knowledge and power and dazzled by his inventions, but despised him for his duplicity and greediness. When at last the Indian saw his world crumble, he was left confused and bewildered, but with the realization that his only hope for survival was to accept the invader's civilization. His chiefs reluctantly urged him to study the white man's culture and to equip himself for a place in this new world.

Today the Indians are taking "the white man's road." In reservation schools they are learning to work and live and think like the white man, but they are also holding fast to the best elements of their native culture.

IX: THE WHITE MAN'S ROAD

MYSTERIOUS MEDICINE OF THE WHITE MAN

OHIYESA—SIOUX

I had heard marvelous things of this people. In some things we despised them; in others we regarded them as *wakan* (mysterious), a race whose power bordered upon the supernatural. I learned that they had made a "fireboat." I could not understand how they could unite two elements which cannot exist together. I thought the water would put out the fire, and the fire would consume the boat if it had the shadow of a chance. This was to me a preposterous thing! But when I was told that the Big Knives had created a "fire-boat-walks-on-mountains" (a locomotive) it was too much to believe.

"Why," declared my informant, "those who saw this monster move said that it flew from mountain to mountain when it seemed to be excited. They said also that they believed it carried a thunderbird, for they frequently heard his unusual war-whoop as the creature sped along!"

Several warriors had observed from a distance one of the first trains on the Northern Pacific, and had gained an exaggerated impression of the wonders of the pale-face. They had seen it go over a bridge that spanned a deep ravine and it seemed to them that it jumped from one bank to the other. I confess that the story almost quenched my ardor and bravery.

Two or three young men were talking together about this fearful invention.

"However," said one, "I understand that this fire-boat-walks-on-mountains cannot move except on the track made for it."

Although a boy is not expected to join in the conversation of his elders, I ventured to ask: "Then it cannot chase us into any rough country?"

"No, it cannot do that," was the reply, which I heard with a great deal of relief.

I had seen guns and various other things brought to us by the French Canadians, so that I already had some notion of the supernatural gifts of the white man; but I had never before heard such tales as I listened to that morning. It was said that they had bridged the Missouri and Mississippi rivers, and that they made immense houses of stone and brick, piled on top of one another until they were as high as high hills. My brain was puzzled with these things for many a day. Finally I asked my uncle why the Great Mystery gave such power to the Washechu (the rich)—sometimes we called them by this name—and not to us Dakotas.

"For the same reason," he answered, "that he gave to Duta the skill to make fine bows and arrows, and to Wachesne no skill to make anything."

"And why do the Big Knives increase so much more in number than the Dakotas?" I continued.

"It has been said, and I think it must be true, that they have larger families than we do. I went into the house of an Eashecha (a German), and I counted no less than nine children. The eldest of them could not have been over fifteen. When my grandfather first visited them, down at the mouth of the Mississippi, they were comparatively few; later my father visited their Great Father at Washington, and they had already spread over the whole country.

"Certainly they are a heartless nation. They have made some of their people servants—yes, slaves! We have never believed in keeping slaves, but it seems that these Washechu do! It is our belief that they painted their servants black a long time ago, to tell them from the rest, and now the slaves have children born to them of the same color!

"The greatest object of their lives seems to be to acquire possessions—to be rich. They desire to possess the whole world. For thirty years they were trying to entice us to sell them our land. Finally the outbreak [Minnesota, 1862] gave them all, and we have been driven away from our beautiful country.

"They are a wonderful people. They have divided the day into hours, like the moons of the year. In fact, they measure everything. Not one of them would let so much as a turnip go from his field unless he received full value for it. I understand that their great men make a feast and invite many, but when the feast is over the guests are required to pay for what they have eaten before leaving the house. I myself saw at White Cliff (the name given to St. Paul, Minnesota) a man who kept a brass drum and a bell to call people to his table; but when he got them in he would make them pay for the food!

"I am also informed," said my uncle, "but this I hardly believe, that their Great Chief (President) compels every man to pay him for the land he lives upon and all his personal goods—even for his own existence—every year!" (This was his idea of taxation.) "I am sure we could not live under such a law.

"In war they have leaders and war-chiefs of different grades. The common warriors are driven forward like a herd of antelopes to face the foe. It is on account of this manner of fighting—from compulsion and not from personal bravery—that we count no *coup* on them. A lone warrior can do much harm to a large army of them in a bad country."

It was this talk with my uncle that gave me my first clear idea of the white man.

THE CHARACTER OF THE WHITE MAN

CHIEF PLENTY-COUPS—CROW

White men with their spotted-buffalo [cattle] were on the plains about us. Their houses were near the water-holes, and their villages on the rivers. We made up our minds to be friendly with them, in spite of all the changes they were bringing. But we found this difficult, because the white men too often promised to do one thing and then, when they acted at all, did another.

They spoke very loudly when they said their laws were made for everybody; but we soon learned that although they expected us to keep them, they thought nothing of breaking them themselves. They told us not to drink whisky, yet they made it themselves and traded it to us for furs and robes until both were nearly gone. Their Wise Ones said we might have their religion, but when we tried to understand it we found that there were too many kinds of religion among white men for us to understand, and that scarcely any two white men agreed which was the right one to learn. This bothered us a good deal until we saw that the white man did not take his religion any more seriously than he did his laws, and that he kept both of them just behind him, like Helpers, to use when they might do him good in his dealings with strangers. These were not our ways. We kept the laws we made and lived our religion. We have never been able to understand the white man, who fools nobody but himself.

HOW THE WHITE MAN FIGHTS

BLACK HAWK—SAUK

On my arrival at the village [after fighting in the War of 1812], I was met by the chiefs and braves, and conducted to a lodge that had been prepared to receive me. I gave an account of what I had seen and done. I explained to them the manner the British and Americans fought. Instead of stealing upon each other, and taking every advantage to kill the enemy and save their own people, as we do, (which, with us, is considered good policy in a war chief,) they march out, in open daylight, and fight, regardless of the number of warriors they may lose! After the battle is over, they retire to feast, and drink wine, as if nothing had happened; after which, they make a statement in writing, of what they have done—each party claiming the victory! and neither giving an account of half the number that have been killed on their own side. They all fought like braves, but would not do to lead a war party with us. Our maxim is, "to kill the enemy and save our own men." Those chiefs would do to paddle a canoe, but not to steer it.

THE SYMBOL OF EXTINCTION

CHIEF STANDING BEAR—SIOUX

I know of no species of plant, bird, or animal that were exterminated until the coming of the white man. For some years after the buffalo disappeared there still remained huge herds of antelope, but the hunter's work was no sooner done in the destruction of the buffalo than his attention was attracted toward the deer. They are plentiful now only where protected. The white man considered natural animal life just as he did the natural man life upon this continent, as "pests." Plants which the Indian found beneficial were also "pests." There is no word in the Lakota vocabulary with the English meaning of this word.

There was a great difference in the attitude taken by the Indian and the Caucasian toward nature, and this difference made of one a conservationist and of the other a non-conservationist of life. The Indian, as well as all other creatures that were given birth and grew, were sustained by the common mother—earth. He was therefore kin to all living things and he gave to all creatures equal rights with himself. Everything of earth was loved and reverenced. The philosophy of the Caucasian was, "Things of the earth, earthy"—to be belittled and despised. Bestowing upon himself the position and title of a superior creature, others in the scheme were, in the natural order of things, of inferior position and title; and this attitude dominated his actions toward all things. The worth and right to live were his, thus he heartlessly destroyed. Forests were mowed down, the buffalo exterminated, the beaver driven to extinction and his wonderfully constructed dams dynamited, allowing flood waters to wreak further havoc, and the very birds of the air silenced. Great grassy plains that sweetened the air have been upturned; springs, streams, and lakes that lived no longer ago than my boyhood have dried, and a whole people harassed to degredation and death. The white man has come to be the symbol of extinction for all things natural to this continent. Between him and the animal there is no rapport and they have learned to flee from his approach, for they cannot live on the same ground.

Because the Indian was unable, and in some cases refused, to accept completely the white man's ways which were so contrary to his heritage and tradition, he earned for himself the reputation of being lazy. He preferred his tribal ways all the more on account of his disappointment with the white man whose deceit and weaknesses filled the Indian soul with distrust. He clung to his native customs and religion, which he could scarcely change if he would; and so the Indian, who had lived the most active of lives and who had developed an unusually high physical perfection, was adjudged the most indolent of characters. And this reputation, false as it is, has become fixed in the mind of the public.

THE WHITE MAN'S LACK OF SENSE

CHIEF KAHKEWAQUONABY—OJIBWAY

The Indian has more sense than the white man. The duellist may possess some *physical* bravery, but he lacks the moral courage of the Indian, who, when he was challenged, replied, "I have two objections to this duel affair; the one is, lest I should hurt *you*, and the other is, lest you should hurt *me*. I do not see any good that it would do me to put a bullet through your body—I could not make any use of you when dead; but I could of a rabbit or turkey. As to myself, I think it more wise to avoid than to put myself in the way of harm; I am under apprehension that you might hit me. That being the case, I think it advisable to keep my distance. If you want to try your pistols, take some object—a tree, or anything about my size; and if you hit that, send me word, and I shall acknowledge, that had I been there you might have hit me."

A TOUR OF THE EAST

BLACK HAWK—SAUK

After his defeat in 1832 Black Hawk was sent on a tour of the East. Everywhere he was cheered by enthusiastic crowds. No doubt much to his amusement, he was treated as a hero rather than a conquered enemy. President Jackson gave him an ornate sword and uniform, Henry Clay presented him with a cane, and John Quincy Adams hung a medal around his neck.

An order came from our Great Father [President Jackson] to the White Beaver [General H. Atkinson], to send us on to Washington. In a little while all were ready, and left Jefferson Barracks on board of a steam boat, under charge of a young war chief, whom the White Beaver sent along as a guide to Washington. He carried with him an interpreter and one soldier. On our way up the Ohio, we passed several large villages, the names of which were explained to me. The first is called Louisville, and is a very pretty village, situate on the bank of the Ohio river. The next is Cincinnati, which stands on the bank of the same river. This is a large and beautiful village, and seemed to be in a thriving condition. The people gathered on the bank as we passed, in great crowds, apparently anxious to see us.

On our arrival at Wheeling, the streets and river's banks were crowded with people, who flocked from every direction to see us. While we remained here, many called upon us, and treated us with kindness—no one offering to molest or misuse us. This village is not so large as either of those before mentioned, but is quite a pretty village.

We left the steam boat here, having travelled a long distance on the prettiest river (except our Mississippi) that I ever saw—and took the stage. Being unaccustomed to this mode of travelling, we soon got tired, and wished ourselves seated in a canoe on one of our own rivers, that we might return to our friends. We had travelled but a short distance, before our carriage turned over, from which I received a slight injury, and the soldier had one arm broken. I was sorry for this accident, as the young man had behaved well.

We had a rough and mountainous country for several days, but had a good trail for our carriage. It is astonishing to see what labor and pains the white people have had to make this road, as it passes over an immense number of mountains, which are generally covered with rocks and timber. Yet it has been made smooth and easy to travel upon.

Rough and mountainous as is this country, there are many wigwams and small villages standing on the roadside. I could see nothing in the country to induce the people to live in it; and was astonished to find so many whites living on the hills.

I have often thought of them since my return to my own people; and am happy to think that they prefer living in their own country to coming out to ours, and driving us from it, that they might live upon and enjoy it—as many of the whites have already done. I think, with them, that wherever the Great Spirit places his people, they ought to be satisfied to remain, and thankful for what He has given them; and not drive others from the country He has given them, because it happens to be better than theirs! This is contrary to our way of thinking, and from my intercourse with the whites, I have learned that one great principle of their religion is, "to do unto others as you wish them to do unto you!" Those people in the mountains seem to act upon this principle, but the settlers on our frontiers and on our lands seem never to think of it, if we are to judge by their actions.

On our arrival at Washington, we called to see our Great Father, the President. He looks as if he had seen as many winters as I have, and seems to be a great brave. I had very little talk with him, as he appeared to be busy, and did not seem much disposed to talk. I think he is a good man; and although he talked but little, he treated us very well. His wigwam is well furnished with everything good and pretty, and is very strongly built.

He said he wished to know the cause of my going to war against his white children. I thought he ought to have known this before, and consequently, said but little to him about it—as I expected he knew as well as I could tell him.

We next started to New York, and on our arrival near the wharf, saw a large collection of people gathered at Castle-Garden. We had seen many wonderful sights in our way—large villages, the great national road over the mountains, the rail roads, steam carriages, ships, steamboats, and many other things. But we were now about to witness a sight more surprising than any of these. We were told that a man was going up into the air in a balloon! We watched with anxiety to see if it could be true, and to our astonishment, saw him ascend into the air until the eye could no longer perceive him. Our people were all surprised, and one of our young men asked if he was going up to see the Great Spirit.

The chiefs of this big village, being desirous that all their people should have an opportunity to see us, fitted up their great council house for this purpose, where we saw an immense number of people; all of whom treated us with friendship, and many with great generosity.

The chiefs were particular in showing us everything that they thought would be pleasing or gratifying to us. We went with them to Castle-Garden to see the fireworks, which was quite an agreeable entertainment—but to the whites who witnessed it, less magnificent than the sight of one of our large prairies would be when on fire.

The squaws presented us many handsome little presents that are said to be valuable. They were very kind, very good, and very pretty—for pale faces!

It has always been our custom to receive all strangers that come to our village or camps, in time of peace, on terms of friendship—to share with them the best provisions we have and give them all the assistance in our power. If on a journey, or lost, to put them on the right trail, and if in want of moccasins, to supply them. I feel grateful to the whites for the kind manner they treated me and my party whilst travelling among them—and from my heart I assure them, that the white man will always be welcome in our village or camps, as a brother. The tomahawk is buried forever!

AT THE ST. LOUIS WORLD'S FAIR

GERONIMO—APACHE

When I was at first asked to attend the St. Louis World's Fair I did not wish to go. Later, when I was told that I would receive good attention and protection, and that the President of the United States said that it would be all right, I consented. I was kept by parties in charge of the Indian Department, who had obtained permission from the President. I stayed in this place for six months. I sold my photographs for twenty-five cents, and was allowed to keep ten cents of this for myself. I also wrote my name for ten, fifteen, or twenty-five cents, as the case might be, and kept all of that money. I often made as much as two dollars a day, and when I returned I had plenty of money—more than I had ever owned before.

Every Sunday the President of the Fair sent for me to go to a wild west show. I took part in the roping contests before the audience. There were many other Indian tribes there, and strange people of whom I had never heard.

When people first came to the World's Fair they did nothing but parade up and down the streets. When they got tired of this they would visit the shows. There were many strange things in these shows. The Government sent guards with me when I went, and I was not allowed to go anywhere without them.

In one of the shows some strange men with red caps [Turks] had some peculiar swords, and they seemed to want to fight. Finally their manager told them they might fight each other. They tried to hit each other over the head with these swords, and I expected both to be wounded or perhaps killed, but neither one was harmed. They would be hard people to kill in a hand-to-hand fight.

In another show there was a strange-looking negro. The manager tied his hands fast, then tied him to a chair. He was securely tied, for I looked myself, and I did not think it was possible for him to get away. Then the manager told him to get loose.

He twisted in his chair for a moment, and then stood up; the ropes were still tied, but he was free. I do not understand how this was done. It was certainly a miraculous power, because no man could have released himself by his own efforts.

In another place a man was on a platform speaking to the audience; they set a basket by the side of the platform and covered it with red calico; then a woman came and got into the basket, and a man covered the basket again with the calico; then the man who was speaking to the audience took a long sword and ran it through the basket, each way, and then down through the cloth cover. I heard the sword cut through the woman's body, and the manager himself said she was dead; but when the cloth was lifted from the basket she stepped out, smiled, and walked off the stage. I would like to know how she was so quickly healed, and why the wounds did not kill her.

One time the guards took me into a little house [Ferris wheel] that had four windows. When we were seated the little house started to move along the ground. Then the guards called my attention to some curious things they had in their pockets. Finally they told me to look out, and when I did so I was scared, for our little house had gone high up in the air, and the people down in the Fair Grounds looked no larger than ants. The men laughed at me for being scared; then they gave me a glass to look through (I often had such glasses which I took from dead officers after battles in Mexico and elsewhere), and I could see rivers, lakes and mountains. But I had never been so high in the air, and I tried to look into the sky. There were no stars, and I could not look at the sun through this glass because the brightness hurt my eyes. Finally I put the glass down, and as they were all laughing at me, I too, began to laugh. Then they said, "Get out!" and when I looked we were on the street again. After we were safe on the land I watched many of these little houses going up and coming down, but I cannot understand how they travel. They are very curious little houses.

We went into one place where they made glassware. I had always thought that these things were made by hand, but they are not. The man had a curious little instrument, and whenever he would blow through this into a little blaze the glass would take any shape he wanted it to. I am not sure, but I think that if I had this kind of an instrument I could make whatever I wished. There seems to be a charm about it. But I suppose it is very difficult to get these little instruments, or other people would have them. The people in this show were so anxious to buy the things the man made that they kept him so busy he could not sit down all day long. I bought many curious things in there and brought them home with me.

At the end of one of the streets some people were getting into a clumsy canoe, upon a kind of shelf, and sliding down into the water [shoot the chute]. They seemed to enjoy it, but it looked too fierce for me. If one of these canoes had gone out of its path the people would have been sure to get hurt or killed.

I am glad I went to the Fair. I saw many interesting things and learned much of the white people. They are a very kind and peaceful people. During all the time I was at the Fair no one tried to harm me in any way. Had this been among the Mexicans I am sure I should have been compelled to defend myself often.

I wish all my people could have attended the Fair.

IMPRESSIONS OF THE ENGLISH

CHIEF KAHKEWAQUONABY—OJIBWAY

The first Indians to visit Europe paraded with Columbus through the streets of Barcelona. During the following centuries, many Indians crossed the "Great Waters." In 1706 Assacumbuit, an Abnaki chief, was knighted and presented with a magnificent sword by Louis XIV. In 1775 and again in 1785, the Mohawk chief Thayendanegea visited England. He was eagerly sought after by Boswell, had his portrait painted by Romney, and dined with the Prince of Wales.

In 1831 Chief Kahkewaquonaby (1802-1856), an educated Ojibway, toured England to raise funds for his people. Kahkewaquonaby was hounded by autograph seekers and pursued by women. On December 30, 1831, he described the English in a letter to his brother.

The English, in general, are a noble, generous-minded people—free to act and free to think; they very much pride themselves on their civil and religious privileges; in their learning, generosity, manufactures, and commerce; and they think that no other nation is equal to them.

I have found them very open and friendly, always ready to relieve the wants of the poor and needy when properly brought before them. No nation, I think, can be more fond of novelties than the English; they will gaze upon a foreigner as if he had just dropped down from the moon; and I have often been amused in seeing what a large number of people a monkey riding upon a dog will collect, where such things may be seen almost every day. When my Indian name, Kahkewaquonaby, is announced to attend any public meeting, so great is the curiosity, the place is sure to be filled. They are truly industrious, and in general very honest and upright. Their close attention to business produces, I think, too much worldly-mindedness, and hence they forget to think about their souls and their God; their motto seems to be "Money, money; get money, get rich, and be a gentleman." With this sentiment they fly about in every direction, like a swarm of bees, in search of the treasure which lies so near their hearts. These remarks refer to the men of the world, and of such there are not a few.

The English are very fond of good living, and many who live on roast beef, plum pudding, and turtle soup, get very fat, and round as a toad. They eat four times in a day. Breakfast at eight or nine, which consists of coffee or tea, bread and butter, and sometimes a little fried bacon, fish, or eggs. Dinner at about two, P.M., when everything that is good is spread before the eater; which winds up with fruit, nuts, and a few glasses of wine. Tea at six, with bread and butter, toast, and sometimes sweet cake. Supper about nine or ten, when the leavings of the dinner again make their appearance, upon which John Bull makes a hearty meal to go to bed upon at midnight.

The fashion in dress varies so much, I am unable to describe it. I will only say, that the ladies of fashion wear very curious bonnets, which look something like a farmer's scoop-shovel; and when they walk in the tiptoe style they put me in mind of the little snipes that run along the shores of the lakes in Canada. They also wear sleeves as big as bushel bags, which make them appear as if they had three bodies with one head. Yet, with all their big bonnets and sleeves, the English ladies, I think, are the best of women.

IMPRESSIONS OF THE FRENCH

MAUNGWADAUS—OJIBWAY

Last Saturday we saw the great chief of France [Napoleon III], and his great chief woman; the great chief of Belgium [Leopold I], and his great chief woman; and some hundreds of their people. These things we did for them:—We played the Indian ball-play, shot at marks with our own bows and arrows, false scalping, war dance, paddled one of our birch-bark canoes in a beautifully made river, among swans, wild geese, and ducks. After the two great chiefs and their great chief women had much talk with us, they thanked us, got into their carriages covered with gold, drawn by six beautiful horses, and drove to the wigwam of the great chief of France. We followed them, and the great chief's servant, who wears a red coat, and much gold and silver, and a hat in the shape of half-night-sun, took us into one of the great rooms to dine. Everything on the table was gold and silver; we had twelve clean plates. Many came in while we were eating, and it was great amusement to them all.

The French people wear much hair about the mouth, which makes them look bold and noble; but our friend Sasagon [an Ojibway who accompanied Maungwadaus], who has no taste for beauty, says that it would puzzle any one of our people to find where the Frenchman's mouth is; and that a person having much hair round his mouth makes him look like one of our Indian dogs in North America when running away with a black squirrel in his mouth.

The French women carry big and heavy loads on their backs, on what we call tetoomaugun [a harness], same as our women do; they do it because they are industrious. Here, again, Sasagon says, "that the French women would make good wives for the Ojebway hunters."

A VISIT TO GRANDMOTHER ENGLAND

BLACK ELK—SIOUX

In 1886, at the age of twenty-three, Black Elk joined Buffalo Bill's Wild West Show. After a tour of the big American cities, the troupe boarded a "fire-boat" and crossed to England.

The following is taken from Black Elk Speaks *by John G. Neihardt.*

One day we were told that Majesty was coming. I did not know what that was at first, but I learned afterward. It was Grandmother England [Queen Victoria], who owned Grandmother's Land [Canada] where we lived awhile after the Wasichus murdered Crazy Horse. [Crazy Horse, Sioux chief, was killed September 7, 1877, "while resisting arrest."]

She came to the show in a big shining wagon, and there were soldiers on both sides of her, and many other shining wagons came too. That day other people could not come to the show—just Grandmother England and some people who came with her.

Sometimes we had to shoot in the show, but this time we did not shoot at all. We danced and sang, and I was one of the dancers chosen to do this for the Grandmother, because I was young and limber then and could dance many ways. We stood right in front of Grandmother England. She was little but fat and we liked her, because she was good to us. After we had danced, she spoke to us. She said something like this: "I am sixty-seven years old. All over the world I have seen all kinds of people; but to-day I have seen the best-looking people I know. If you belonged to me, I would not let them take you around in a show like this." She said other good things too, and then she said we must come to see her, because she had come to see us. She shook hands with all of us. Her hand was very little and soft. We gave a big cheer for her, and then the shining wagons came in and she got into one of them and they all went away.

In about a half-moon after that we went to see the Grandmother. They put us in some of those shining wagons and took us to a very beautiful place where there was a very big house with sharp, pointed towers on it. There were many seats built high in a circle, and these were just full of Wasichus who were all pounding their heels and yelling: "Jubilee! Jubilee! Jubilee!" I never heard what this meant.

They put us together in a certain place at the bottom of the seats. First there appeared a beautiful black wagon with two black horses, and it went all around the show place. I heard that the Grandmother's grandson, a little boy, was in that wagon. Next came a beautiful black wagon with four gray horses. On each of the two right hand horses there was a rider, and a man walked, holding the front left hand horse. I heard that some of Grandmother's relatives were in this wagon. Next came eight buckskin horses, two by two, pulling a shining black wagon. There was a rider on each right hand horse and a man walked, holding the front left hand horse. There were soldiers, with bayonets, facing outward all around this wagon. Now all the people in the seats were roaring and yelling "Jubilee!" and "Victoria!" Then we saw Grandmother England again. She was sitting in the back of the wagon and two women sat in the front, facing her. Her dress was all shining and her hat was all shining and her wagon was all shining and so were the horses. She looked like a fire coming.

Afterward I heard that there was yellow and white metal all over the horses and the wagon.

When she came to where we were, her wagon stopped and she stood up. Then all those people stood up and roared and bowed to her; but she bowed to us. We sent up a great cry and our women made the tremolo. The people in the crowd were so excited that we heard some of them got sick and fell over. Then when it was quiet, we sang a song to the Grandmother.

That was a very happy time.

We liked Grandmother England, because we could see that she was a fine woman, and she was good to us. Maybe if she had been our Grandmother, it would have been better for our people.

A SIOUX AT DARTMOUTH

OHIYESA—SIOUX

Samson Occom, an educated Mohegan, traveled to England in 1765 to raise money for Dr. Wheelock's Indian charity school at Lebanon. He was lionized in London where he met King George and dined with Lord Dartmouth. He spent a year and a half preaching in England and Scotland and raised £12,000, an enormous sum for those days.

With the money collected by Occom for Indian education, Dr. Wheelock founded Dartmouth College, but only a few Indians were admitted during the nineteenth century under the provisions of its charter. One who benefited was Ohiyesa (Charles A. Eastman), who entered the freshman class in the fall of 1883.

When I reached Boston, I was struck with the old, mossy, granite edifices, and the narrow, crooked streets. Here the people hurried along as if the gray wolf were on their trail. Their ways impressed me as cold, but I forgot that when I had learned to know some of them better.

I went on to Dartmouth College, away up among the granite hills. The country around it is rugged and wild; and thinking of the time when red men lived here in plenty and freedom, it seemed as if I had been destined to come view their graves and bones. No, I said to myself, I have come to continue that which in their last struggle they proposed to take up, in order to save themselves from extinction; but alas! it was too late. Had our New England tribes but followed the example of that great Indian, Samson Occom, and kept up with the development of Dartmouth College, they would have brought forth leaders and men of culture. This was my ambition—that the Sioux should accept civilization before it was too late! I wished that our young men might at once take up the white man's way, and prepare themselves to hold office and wield influence in their native states. Although this hope has not been fully realized, I have the satisfaction of knowing that not a few Indians now hold positions of trust and exercise some political power.

On the evening of our first class meeting, lo! I was appointed football captain for my class. My supporters orated quite effectively on my qualifications as a frontier warrior, and some went so far as to predict that I would, when warmed up, scare all the Sophs off the premises! These representations seemed to be confirmed when, that same evening after supper, the two classes met in a first "rush," and as I was not acquainted with the men, I held up the professor of philosophy, mistaking him for one of the sophomores. Reporters for the Boston dailies made the most of their opportunity to enlarge upon this incident.

I was a sort of prodigal son of old Dartmouth, and nothing could have exceeded the heartiness of my welcome. The New England Indians, for whom it was founded, had departed well-nigh a century earlier, and now a warlike Sioux, like a wild fox, had found his way into this splendid seat of learning! Though poor, I was really better off than many of the students, since the old college took care of me under its ancient charter. I was treated with the greatest kindness by the president and faculty, and often encouraged to ask questions and express my own ideas. My uncle's observations in natural history, for which he had a positive genius, the Indian standpoint in sociology and political economy, these were the subject of some protracted discussions in the class room. This became so well understood, that some of my classmates who had failed to prepare their recitations would induce me to take up the time by advancing a native theory or first hand observation.

For the first time, I became really interested in literature and history. Here it was that civilization began to loom up before me colossal in its greatness, when the fact dawned upon me that nations and tongues, as well as individuals, have lived and died. There were two men of the past who were much in my thoughts: my countryman Occom, who matriculated there a century before me, and the great Daniel Webster (said to have a strain of Indian blood), who came to Dartmouth as impecunious as I was. It was under the Old Pine Tree that the Indians were supposed to have met for the last time to smoke the pipe of peace, and under its shadow every graduating class of my day smoked a parting pipe.

I was anxious to help myself as much as possible and gain practical experience at the same time, by working during the long summer vacations. One summer I worked in a hotel, at another time I canvassed for a book, I think it was the "Knights of Labor," published in Boston. Such success as I attained was due less to any business sagacity than to a certain curiosity I seemed to excite, and which often resulted in the purchase of the book, whether the subscriber really cared for it or not. Another summer, an old school friend, an Armenian, conceived the scheme of dressing me in native costume and sending me out to sell his goods. When I wore a jacket and fez, and was well scented with attar of rose, no dog would permit me on his master's premises if he could help it; nevertheless I did very well. For business purposes I was a Turk, but I never answered any direct questions on the subject of my nativity.

At the seaside hotels, I met society people of an entirely different sort to those I had hitherto taken as American types. I was, I admit, particularly struck with the audacity and forwardness of the women. Among our people the man always leads. I was astonished to learn that some women whom I had observed to accept the most marked attentions from the men were married ladies. Perhaps my earlier training had been too Puritanical, or my aesthetic sense was not then fully developed, for I was surprised when I entered the ballroom to see the pretty women clad so scantily.

One summer at Nantasket beach, I recall that I had somehow been noted by an enterprising representative of a Boston daily, who printed a column or so of my doings, which were innocent enough. He good-naturedly remarked that "the hero of the Boston society girls just now is a Sioux brave," etc. and described all the little gifts of sofa cushions, pictures, and so on, that I had ever received from my girl friends, as well as the medals won in college. I never knew who had let him into my room!

EARLY DAYS AT CARLISLE

CHIEF STANDING BEAR—SIOUX

The Indian school at Carlisle, Pennsylvania, was established in 1879 under the guidance of General R. H. Pratt. It opened with an enrollment of 147 Indians, and the first student to step inside the grounds was an eleven year old Sioux boy—Standing Bear. Together with other Sioux boys and girls, Standing Bear had volunteered to leave the reservation in South Dakota. The Indian children had traveled fifty miles by wagon and boarded a steamboat at Black Pole.

It did not occur to me at that time that I was going away to learn the ways of the white man. My idea was that I was leaving the reservation and going to stay away long enough to do some brave deed, and then come home again alive. If I could just do that, then I knew my father would be so proud of me.

About noon the next day, the interpreter came around and told us we must get ready to leave the boat. Finally it stopped close to the shore and they put out the little bridge and we all got off. We walked quite a distance until we came to a long row of little houses standing on long pieces of iron which stretched away as far as we could see. The little houses were all in line, and the interpreter told us to get inside. So we climbed up a little stairway into one of the houses, and found ourselves in a beautiful room, long but narrow, in which were many cushioned seats.

I took one of these seats, but presently changed to another. I must have changed my seat four or five times before I quieted down. We admired the beautiful room and the soft seats very much. While we were discussing the situation, suddenly the whole house started to move away with us. We boys were in one house and the girls in another. I was glad my sister was not there. We expected every minute that the house would tip over, and that something terrible would happen. We held our blankets between our teeth, because our hands were both busy hanging to the seats, so frightened were we.

We were in our first railway train, but we did not know it. We thought it was a house. I sat next to the window, and observed the poles that were stuck up alongside the iron track. It seemed to me that the poles almost hit the windows, so I changed my seat to the other side.

We rode in this manner for some distance. Finally the interpreter came into the room and told us to get ready to leave it, as we were going to have something to eat. Those who carried bundles were told to leave them in their seats. Some of the older boys began fixing feathers in their hair and putting more paint on their faces.

When the train stopped at the station there was a great crowd of white people there. It was but three years after the killing of Custer by the Sioux, so the white people were anxious to see some Sioux Indians. I suppose many of these people expected to see us coming with scalping-knives between our teeth, bows and arrows in one hand and tomahawk in the other, and to hear a great war-cry as we came off that Iron Horse. The Sioux name for railroad was Maza Canku, or Iron Road. The term "Iron Horse" is merely a white man's name for a moving-picture play.

The place where we stopped was called Sioux City. The white people were yelling at us and making a great noise. When the train stopped, we raised the windows to look out. Soon they started to throw money at us. We little fellows began to gather up the money, but the larger boys told us not to take it, but to throw it back at them. They told us if we took money the white people would put our names in a big book. We did not have sense enough then to understand that those white people had no way of discovering what our names were. However, we threw the money all back at them. At this, the white people laughed and threw more money at us. Then the big boys told us to close the windows. That stopped the money-throwing.

The interpreter then came in and told us we were to get off here. As we left the little house, we saw that there were lots of what we took to be soldiers lined up on both sides of the street. I expect these were policemen, but as they had on uniforms of some sort, we called them soldiers. They formed up a line and we marched between them to the eating-place.

Many of the little Indian boys and girls were afraid of the white people. I really did not blame them, because the whites acted so wild at seeing us. They tried to give the war-whoop and mimic the Indian and in other ways got us all wrought up and excited, and we did not like this sort of treatment.

When we got inside the restaurant, there were two long tables with white covers on. There was plenty of fine silverware and all kinds of good food. We all sat down around the table, but we did not try to eat. We just helped ourselves to all the food, scooping it into our blankets, and not missing all the lump sugar. The white people were all crowded up close to the windows on the outside, watching us and laughing their heads off at the way we acted. They were waiting to see how we ate, but we fooled them, for we carried everything back to the iron road, and inside the little houses we sat down in peace and enjoyed our meal.

Then the train started up again, and we traveled all that night. The next day we reached Sotoju Otun Wake, which, translated into Sioux, means "smoky city" or your great city of Chicago. Here we saw so many people and such big houses that we began to open our eyes in astonishment. The big boys said, "The white people are like ants; they are all over—everywhere." We Indians do not call the Caucasian race "white people," but "Wasicun" or "Mila Hanska." This latter means "long knife."

In the evening we were loaded on to another iron road, traveling all night, the next day and then another night came. By this time we were all beginning to feel very restless. We had been sitting up all the way from Dakota in those straight seats and were getting very tired. The big boys began to tell us little fellows that the white people were taking us to the place where the sun rises, where they would dump us over the edge of the earth, as we had been taught that the earth was flat, with four corners, and when we came to the edge, we would fall over.

Now the full moon was rising, and we were traveling toward it. The big boys were singing brave songs, expecting to be killed any minute. We all looked at the moon, and it was in front of us, but we felt that we were getting too close to it for comfort. We were very tired, and the little fellows dozed off. Presently the big boys woke everybody. They said they had made a discovery. We were told to look out the window and see what had happened while we were dozing. We did so, and the moon was now behind us! Apparently we had passed the place where the moon rose!

This was quite a mystery. The big boys were now singing brave songs again, while I was wide awake and watchful, waiting to see what was going to happen. But nothing happened.

We afterward learned that at Harrisburg, Pennsylvania, the train turned due west to Carlisle, which placed the moon in our rear. And to think we had expected to be killed because we had passed the moon!

At last the train arrived at a junction where we were told we were at the end of our journey. Here we left the train and walked about two miles to the Carlisle Barracks. Soon we came to a big gate in a great high wall. The gate was locked, but after quite a long wait, it was unlocked and we marched in through it. I was the first boy inside. At that time I thought nothing of it, but now I realize that I was the first Indian boy to step inside the Carlisle Indian School grounds. . . .

Although we were yet wearing our Indian clothes, the interpreter came to us and told us we must go to school. We were marched into a schoolroom, where we were each given a pencil and slate. We were seated at single desks. We soon discovered that the pencils made marks on the slates. So we covered our heads with our blankets, holding the slate inside so the other fellow would not know what we were doing. Here we would draw a man on a pony chasing buffalo, or a boy shooting birds in a tree, or it might be one of our Indian games, or anything that suited our fancy to try and portray.

When we had all finished, we dropped our blankets down on the seat and marched up to the teacher with our slates to show what we had drawn. Our teacher was a woman. She bowed her head as she examined the slates and smiled, indicating that we were doing pretty well—at least we interpreted it that way.

One day when we came to school there was a lot of writing on one of the blackboards. We did not know what it meant, but our interpreter came into the room and said, "Do you see all these marks on the blackboard? Well, each word is a white man's name. They are going to give each one of you one of these names by which you will hereafter be known." None of the names were read or explained to us, so of course we did not know the sound or meaning of any of them.

The teacher had a long pointed stick in her hand, and the interpreter told the boy in the front seat to come up. The teacher handed the stick to him, and the interpreter then told him to pick out any name he wanted. The boy had gone up with his blanket on. When the long stick was handed to him, he turned to us as much as to say, "Shall I—or will you help me—to take one of these names? Is it right for me to take a white man's name?" He did not know what to do for a time, not uttering a single word—but he acted a lot and was doing a lot of thinking.

Finally he pointed out one of the names written on the blackboard. Then the teacher took a piece of white tape and wrote the name on it. Then she cut off a length of the tape and sewed it on the back of the boy's shirt. Then that name was erased from the board. There was no duplication of names in the first class at Carlisle School!

Then the next boy took the pointer and selected a name. He was also labeled in the same manner as Number One. When my turn came, I took the pointer and acted as if I were about to touch an enemy. Soon we all had the names of white men sewed on our backs. When we went to school, we knew enough to take our proper places in the class, but that was all. When the teacher called the roll, no one answered his name. Then she would walk around and look at the back of the boys' shirts. When she had the right name located, she made the boy stand up and say "Present." She kept this up for about a week before we knew what the sound of our new names was.

I was one of the "bright fellows" to learn my name quickly. How proud I was to answer when the teacher called the roll! I would put my blanket down and half raise myself in my seat, all ready to answer to my new name. I had selected the name "Luther"—not "Lutheran" as many people call me. "Lutheran" is the name of a church denomination, not a person.

Next we had to learn to write our names. Our good teacher had a lot of patience with us. She is now living in Los Angeles, California, and I still like to go and ask her any question which may come up in my mind. She first wrote my name on the slate for me, and then, by motions, indicated that I was to write it just like that. She held the pencil in her hand just so, then made first one stroke, then another, and by signs I was given to understand that I was to follow in exactly the same way.

The first few times I wrote my new name, it was scratched so deeply into the slate that I was never able to erase it. But I copied my name all over both sides of the slate until there was no more room to write. Then I took my slate up to show it to the teacher, and she indicated, by the expression of her face, that it was very good. I soon learned to write it very well; then I took a piece of chalk downstairs and wrote "Luther" all over everything I could copy it on.

Next the teacher wrote out the alphabet on my slate and indicated to me that I was to take the slate to my room and study. I was pleased to do this, as I expected to have a lot of fun. I went up to the second floor, to the end of the building, where I thought nobody would bother me. There I sat down and looked at those queer letters, trying hard to figure out what they meant. No one was there to tell me that the first letter was "A" the next "B" and so on. This was the first time in my life that I was really disgusted. It was something I could not decipher, and all this study business was not what I had come East for anyhow—so I thought.

How lonesome I felt for my father and mother! I stayed upstairs all by myself, thinking of the good times I might be having if I were only back home, where I could ride my ponies, go wherever I wanted to and do as I pleased, and, when it came night, could lie down and sleep well. Right then and there I learned that no matter how humble your home is, it is yet home.

So it did me no good to take my slate with me that day. It only made me lonesome. The next time the teacher told me by signs to take my slate to my room, I shook my head, meaning "no." She came and talked to me in English, but of course I did not know what she was saying.

A few days later, she wrote the alphabet on the blackboard, then brought the interpreter into the room. Through him she told us to repeat each letter after her, calling out "A," and we all said "A"; then "B," and so on. This was our real beginning. The first day we learned the first three letters of the alphabet, both the pronunciation and the reading of them.

Next, we heard that we were soon to have white men's clothes. We were all very excited and anxious when this was announced to us. One day some wagons came in, loaded with big boxes, which were unloaded in front of the office. Of course we were all very curious, and gathered around to watch the proceedings and see all we could.

Here, one at a time, we were "sized up" and a whole suit handed to each of us. The clothes were some sort of dark heavy gray goods, consisting of coat, pants, and vest. We were also given a dark woolen shirt, a cap, a pair of suspenders, socks, and heavy farmer's boots.

Up to this time we had all been wearing our thin shirts, leggings, and a blanket. Now we had received new outfits of white men's clothes, and to us it seemed a whole lot of clothing to wear at once, but even at that, we had not yet received any underwear.

As soon as we had received our outfits, we ran to our rooms to dress up. Although the suits were too big for many of us, we did not know the difference. I remember that my boots were far too large, but as long as they were "screechy" or squeaky, I didn't worry about the size! I liked the noise they made when I walked, and the other boys were likewise pleased.

How proud we were with clothes that had pockets and with boots that squeaked! We walked the floor nearly all that night. Many of the boys even went to bed with their clothes all on. But in the morning, the boys who had taken off their pants had a most terrible time. They did not know whether they were to button up in front or behind. Some of the boys said the open part went in front; others said, "No, it goes at the back." There is where the boys who had kept all their clothes on came in handy to look at. They showed the others that the pants buttoned up in front and not at the back. So here we learned something again.

A short time later, some boys, myself among the number, were called into one of the schoolrooms. There we found a little white woman. There was a long table in front of her, on which were many packages tied in paper. She opened up one package and it contained a bright, shining horn. Other packages disclosed more horns, but they seemed to be of different sizes.

The little white woman picked up a horn and then looked the boys over. Finally she handed it to a boy who she thought might be able to use it. Then she picked out a shorter horn and gave it to me. I learned afterward that it was a B-flat cornet. When she had finished, all the boys had horns in their hands. We were to be taught how to play on them and form a band.

The little woman had a black case with her, which she opened. It held a beautiful horn, and when she blew on it it sounded beautiful. Then she motioned to us that we were to blow our horns. Some of the boys tried to blow from the large end. Although we tried our best, we could not produce a sound from them. She then tried to talk to us, but we did not understand her. Then she showed us how to wet the end of the mouthpiece. We thought she wanted us to spit into the horns, so we did. She finally got so discouraged with us that she started crying.

We just stood there and waited for her to get through, then we all tried again. Finally, some of the boys managed to make a noise through their horns. But if you could have heard it! It was terrible! But we thought we were doing fine.

So now I had more to occupy my attention. In the morning I had one hour to practice for the band. Then I must run to my room and change my clothes and go to work in the tin shop. From there I had to run again to my room and change my clothes and get ready for dinner. After that, I had a little time to study my lessons.

Then the school bell would ring and it was time for school. After that, we played or studied our music. Then we went to bed. All lights had to be out at nine o'clock. The first piece of music our band was able to play was the alphabet, from "a" to "z." It was a great day for us when we were able to play this simple little thing in public. But it was a good thing we were not asked to give an encore, for that was all we knew!

After I had learned to play a little, I was chosen to give all the bugle calls. I had to get up in the morning before the others and arouse everybody by blowing the morning call. Evenings at ten minutes before nine o'clock I blew again. Then all the boys would run for their rooms. At nine o'clock the second call was given, when all lights were turned out and we were supposed to be in bed. Later on I learned the mess call, and eventually I could blow all the calls of the regular army.

RED JACKET DENOUNCES THE BLACK-COATS

RED JACKET—SENECA

Although the early missionaries won many quick converts in New England and the Old Northwest, the Senecas of New York, led by Red Jacket (died 1830), stood fast by the religion of their fathers. Once, after listening patiently to a black-coat's harangue, Red Jacket said calmly: "If you white people murdered 'the Saviour,' make it up yourselves. We had nothing to do with it. If he had come among us we should have treated him better." Red Jacket was bitterly opposed to reform or change. To a young Indian who had been educated among the whites, he said: "What have we here? You are neither a white man nor an Indian; for heaven's sake tell us, what are you?"

At the request of a missionary from Massachusetts, the Senecas called a council at Buffalo. The black-coat said that he wanted no money or lands from the Indians, but only their acceptance of the true God. In a masterful reply, Red Jacket summarized the objections of the Indians to the white man's religion.

Friend and Brother! It was the will of the Great Spirit that we should meet together this day. He orders all things, and he has given us a fine day for our council. He has taken his garment from before the sun, and caused it to shine with brightness upon us. Our eyes are opened that we see clearly. Our ears are unstopped that we have been able to hear distinctly the words you have spoken. For all these favors we thank the Great Spirit, and him only.

Brother! This council fire was kindled by you. It was at your request that we came together at this time. We have listened with attention to what you have said. You requested us to speak our minds freely. This gives us great joy, for we now consider that we stand upright before you, and can speak what we think. All have heard your voice, and all speak to you as one man. Our minds are agreed.

Brother! You say you want an answer to your talk before you leave this place. It is right you should have one, for you are a great distance from home, and we do not wish to detain you. But we will first look back a little, and tell you what our fathers have told us, and what we have heard from the white people.

From Catlin Sketchbook
Courtesy of Gilcrease Institute

INDIAN FEMALE
Missisauga Tribe
George Catlin
ca. 1830–40

Brother! Listen to what we say. There was a time when our forefathers owned this great island. Their lands extended from the rising to the setting sun. The Great Spirit had made it for the use of Indians. He had created the buffalo, the deer, and other animals for food. He made the bear and the beaver, and their skins served us for clothing. He had scattered them over the country, and taught us how to take them. He had caused the earth to produce corn for bread. All this he had done for his red children because he loved them. If we had any disputes about hunting grounds, they were generally settled without the shedding of much blood. But an evil day came upon us. Your forefathers crossed the great waters, and landed on this island. Their numbers were small. They found friends and not enemies. They told us they had fled from their own country for fear of wicked men, and come here to enjoy their religion. They asked for a small seat. We took pity on them, granted their request, and they sat down amongst us. We gave them corn and meat. They gave us poison in return. The white people had now found our country. Tidings were carried back, and more came amongst us. Yet we did not fear them. We took them to be friends. They called us brothers. We believed them, and gave them more lands. At length their numbers had greatly increased. They wanted more land. They wanted our country. Our eyes were opened, and our minds became uneasy. Wars took place. Indians were hired to fight against Indians, and many of our people were destroyed. They also brought strong liquors among us. It was strong and powerful, and has slain thousands.

Brother! Our lands were once large, and yours were very small. You have now become a great people, and we have scarcely a place left to spread our blankets. You have got our country, but are not satisfied. You want to force your religion upon us.

Brother! Continue to listen. You say that you are sent to instruct us how to worship the Great Spirit agreeably to his mind; and if we do not take hold of the religion which you white people teach, we shall be unhappy hereafter. You say that you are right and we are lost. How do we know this to be true? We understand that your religion is written in a book. If it was intended for us as well as for you, why had not the Great Spirit given it to us; and not only to us, but why did he not give to our forefathers the knowledge of that book, with the means of understanding it rightly? We only know what you tell us about it. How shall we know when to believe, being so often deceived by the white people?

Brother! You say there is but one way to worship and serve the Great Spirit. If there is but one religion, why do you white people differ so much about it? Why not all agree, as you can all read the book?

Brother! We do not understand these things. We are told that your religion was given to your forefathers, and has been handed down from father to son. We also have a religion which was given to our forefathers, and has been handed down to us their children. We worship that way. It teaches us to be thankful for all the favors we receive, to love each other, and to be united. We never quarrel about religion.

Brother! The Great Spirit has made us all. But he has made a great difference between his white and red children. He has given us a different complexion and different customs. To you he has given the arts; to these he had not opened our eyes. We know these things to be true. Since he has made so great a difference between us in other things, why may we not conclude that he has given us a different religion, according to our understanding? The Great Spirit does right. He knows what is best for his children. We are satisfied.

Brother! We do not wish to destroy your religion, or take it from you. We only want to enjoy our own.

Brother! You say you have not come to get our land or our money, but to enlighten our minds. I will now tell you that I have been at your meetings and saw you collecting money from the meeting. I cannot tell what this money was intended for, but suppose it was for your minister; and if we should conform to your way of thinking, perhaps you may want some from us.

Brother! We are told that you have been preaching to white people in this place. These people are our neighbors. We are acquainted with them. We will wait a little while, and see what effect your preaching has upon them. If we find that it does them good and makes them honest and less disposed to cheat Indians, we will then consider again what you have said.

Brother! You have now heard our answer to your talk, and this is all we have to say at present. As we are going to part, we will come and take you by the hand, and hope the Great Spirit will protect you on your journey, and return you safe to your friends.

As he finished his speech, Red Jacket came forward to bid farewell to the black-coat; but the missionary turned away quickly rather than shake hands with a pagan who advocated tolerance.

MURDER OF AN INDIAN SEMINARIST

CHIEF ANDREW J. BLACKBIRD—OTTAWA

William Blackbird was the first Indian selected for seminar studies by the Roman Catholic Church. He was sent to Rome in 1832, where two years later he died suddenly on the eve of his ordination. Contemporary newspapers mentioned nothing unusual about his death, but in 1885, his brother wrote that William was murdered.

The first full-blood Indian priest was Albert Negahnquet, a Pottawattami ordained in 1903.

When my brother William was about twelve or thirteen years of age the Protestant Mission School started at Mackinac Island, and my father thought best to put him to that school. After being there less than a year, he was going around with his teachers, acting as interpreter among the Indian camps at the Island of Mackinac. I was perfectly astonished to see how quick he had acquired the English language. After the mission broke up at the island, about the time the Catholic mission was established at Little Traverse, William came home and stayed with us for about two years, when he was taken by Bishop Reese to Cincinnati, Ohio, and there my brother attained the highest degree of education, or graduation as it is called.

From thence he was taken across the ocean to the city of Rome, to study for the priesthood. It is related that he was a very eloquent and powerful orator, and was considered a very promising man by the people of the city of Rome, and received great attention from the noble families, on account of his wisdom and talent and his being a native American.

He died almost the very day when he was to be ordained a priest. He received a long visit from his cousin Hamlin that evening, and they sat late in the night, talking on various subjects, and particularly on American matters and his ordination. My brother was perfectly well and robust at that time, and full of lively spirits. He told his cousin that night, that if he ever set his foot again on American soil, his people, the Ottawas and Chippewas of Michigan, should always remain where they were. The United States would never be able to compel them to go west of the Mississippi, for he knew the way to prevent them from being driven off from their native land. He also told his cousin that as soon as he was ordained and relieved from Rome, he would at once start for America, and go straight to Washington to see the President of the United States, in order to hold conference with him on the subject of his people and their lands. There was a great preparation for the occasion of his ordination. A great ceremony was to be in St. Peter's Church, because a native American Indian, son of the chief of the Ottawa tribe of Indians, a prince of the forests of Michigan, was to be ordained a priest, which had never before happened since the discovery of the aborigines in America. In the morning, at the breakfast table, my brother William did not appear, and everyone was surprised not to see him at the table. After breakfast, a messenger was sent to his room. He soon returned with the shocking news that he was dead. Then the authorities of the college arose and rushed to the scene, and there they found him on the floor, lying in his own blood. When Hamlin, his cousin heard of it, he too rushed to the room; and after his cousin's body was taken out, wrapped up in a cloth, he went in, and saw at once enough to tell him that it was the work of an assassin.

No motive for the assassination has ever been developed, and it remains to this day a mystery. There were several American students at Rome at that time, and it was claimed by the Italians that my brother's death came through some of the American students from a secret plot originating in this country to remove this Indian youth who had attained the highest pinnacle of science and who had become their equal in wisdom, and in all the important questions of the day, both in temporal and spiritual matters. He was slain, it has been said, because it was found out that he was counseling his people on the subject of their lands and their treaties with the government of the United States. His death deprived the Ottawa and Chippewa Indians of a wise counselor and adviser, one of their own native countrymen; but it seems that it would be impossible for the American people in this Christian land to make such a wicked conspiracy against this poor son of the forest. Yet it might be possible, for we have learned that we cannot always trust the American people as to their integrity and stability in well doing with us.

It is said the stains of my brother's blood can be seen to this day in Rome, as the room has been kept as a memorial, and is shown to travelers from this country. His statue in full size can also be seen there, which is said to be a perfect image of him.

CONFUSION OF THE WHITE MAN'S RELIGION

CHIEF SPOTTED TAIL—SIOUX

I am bothered what to believe. Some years ago a good man, as I think, came to us. He talked me out of all my old faith; and after a while, thinking that he must know more of these matters than an ignorant Indian, I joined his church, and became a Methodist. After a while he went away; another man came and talked, and I became a Baptist; then another came and talked, and I became a Presbyterian. Now another one has come, and wants me to be an Episcopalian. All these people tell different stories, and each wants me to believe that his special way is the only way to be good and save my soul. I have about made up my mind that either they all lie, or that they don't know any more about it than I did at first. I have always believed in the Great Spirit, and worshipped him in my own way. These people don't seem to want to change my belief in the Great Spirit, but to change my way of talking to him. White men have education and books, and ought to know exactly what to do, but hardly any two of them agree on what should be done.

SEQUOYAH AND THE CHEROKEE ALPHABET

JOHN RIDGE—CHEROKEE

The Cherokees are the only modern nation who can claim the honour of having invented an alphabet. George Guess [Sequoyah], a Cherokee Indian, who did not understand a single letter within a few years, had invented an alphabet in which a newspaper is published in the Cherokee nation, and their children taught to read and write. He was a poor man, living in a retired part of the nation, and he told the head men one day that he could make a book. The chiefs replied it was impossible, because, they said, the Great Spirit at first made a red and a white boy; to the red boy he gave a book, and to the white boy a bow and arrow, but the white boy came round the red boy, stole his book, and went off, leaving him the bow and arrow, and therefore an Indian could not make a book. But George Guess thought he could. He shut himself up to study; his corn was left to weeds, and he was pronounced a crazy man by the tribe. His wife thought so too, and burnt up his manuscripts whenever she could find them. But he persevered. He first attempted to form a character for every word in the Cherokee language, but was forced to abandon it. He then set about discovering the number of sounds in the language, which he found to be sixty-eight, and for each of these he adopted a character, which forms the alphabet, and these characters combined like letters form words. Having accomplished this he called together six of his neighbours, and said, "Now I can make a book." They did not believe him. To convince them, he asked each to make a speech, which he wrote down as they spoke, and then read to them, so that each knew his own speech, and they then acknowledged he could make a book, and from this invention of this great man, the Cherokees have become a reading people.

The first Indian newspaper, the Cherokee Phoenix, *was published in 1828 and was edited by Elias Boudinott, an educated Cherokee. The* Cherokee Phoenix *was printed in English and Cherokee and was, wrote its editor, "sacred to the cause of the Indians."*

When the Cherokees became prosperous, the white men in Georgia coveted their farms and lands. In 1835, several Cherokee leaders, including Elias Boudinott and John Ridge, signed away the Cherokee possessions in Georgia and agreed to move to Oklahoma. Boudinott and Ridge believed they had obtained the best possible terms for the Cherokees, but they had acted without the authority of their nation. Despite efforts of the great Cherokee chief, John Ross, to prevent the government from carrying out the treaty, the Cherokees were evicted from their homes at bayonet point and started down the "trail of tears" to Oklahoma. During the journey one-fourth of the tribe died from exposure or starvation.

In 1839 the followers of John Ross attacked and murdered the chiefs who had signed the treaty of 1835. Among the murdered men were Elias Boudinott and John Ridge. Ridge's murder, one of the most dramatic events in Cherokee history, was described by his son, John R. Ridge: "On the morning of the 22d of June, 1839, about day-

break, our family was aroused from sleep by a violent noise. The doors were broken down, and the house was full of armed men. I saw my father in the hands of assassins. He endeavored to speak to them, but they shouted and drowned his voice, for they were instructed not to listen to him for a moment, for fear they would be persuaded not to kill him. They dragged him into the yard, and prepared to murder him. Two men held him by the arms, and others by the body, while another stabbed him deliberately with a dirk twenty-nine times. My mother rushed out to the door, but they pushed her back with their guns into the house, and prevented her egress until their act was finished, when they left the place quietly. My father fell to the earth, but did not immediately expire. My mother ran out to him. He raised himself on his elbow and tried to speak, but the blood flowed into his mouth and prevented him. In a few moments more he died, without speaking that last word which he wished to say. Then succeeded a scene of agony the sight of which might make one regret that the human race had ever been created. It has darkened my mind with an eternal shadow. In a room prepared for the purpose, lay pale in death the man whose voice had been listened to with awe and admiration in the councils of his Nation, the blood oozing through his winding sheet, and falling drop by drop on the floor."

THE INDIAN PROBLEM

CHIEF STANDING BEAR—SIOUX

The white man does not understand the Indian for the reason that he does not understand America. He is too far removed from its formative processes. The roots of the tree of his life have not yet grasped the rock and soil. The white man is still troubled with primitive fears; he still has in his consciousness the perils of this frontier continent, some of its fastnesses not yet having yielded to his questing footsteps and inquiring eyes. He shudders still with the memory of the loss of his forefathers upon its scorching deserts and forbidding mountain-tops. The man from Europe is still a foreigner and an alien. And he still hates the man who questioned his path across the continent.

But in the Indian the spirit of the land is still vested; it will be until other men are able to divine and meet its rhythm. Men must be born and reborn to belong. Their bodies must be formed of the dust of their forefathers' bones.

The attempted transformation of the Indian by the white man and the chaos that has resulted are but the fruits of the white man's disobedience of a fundamental and spiritual law. The pressure that has been brought to bear upon the native people, since the cessation of armed conflict, in the attempt to force conformity of custom and habit has caused a reaction more destructive than war, and the injury has not only affected the Indian, but has extended to the white population as well. Tyranny, stupidity, and lack of vision have brought about the situation now alluded to as the "Indian Problem."

There is, I insist, no Indian problem as created by the Indian himself. Every problem that exists today in regard to the native population is due to the white man's cast of mind, which is unable, at least reluctant, to seek understanding and achieve adjustment in a new and a significant environment into which it has so recently come.

THE INDIANS' APPEAL FOR JUSTICE

CHIEF JOSEPH—NEZ PERCE

I do not understand why nothing is done for my people. I have heard talk and talk, and nothing is done. Good words do not last long unless they amount to something. Words do not pay for my dead people. They do not pay for my country, now overrun by white men. They do not protect my father's grave. They do not pay for all my horses and cattle. Good words will not give me back my children. Good words will not give my people good health and stop them from dying. Good words will not get my people a home where they can live in peace and take care of themselves. I am tired of talk that comes to nothing. It makes my heart sick when I remember all the good words and all the broken promises. There has been too much talking by men who had no right to talk. Too many misrepresentations have been made, too many misunderstandings have come up between the white men about the Indians.

Treat all men alike. Give them all the same law. Give them all an even chance to live and grow. All men were made by the same Great Spirit Chief. They are all brothers. The earth is the mother of all people, and all people should have equal rights upon it. You might as well expect the rivers to run backward as that any man who was born a free man should be contented when penned up and denied liberty to go where he pleases. If you tie a horse to a stake, do you expect he will grow fat? If you pen an Indian up on a small spot of earth, and compel him to stay there, he will not be contented, nor will he grow and prosper. I have asked some of the great white chiefs where they get their authority to say to the Indian that he shall stay in one place, while he sees white men going where they please. They can not tell me.

When I think of our condition my heart is heavy. I see men of my race treated as outlaws and driven from country to country, or shot down like animals.

I know my race must change. We can not hold our own with the white men as we are. We only ask an even chance to live as other men live. We ask to be recognized as men. We ask that the same law shall work alike on all men. If the Indian breaks the law, punish him by the law. If the white man breaks the law, punish him also.

Let me be a free man—free to travel, free to stop, free to work, free to trade where I choose, free to choose my own teachers, free to follow the religion of my fathers, free to think and talk and act for myself—and I will obey every law, or submit to the penalty.

Whenever the white man treats the Indian as they treat each other, then we will have no more wars. We shall all be alike—brothers of one father and one mother, with one sky above us and one country around us, and one government for all. For this time the Indian race is waiting and praying.

THE FUTURE OF THE INDIAN

CHIEF STANDING BEAR—SIOUX

There certainly can be no doubt in the public mind today as to the capacity of the younger Indians in taking on white modes and manners. For many years, and particularly since the days of General Pratt, the young Indian has been proving his efficiency when entering the fields of white man's endeavor and has done well in copying and acquiring the ways of the white man.

The Indian liked the white man's horse and straightway became an expert horseman; he threw away his age-old weapons, the bow and arrow, and matched the white man's skill with gun and pistol; in the field of sports—games of strength and skill—the Indian enters with no shame in comparison; the white man's beads the Indian woman took, developed a technique and an art distinctly her own with no competitor in design; and in the white man's technique of song and dance the Indian has made himself a creditable exponent.

However, despite the fact that Indian schools have been established over several generations, there is a dearth of Indians in the professions. It is most noticeable on the reservations where the numerous positions of consequence are held by white employees instead of trained Indians. For instance, why are not the stores, post-offices, and Government office jobs on the Sioux Reservation held by trained Indians? Why cannot Sioux be reservation nurses and doctors; and road-builders too? Much road work goes on every summer, but the complaint is constant that it is always done by white workmen, and in such a manner as to necessitate its being done again in a short time. Were these numerous positions turned over to trained Indians, the white population would soon find reservation life less attractive and less lucrative.

With school facilities already fairly well established and the capability of the Indian unquestioned, every reservation could well be supplied with Indian doctors, nurses, engineers, road- and bridge-builders, draughtsmen, architects, dentists, lawyers, teachers, and instructors in tribal lore, legends, orations, song, dance, and ceremonial ritual. The Indian, by the very sense of duty, should become his own historian, giving his account of the race—fairer and fewer accounts of the wars and more of statecraft, legends, languages, oratory, and philosophical conceptions. No longer should the Indian be dehumanized in order to make material for lurid and cheap fiction to embellish street-stands. Rather, a fair and correct history of the native American should be incorporated in the curriculum of the public school.

Caucasian youth is fed, and rightly so, on the feats and exploits of their old-world heroes, their revolutionary forefathers, their adventurous pioneer trail-blazers, and in our Southwest through pageants, fiestas, and holidays the days of the Spanish *conquistador* is kept alive.

But Indian youth! They, too, have fine pages in their past history; they, too, have patriots and heroes. And it is not fair to rob Indian youth of their history, the stories of their patriots, which, if impartially written, would fill them with pride and dignity. Therefore, give back to Indian youth all, everything in their heritage that belongs to them and augment it with the best in the modern schools. I repeat, doubly educate the Indian boy and girl.

What a contrast this would make in comparison with the present unhealthy, demoralized place the reservation is today, where the old are poorly fed, shabbily clothed, divested of pride and incentive; and where the young are unfitted for tribal life and untrained for the world of white man's affairs except to hold an occasional job!

Why not a school of Indian thought, built on the Indian pattern and conducted by Indian instructors? Why not a school of tribal art?

Why should not America be cognizant of itself; aware of its identity? In short, why should not America be preserved?

There were ideals and practices in the life of my ancestors that have not been improved upon by the present-day civilization; there were in our culture elements of benefit; and there were influences that would broaden any life. But that almost an entire public needs to be enlightened as to this fact need not be discouraging. For many centuries the human mind labored under the delusion that the world was flat; and thousands of men have believed that the heavens were supported by the strength of an Atlas. The human mind is not yet free from fallacious reasoning; it is not yet an open mind and its deepest recesses are not yet swept free of errors.

But it is now time for a destructive order to be reversed, and it is well to inform other races that the aboriginal culture of America was not devoid of beauty. Furthermore, in denying the Indian his ancestral rights and heritages the white race is but robbing itself. But America can be revived, rejuvenated, by recognizing a native school of thought.

EPILOGUE

WILLIAM J. HARSHA

My brothers, the Indians must always be remembered in this land. Out of our languages we have given names to many beautiful things which will always speak of us. Minnehaha will laugh of us, Seneca will shine in our image, Mississippi will murmur our woes. The broad Iowa and the rolling Dakota and the fertile Michigan will whisper our names to the sun that kisses them. The roaring Niagara, the sighing Illinois, the singing Delaware, will chant unceasingly our Dta-wa-e [Death Song]. Can it be that you and your children will hear that eternal song without a stricken heart? We have been guilty of only one sin—we have had possessions that the white man coveted. We moved away toward the setting sun; we gave up our homes to the white man.

My brethren, among the legends of my people it is told how a chief, leading the remnant of his people, crossed a great river, and striking his tepee-stake upon the ground, exclaimed, "A-la-ba-ma!" This in our language means "Here we may rest!" But he saw not the future. The white man came: he and his people could not rest there; they were driven out, and in a dark swamp they were thrust down into the slime and killed. The word he so sadly spoke has given a name to one of the white man's states. There is no spot under those stars that now smile upon us, where the Indian can plant his foot and sigh "A-la-ba-ma."

NOTES

Biographical information on each author is given under the author's first entry in these Notes, except for authors who are discussed in the introductions to selections.

PART I. AROUND THE CAMPFIRE

A SIOUX COURTSHIP from *Black Elk Speaks*, as told to John G. Neihardt, pp. 67–76. Born in "the Moon of Popping Trees on the Little Powder River in the Winter When the Four Crows Were Killed" (December, 1863), Black Elk was old and nearly blind when he dictated the story of his life as a visionary and medicine man of the Oglala Sioux. "Now that I can see it all as from a lonely hilltop," he said, "I know it was the story of a mighty vision given to a man too weak to use it; of a holy tree that should have flourished in a people's heart with flowers and singing birds, and now is withered; and of a people's dream that died in bloody snow."

The courting adventures of High Horse probably took place on the Great Plains about the middle of the nineteenth century.

THE MAIDENS' FEAST from *Indian Boyhood* by Ohiyesa (Dr. Charles A. Eastman), pp. 181 ff. Most famous of American Indian authors, Ohiyesa was born in 1858 near Redwood Falls, Minnesota, but fled with his uncle to Canada after the Minnesota Massacre of 1862. Until he was fifteen he lived among the Santee band of Sioux. He began his education in the mission school at Santee, Nebraska. Graduated from Dartmouth in 1887, Ohiyesa received his M.D. from Boston University three years later; and after a disillusioning experience as government physician at Pine Ridge Agency, South Dakota, he began the private practice of medicine. Encouraged by his wife (Elaine Goodale), Ohiyesa turned to writing and lecturing, and with the publication of his first book, *Indian Boyhood* (1902), was accepted as a leading authority on the Sioux. Until his death in 1939, Ohiyesa continued to write books and articles distinguished for their fluent and graceful style.

SONGS OF OJIBWAY LOVERS. "The Brave to the Maiden" from *Path on the Rainbow*, pp. 12–13, translated by Charles Fenno Hoffman; "The Maiden to the Brave" from *Information Respecting the Indian Tribes of the United States* by Henry R. Schoolcraft, Vol. V, pp. 560–561. Like most Indian poetry, these Ojibway songs were intended to be sung or chanted to music. The holophrastic character of Indian verse often makes literal translation impractical. These songs are no doubt very free translations, and were probably composed in the Northeast woodlands in the eighteenth century, at a time when the New England literati were turning out sterile and imitative doggerel.

TRADITIONAL ADVICE ON GETTING MARRIED from *The Winnebago Tribe* by Paul Radin, 37th Annual Report of the Bureau of American Ethnology, pp. 175 ff. These marriage traditions were furnished by Winnebago informants in Wisconsin between 1908 and 1913.

HOME AND FAMILY from *Land of the Spotted Eagle* by Chief Luther Standing Bear, pp. 84 ff. Born in 1868, Standing Bear passed his boyhood on the plains of Nebraska and South Dakota. At the age of eleven he was sent to the Carlisle Indian School in Pennsylvania, where he stayed four years. After a brief experience clerking in Wanamaker's, he became a teacher in the Indian school at Rosebud Agency, South Dakota. In 1898 he joined Buffalo Bill's Wild West Show as interpreter. In his later years he acted in motion pictures, lectured, and wrote the books which brought him fame.

Chief Standing Bear describes the home life of the Oglala band of Sioux in the era just preceding the Custer Battle (1876).

EDUCATION OF CHILDREN from *Indian Boyhood* by Ohiyesa (Dr. Charles A. Eastman), pp. 49 ff. The customs depicted are those of the Santee Sioux, living in British Columbia in the late 1860's.

A HOPI CHILDHOOD from *Sun Chief: The Autobiography of a Hopi* by Don C. Talayesva, edited by Leo W. Simmons, pp. 56–59. Talayesva, owner of his tribe's Sun Hill kiva, was born in 1890 and raised among the Hopi at Oraibi, Arizona. At ten, he began the study of English. "I learned little at school the first year," he wrote later, "except 'bright boy,' 'smart boy,' 'yes' and 'no,' 'nail,' and 'candy.'" Eventually, he acquired a knowledge of English and accepted the ways of the white man, but later he returned to his people in the ancient village of Oraibi. Between 1938 and 1941, aided by Leo W. Simmons, he wrote the story of his life.

BLANKET SIGNALS from *Land of the Spotted Eagle* by Chief Luther Standing Bear, pp. 80–81.

OJIBWAY PICTURE WRITING from *Traditional History and Characteristic Sketches of the Ojibway Nation* by Chief Kah-ge-ga-gah-bowh (George Copway), pp. 126–136. Born in central Canada in 1818, Kah-ge-ga-gah-bowh described himself as "one of Nature's children." He was distinguished as a great hunter and a man of prodigious strength. Once he carried more than 200 pounds of flour, shot, coffee, and sugar on his back for nearly a quarter of a mile without resting. In the spring of 1841 he struck out across Wisconsin to warn the Ojibways against a Sioux war party. "I went at the rate of about seventy-five miles per day," he wrote, "and arrived at noon on the fourth day; having walked two hundred and forty miles, forded eight large streams, and crossed the broad Mississippi twice." In 1830 he was converted to Methodism and passed two years at the Ebenezer Academy near Jacksonville, Illinois. Until his death in Michigan about 1863, most of his time was occupied with writing and lecturing on Indian problems.

TELLING OF LEGENDS from *Legends, Traditions, and Laws of the Iroquois or Six Nations* by Chief Elias Johnson, p. 220. Chief Johnson, an educated Tuscarora, published his legendary account of the Iroquois in 1881. The customs described existed among the New York Iroquois in the nineteenth century and earlier.

PART II. GAME TRAILS

BOYHOOD TRAINING IN WOODCRAFT and THE BOY HUNTER from *Indian Boyhood* by Ohiyesa (Dr. Charles A. Eastman), pp. 52–56, 86–95. Ohiyesa received his boyhood training among the Santee Sioux in British Columbia during the 1860's.

HUNTING LAWS from *The Life, Letters and Speeches* by Chief Kah-ge-ga-gah-bowh (George Copway), pp. 20 ff. These were the hunting laws of the Ojibway in Michigan and southeastern Canada during the first half of the nineteenth century.

DEER HUNTING RITUAL from *Flaming Arrow's People* by Flaming Arrow (James Paytiamo), pp. 69—79. A full-blood Pueblo Indian, Flaming Arrow was born and raised among his people in the sky city of Acoma, New Mexico. The ritual he describes has existed almost unchanged since pre-Columbian days.

WAYS OF HUNTING THE DEER from Chief Kah-ge-ga-gah-bowh's *Life, Letters and Speeches*, pp. 25–26, and *Traditional History and Characteristic Sketches of the Ojibway Nation*, pp. 34–35. Most of the Northeast tribes used similar methods of deer hunting during the early and middle nineteenth century.

A BUFFALO HUNT from *My People, the Sioux* by Chief Luther Standing Bear, pp. 61–66. This way of hunting buffalo, known as "the surround," was used by most of the Plains Indians during the nineteenth century. The Oglala Sioux hunt took place in northern Nebraska about 1875.

KILLING A BEAR from *The Life, Letters and Speeches* by Chief Kah-ge-ga-gah-bowh (George Copway), pp. 26–27. This incident occurred about 1829 in southern Canada.

PART III. WILDERNESS SPORTS

GAMES OF SIOUX CHILDREN from *Indian Boyhood* by Ohiyesa (Dr. Charles A. Eastman), pp. 63–75. The locale was British Columbia, between 1865 and 1870.

HOPI CHILDREN AT PLAY from *Sun Chief: The Autobiography of a Hopi* by Don C. Talayesva, edited by Leo W. Simmons, p. 62. Talayesva passed his boyhood at Oraibi, Arizona, in the 1890's.

GAMES OF THE EASTERN TRIBES from *Traditional History and Characteristic Sketches of the Ojibway Nation* by Chief Kah-ge-ga-gah-bowh (George Copway), pp. 47–56. These games were popular among most tribes in the Old Northwest during the seventeenth and eighteenth centuries.

OUTDOOR SPORTS OF THE PLAINS INDIANS from *A Warrior Who Fought Custer*, interpreted by Thomas B. Marquis, pp. 39–45. In 1930, Marquis recorded the autobiography of Wooden Leg, a Northern Cheyenne born in the Black Hills in 1858. Wooden Leg, who fought in the Custer battle in 1876, dictated his story in the sign language, supplemented with occasional drawings and a few words of English. He was aided by a group of fellow tribesmen who checked or corroborated his assertions.

The Cheyenne sports described were played by most of the Plains Indians during the nineteenth century.

WHISKY SPREES from *The Life, Letters and Speeches* by Chief Kah-ge-ga-gah-bowh (George Copway), pp. 41–42. Whisky sprees were common among most tribes exposed to white civilization.

TEMPERANCE LESSONS from *O-Gi-Maw-Kwe Mit-I-Gwa-Ki (Queen of the Woods)* by Chief Simon Pokagon, pp. 135–136. Chief Pokagon (1830–1899) was the son of Leopold Pokagon, who in 1833 sold the site of Chicago to the white men. Until Simon was fourteen, he spoke only the Pottawattami language. He began the study of English at Notre Dame and later attended Oberlin College, where he studied Latin and Greek. He wrote his autobiographical romance in the Pottawattami language, then translated it into English. Most of his characters, like Ash-taw, the temperance worker, were actual persons whom he knew in Michigan about the middle of the nineteenth century.

FIRESIDE HUMOR from *Indian Boyhood* by Ohiyesa (Dr. Charles A. Eastman), pp. 274–276. This incident occurred while the Santee Sioux were living in Minnesota, probably during the first half of the nineteenth century.

PART IV. THE GREAT SPIRIT

SEARCHING FOR A SPIRITUAL GUIDE from *Goodbird the Indian, His Story*, pp. 27–33. Born in 1869 near the mouth of the Yellowstone River, Edward Goodbird moved with his father to the Indian reservation at Independence, North Dakota, when the buffalo and deer became scarce. He became a successful farmer and was appointed assistant in farming procedures to the Indian agent. In 1913, while living on the Fort Berthold Reservation, he dictated the story of his life and a brief history of the Hidatsa tribe to his adopted white brother, Gilbert L. Wilson.

The vision of Bush was characteristic of the widespread Indian belief in supernatural guidance. Many Indians of the Plains and the Northwest have recorded similar spiritual experiences.

THE GODS OF THE OJIBWAYS from *Traditional History and Characteristic Sketches of the Ojibway Nation* by Chief Kah-ge-ga-gah-bowh (George Copway), pp. 147–149. Kah-ge-ga-gah-bowh is probably mistaken in assuming that the Ojibways "believed in a Great Good Spirit, and in a Bad Spirit." Most Indians had no clear notion of religion, and the concept of two major controlling deities (God and the Devil) was doubtless acquired from early missionaries.

SACRED SONG TO THE MORNING STAR from *The Hako: A Pawnee Ceremony*, edited by Alice C. Fletcher, 22nd Annual Report of the Bureau of American Ethnology, Part 2, pp. 129–130, 323. This song is a part of the Hako, a series of ancient rites in praise of the supernatural. Tahirussawichi, a Chaui-Pawnee ceremonial leader, was about seventy years old when he explained the Hako rites in 1898: "When I think of all the people of my own tribe who have died during my lifetime and then of those in other tribes that have fallen by our hands, they are so many that they make a vast cover over Mother Earth. I did not fall but I passed on, wounded sometimes but not to death, until I am here to-day doing this thing, singing these sacred songs into that great pipe [the phonograph] and telling you of these ancient rites of my people. It must be that I have been preserved for this purpose, otherwise I should be lying back there among the dead."

Ceremonies similar to the Hako were observed by other Plains Indians as recently as the last quarter of the nineteenth century.

THE SUN DANCE from *Long Lance* by Chief Buffalo Child Long Lance (Sylvester Long), pp. 129–133. Until about seventy years ago the Sun Dance was observed in some form by most of the Plains Indians. Long Lance's description of the Blackfoot Sun Dance, based largely upon information obtained from the Venerable Archdeacon S. H. Middleton, a missionary to the Blackfeet, is substantially correct.

GETTING IN TOUCH WITH THE SPIRITS from *Long Lance* by Chief Buffalo Child Long Lance, pp. 51–57. Long Lance, a mixed-blood Croatan, never actually witnessed the ritual performed in contacting spirits; but white travelers observed similar ceremonies among the Blackfeet and other plains tribes and were unable to offer an adequate explanation for the feats of the medicine men. It is said that medicine men were adept at sleight of hand, hypnosis, and ventriloquism.

CURING A WOUNDED WARRIOR from *American: The Life Story of a Great Indian* (Plenty-coups) by Frank B. Linderman, pp. 213–215. The incident occurred about 1868 in Montana. Plenty-coups, greatest of Crow chiefs, was born in 1848 near the present site of Billings, Montana. Before he was twenty-six, he had counted so many coups against enemy warriors that he was made a chief. Later, he served with the American army during the campaigns against the warring Sioux and Cheyenne. At eighty, he dictated the story of his life to Frank B. Linderman. "I know that your writing will be straight like your tongue," he said, "and I sign your paper with my thumb so that your people and mine will know I told you the things you have written down."

MARKSMANSHIP OF A MEDICINE MAN from *A Warrior Who Fought Custer*, interpreted by Thomas B. Marquis, pp. 45–47. This incident took place in Montana about 1875.

WITCHCRAFT from *History of the Ojebway Indians* by Chief Kahkewaquonaby (Peter Jones), pp. 145–147. Chief Kahkewaquonaby (1802–1856), a mixed-blood, was born in Ontario and passed his first fourteen years with the Missisaugas, a subtribe of the Ojibways. In 1816, he attended an English school at Saltfleet for about nine months, where he was taught to "read, write, and cypher." He was converted to Methodism at a camp meeting in 1823 and devoted the remainder of his life to missionary activities and writing.

Witchcraft was widely practiced among the Indians of the Northeast and Old Northwest.

CANNIBALISM AMONG MEDICINE MEN from *History of the Ojibways* by William W. Warren, pp. 109–110. A mixed-blood Ojibway, Warren (1825–1853) passed his youth in the tribe at La Pointe and Mackinac, Michigan. His schooling began at the Indian School at La Pointe and was continued at the Oneida Institute at Whitesboro, near Utica. In the Preface to his *History of the Ojibways,* published long after his early death from tuberculosis, he wrote: "The following work may not claim to be well and elaborately written, as it cannot be expected that a person who has passed most of his life among the wild Indians can wield the pen of an Irving or a Schoolcraft. But the work does claim to be one of truth, and the first work written from purely Indian sources."

The cannibalism described by Warren presumably occurred in the seventeenth century, but there is no evidence to substantiate Warren's claim that an early band of Ojibways lived at La Pointe.

THE PEYOTE CULT from *The Winnebago Tribe* by Paul Radin, 37th Annual Report of the Bureau of American Ethnology, pp. 389–392.

BURIAL CUSTOMS from *History of the Ojebway Indians* by Chief Kahkewaquonaby (Peter Jones), pp. 98–100. Similar burial customs existed among most of the Northeast Indians during the eighteenth and nineteenth centuries.

THE HAPPY HUNTING GROUNDS from *History of the Ojibways* by William W. Warren, pp. 72–73. The ancient Ojibway belief in a westward heaven supports the theory that the Ojibways came to America from Asia and anticipated a return to their original home after death.

PART V. ON THE WARPATH

BOYHOOD PREPARATION FOR THE WARPATH from *Indian Boyhood* by Ohiyesa (Dr. Charles A. Eastman), pp. 56–58. Ohiyesa's training among the Santee Sioux in British Columbia was similar to the schooling of other Plains Indians.

COUNTING COUP ON A WOUNDED BUFFALO from *American: The Life Story of a Great Indian* (Plenty-coups) by Frank B. Linderman, pp. 29–31. The setting is the Great Plains, probably Montana, about 1857.

MAKING A WAR CLUB AND WAR WHISTLE from *Yellow Wolf: His Own Story,* edited by Lucullus Virgil McWhorter. Yellow Wolf (1855–1935) was born in the Wallowa valley in Oregon and fought under Chief Joseph in the Nez Perce War of 1877. At intervals during the last twenty-seven years of his life he dictated the story of the Nez Perce campaign in which he used this war club and whistle.

SCOUTING OUT THE ENEMY from *Land of the Spotted Eagle* by Chief Luther Standing Bear, pp. 75–77. Most of the Indian tribes on the Great Plains used scouts who were as expertly trained as these Oglala Sioux.

PREPARATION FOR BATTLE from *A Warrior Who Fought Custer* (Wooden Leg), interpreted by Thomas B. Marquis, pp. 83–87.

BATTLE TACTICS from *History of the Ojebway Indians* by Chief Kahkewaquonaby (Peter Jones), pp. 130–131. These were the familiar tactics of the Northeast and Old Northwest tribes, also utilized by early frontiersmen.

A HORSE STEALING RAID from *American: The Life Story of a Great Indian* (Plenty-coups) by Frank B. Linderman, pp. 125–133. The raid took place on the Great Plains about 1865.

BURNING AT THE STAKE from *History of the Ojibways* by William W. Warren, pp. 106–107. This legendary incident may have taken place about 1600, during the wars between the Foxes and the Ojibways. Warren's surmise that the word "Ojibway" originated from this episode is not accepted by most authorities, who contend that "to roast till puckered up with fire" refers to the puckered seam on Ojibway moccasins.

STRATAGEM OF A WYANDOTT CHIEF from *Origin and Traditional History of the Wyandotts* by Peter D. Clarke, pp. 7–9. Historian of the Wyandott (or Huron) Indians, Clarke (about 1810–1870) was the son of a Wyandott woman and an officer in the British Indian Department. In explaining the sources of his history, Clarke wrote: "The lapse of ages has rendered it difficult to trace the origin of the Wyandotts. Nothing now remains to tell whence they came, but a tradition that lives only in the memory of a few among the remnant of this tribe. Of this I will endeavour to give a sketch as I had it from the lips of such, and from some of the tribe who have since passed away."

CHIVALRY OF THE IOWAYS from *Life of Ma-ka-tai-me-she-kia-kiak or Black Hawk*, dictated by himself, pp. 82–83. This incident probably occurred in Illinois in the first quarter of the nineteenth century.

THE COURAGE OF AN OLD WARRIOR from *History of the Ojibways* by William W. Warren, pp. 127–129. The locale was Michigan, about 1600.

ORIGIN OF THE FIVE NATIONS from *Legends, Traditions, and Laws of the Iroquois or Six Nations* by Chief Elias Johnson, pp. 50–53.

PART VI. WAR BELTS ON THE OLD FRONTIER

THE WARNING OF THE BEES from *Origin and Traditional History of the Wyandotts* by Peter D. Clarke, p. 6.

ARRIVAL OF THE WHITE MEN from *Life and Traditions of the Red Men* by Joseph Nicolar, p. 128. Nicolar's history of the Penobscots is largely devoted to pre-Columbian traditions.

CAPTAIN JOHN SMITH AND POWHATAN from *Firewater and Forked Tongues,* dictated to M. I. McCreight by Flying Hawk, pp. 20–21.

THE PILGRIM INVASION and KING PHILIP'S WAR from *Eulogy on King Philip* by William Apes, pp. 10 ff., 35 ff.

GERM WARFARE AGAINST THE INDIANS from *History of the Ottawa and Chippewa Indians of Michigan* by Chief Andrew J. Blackbird, pp. 9–10. Chief Blackbird (about 1825–1898) was taught to read and write by the Catholic missionaries in Michigan. Aided by a small government subsidy, he attended the Ypsilanti State Normal School for two and one-half years. During the Civil War, he was the United States interpreter for the Ottawa Indians, and on at least one occasion persuaded his tribe not to secede from the Union! His account of germ warfare against the Indians was questioned by William W. Warren, who contended that smallpox spread among the Ojibways and Ottawas after a war party of Assiniboins and Ojibways attacked an encampment of infected Gros Ventres and brought the diseased scalps back to their village.

THE CAPTURE OF FORT MICHILIMACKINAC from *History of the Ojibways* by William W. Warren, pp. 199–204.

LOGAN DEFENDS HIS CONDUCT from *Indian Life and Battles* by B. B. Thatcher, p. 187. The authenticity of this famous speech by Chief James (or John?) Logan has been questioned by Brantz Mayer and other historians. It is now believed that Greathouse and not Colonel Michael Cresap led the settlers in the massacre at Yellow Creek, that Logan's sister was killed, and that Logan had neither wife nor children. However, the speech was probably dictated by Logan and read before the treaty conference at Chillicothe which he refused to attend. Despite its minor inconsistencies, the speech is almost certainly authentic and as accurately recorded as most Indian speeches of the eighteenth century.

PART VII. FIGHTING THE LONG KNIVES

WITH THE BRITISH IN THE REVOLUTION from *Indian Life and Battles* by B. B. Thatcher, pp. 158–160.

COLONEL CRAWFORD BURNED AT THE STAKE and AN ATTACK ON A FLATBOAT from *Origin and Traditional History of the Wyandotts* by Peter D. Clarke, pp. 69–71, 76–78, and 57–59. Chief Hopocan probably led the Delawares in their victory over Colonel Crawford.

THE BRITISH CAMPAIGN IN THE NORTHWEST from *Life of Ma-ka-tai-me-she-kia-kiak or Black Hawk, Dictated by Himself*, pp. 33–34.

THE INVASION OF CANADA from *A Son of the Forest* by William Apes, pp. 53–62.

THE OJIBWAYS REMAIN NEUTRAL from *History of the Ojibways* by William W. Warren, pp. 376–377.

"WE ARE DETERMINED TO DEFEND OUR LANDS" from *Indian Life and Battles* by B. B. Thatcher, pp. 263–265.

THE SURRENDER OF WILLIAM WEATHERFORD from *Adventures Among the Indians* by W. H. G. Kingston, pp. 17–18.

THE BLACK HAWK WAR from *Life of Ma-ka-tai-me-she-kia-kiak or Black Hawk, Dictated by Himself*, pp. 83–136.

PART VIII. COVERED WAGONS AND IRON HORSES

ATTACKING THE UNION PACIFIC from *My People, the Sioux* by Chief Luther Standing Bear, pp. 6–8.

THE WAGON BOX FIGHT from *Black Elk Speaks*, as told to John G. Neihardt, pp. 16–17.

FIGHTING THE MEXICANS from *Geronimo's Story of His Life*, pp. 43–54.

THE RETREAT OF THE NEZ PERCES from "An Indian's View of Indian Affairs," *North American Review*, Vol. 128, pp. 415–433 (April, 1879). The name Nez Perce (Nez Percé) is usually pronounced *Nez Pers* (plural, *Nez Perses*) to rhyme with "verse." This pronunciation is used by the Indians and has also been approved by the U.S. Geographic Board.

THE LAST STAND OF THE NEZ PERCES from *Yellow Wolf: His Own Story* by Lucullus Virgil McWhorter, pp. 210–212.

THE SURRENDER SPEECH OF CHIEF JOSEPH from *The Ghost Dance Religion* by James Mooney, 14th Annual Report of the Bureau of American Ethnology, p. 715.

THE COURAGE OF SITTING BULL from *Indian Heroes and Great Chieftains* by Ohiyesa (Dr. Charles A. Eastman), pp. 112–114.

SITTING BULL DEFENDS HIS CHARACTER from *Life of Sitting Bull* by W. Fletcher Johnson, p. 201.

CUSTER WARNED BY HIS INDIAN SCOUTS from *American: The Life Story of a Great Indian* (Plenty-coups) by Frank B. Linderman, p. 175.

THE CUSTER BATTLE from *Black Elk Speaks,* as told to John G. Neihardt, pp. 122–129.

LOOTING AFTER THE CUSTER BATTLE from *A Warrior Who Fought Custer* (Wooden Leg), interpreted by Thomas B. Marquis, pp. 238–241, 263–267.

WHY THE INDIANS FOUGHT CUSTER and THE GHOST DANCE RELIGION from *Life of Sitting Bull* by W. Fletcher Johnson, pp. 153–154, 267–269.

THE MASSACRE AT WOUNDED KNEE from *The Ghost Dance Religion* by James Mooney, 14th Annual Report of the Bureau of American Ethnology, pp. 885–886.

PART IX. THE WHITE MAN'S ROAD

MYSTERIOUS MEDICINE OF THE WHITE MAN from *Indian Boyhood* by Ohiyesa (Dr. Charles A. Eastman), pp. 281–284.

THE CHARACTER OF THE WHITE MAN from *American: The Life Story of a Great Indian* (Plenty-coups) by Frank B. Linderman, pp. 227–228.

HOW THE WHITE MAN FIGHTS from *Life of Ma-ka-tai-me-she-kia-kiak or Black Hawk, Dictated by Himself*, p. 47. During the War of 1812, Black Hawk served as brevet brigadier general in the British army on the Northwest frontier.

THE SYMBOL OF EXTINCTION from *Land of the Spotted Eagle* by Chief Luther Standing Bear, pp. 165–166. The great buffalo herds on the plains were almost exterminated by white hunters between 1870 and 1880.

THE WHITE MAN'S LACK OF SENSE from *History of the Ojebway Indians* by Chief Kahkewaquonaby (Peter Jones), p. 230.

A TOUR OF THE EAST from *Life of Ma-ka-tai-me-she-kia-kiak or Black Hawk, Dictated by Himself*, pp. 140–147.

AT THE ST. LOUIS WORLD'S FAIR from *Geronimo's Story of His Life*, pp. 197–206. The Louisiana Purchase Exposition was held in St. Louis in 1904.

IMPRESSIONS OF THE ENGLISH and IMPRESSIONS OF THE FRENCH from *History of the Ojebway Indians* by Chief Kahkewaquonaby (Peter Jones), pp. 221–222, 219–220. Maungwadaus, an educated Ojibway chief, wrote the description of the French for his friend Kahkewaquonaby in 1854.

A VISIT TO GRANDMOTHER ENGLAND from *Black Elk Speaks*, as told to John G. Neihardt, pp. 224–227.

A SIOUX AT DARTMOUTH from *From the Deep Woods to Civilization* by Ohiyesa (Dr. Charles A. Eastman), pp. 64 ff.

EARLY DAYS AT CARLISLE from *My People, the Sioux* by Chief Luther Standing Bear, pp. 128–149.

RED JACKET DENOUNCES THE BLACK-COATS from *Indian Life and Battles* by B. B. Thatcher, pp. 325–329.

MURDER OF AN INDIAN SEMINARIST from *History of the Ottawa and Chippewa Indians of Michigan* by Chief Andrew J. Blackbird, pp. 41–43.

CONFUSION OF THE WHITE MAN'S RELIGION from *Our Wild Indians* by Colonel Richard I. Dodge, pp. 111–112. Chief Spotted Tail (1833?–1881) was one of the first of the hostile Sioux to advocate acceptance of the white man's way of life.

SEQUOYAH AND THE CHEROKEE ALPHABET from a speech by John Ridge quoted in *History of the Ojebway Indians* by Chief Kahkewaquonaby (Peter Jones), pp. 187–188.

THE INDIAN PROBLEM from *Land of the Spotted Eagle* by Chief Luther Standing Bear, pp. 248–249.

THE INDIANS' APPEAL FOR JUSTICE from "An Indian's View of Indian Affairs," *North American Review*, Vol. 128, pp. 415–433 (April, 1879).

THE FUTURE OF THE INDIAN from *Land of the Spotted Eagle* by Chief Luther Standing Bear, pp. 252–255.

A SELECTED BIBLIOGRAPHY

BOOKS AND PAMPHLETS WRITTEN OR DICTATED BY AMERICAN INDIANS

This bibliography is intended as a guide for those who wish to explore Indian literature and history. Writings such as treaty minutes, memorials to Congress, speeches, military reports, political documents, and collections of myths and folklore are excluded with a few exceptions. Also omitted are certain scholarly publications by educated Indians like A. C. Parker, J. N. B. Hewitt, Francis LaFlesche, and Ella Deloria, specialized works such as Oronhyatekha's *History of the Independent Order of Foresters*, and unpublished typescripts and manuscripts. A few books on art and music are included because they possess special interest.

ABEITA, LOUISE (E-YEH-SHURE), *I Am a Pueblo Indian Girl*. New York, 1939.

ALFORD, THOMAS WILDCAT, *Civilization*, as told to Florence Drake. Norman, Okla., 1936.

By a great-grandson of Tecumseh. Contains an eyewitness account of the opening and settlement of Oklahoma.

APES, WILLIAM, *Eulogy on King Philip*. Boston, 1836.

———, *Increase of the Kingdom of Christ*. New York, 1831.

———, *A Son of the Forest*, 2nd ed., rev. and cor. New York, 1831.

Autobiography of an Acoma Indian, ed. by Leslie A. White. Bureau of American Ethnology, Bulletin 136. Washington, 1943.

Autobiography of a Papago Woman, ed. by Ruth Underhill. Memoirs of the American Anthropological Association, No. 46. Menasha, Wis., 1936.

BENT, GEORGE, "Forty Years with the Cheyennes." *The Frontier*. Colorado Springs, Oct.-Dec., 1905, Jan.-Mar., 1906.

[BLACK ELK], *Black Elk Speaks*, as told to John G. Neihardt. New York, 1932.

[BLACK HAWK], *Life of Ma-ka-tai-me-she-kia-kiak or Black Hawk, Dictated by Himself*. Boston, 1834.

Blackbird, Chief Andrew J., *Education of Indian Youth.* Philadelphia, 1856.

———, *History of the Ottawa and Chippewa Indians of Michigan.* Ypsilanti, Mich., 1887.

Boudinott, Elias, *Address to the Whites.* Philadelphia, 1826.

A plea for funds with which to establish a Cherokee printing press.

[Boudinott, Elias], *Documents in Relation to the Validity of the Cherokee Treaty of 1835.* Washington, 1838.

Cherokee Cavaliers: Forty Years of Cherokee History as Told in the Correspondence of the Ridge-Watie-Boudinot Families, ed. by Edward E. Dale and G. L. Litton. Norman, Okla., 1939.

"A Chiricahua Apache's Account of the Geronimo Campaign," ed. by M. E. Opler. *New Mexico Historical Review,* Vol. 13, pp. 360–386 (Oct., 1938).

[Clarke, Peter Dooyentate], *Origin and Traditional History of the Wyandotts.* Toronto, 1870.

An important source of information on Tecumseh and the Indians of the Old Northwest.

Commuck, Thomas, *Indian Melodies,* with a Preface by the Composer. New York, 1845.

A collection of 120 original hymns named after Indian tribes and famous chiefs. The author, a Narraganset Indian, also wrote "A Sketch of the Brothertown Indians," in Vol. 4 of the Wisconsin Historical Society Collections. The Rev. G. Cole said of *Indian Melodies:* "In the first strain of the first tune there is something worthy of Handel, and in the whole there is something equal to anything we ever saw in the productions of Haydn."

Cornplanter, Jesse, *Iroquois Indian Games and Dances.* N.p., n.d. [c. 1903].

A series of fifteen full-page drawings illustrating the games and dances of the Seneca Indians.

[Crashing Thunder], *Crashing Thunder: The Autobiography of an American Indian,* ed. by Paul Radin. New York, 1926.

Based upon "Reminiscences of a Winnebago," ed. by Radin. *Journal of American Folklore,* Vol. 26 (1913).

[Cuffe, Paul], *Narrative of the Life and Adventures of Paul Cuffe.* Vernon, N.Y., 1839.

The author, of mixed Pequod and Negro blood, was the son of Paul Cuffe (1759–1818), the famous colonizer of Sierra Leone. The younger Cuffe was a harpooner. Possibly he knew Herman Melville, and if so he may have served as the prototype for Queequeg, the aboriginal harpooner in *Moby Dick.*

CUSICK, DAVID, *Ancient History of the Six Nations.* New York, 1848.
A quaint pre-Columbian history of the Tuscaroras.

DELORIA, ELLA C., *Speaking of Indians.* New York, 1944.

[EN-ME-GAH-BOWH], *En-me-gah-bowh's Story: An Account of the Disturbances of the Chippewa Indians at Gull Lake in 1857 and 1862 and Their Removal in 1868.* Minneapolis, Minn., 1904.
Contains material on the famous Sioux chief Little Crow (d. 1863), leader in the Minnesota Massacre of 1862.

[FIELDING, MRS.], *A Mohegan-Pequot Diary,* ed. by Frank G. Speck. Bureau of American Ethnology, 43rd Annual Report, 1925–1926. Washington, 1928.

[FLAMING ARROW], *Flaming Arrow's People,* by an Acoma Indian, James Paytiamo. New York, 1932.
Illustrated by the author.

[FLYING HAWK], *Firewater and Forked Tongues,* dictated to M. I. McCreight. Pasadena, 1947.
Comments on American history. Portions of this volume were published earlier as *Chief Flying Hawk's Tales* (1936) and *The Wigwam: Puffs from the Peace Pipe* (1943).

[GERONIMO], *Geronimo's Story of His Life,* ed. by S. M. Barrett. New York, 1906.

[GOODBIRD, EDWARD], *Goodbird the Indian: His Story,* ed. by Gilbert L. Wilson. New York, 1914.

The Hako: A Pawnee Ceremony, ed. by Alice C. Fletcher. Bureau of American Ethnology, 22nd Annual Report, Pt. 2, 1900–1901. Washington, 1904.

Indian Legends and Superstitions, as told by pupils of Haskell Institute. Lawrence, Kans., 1932.

The Iroquois Book of Rites, ed. by Horatio Hale. Philadelphia, 1883.

JACOBS, PETER (PAH-TAH-SE-GA), *Journal from Rice Lake to the Hudson's Bay Territory, and Returning, Commencing May, 1852.* Toronto, 1853.

JOHNSON, E. PAULINE (TEKAHIONWAKE), *Flint and Feather,* rev. and enl. ed. Toronto, 1914.
The collected poems of a talented Mohawk woman.

JOHNSON, CHIEF ELIAS, *Legends, Traditions, and Laws of the Iroquois or Six Nations and History of the Tuscarora Indians.* Lockport, N.Y., 1881.

JOSEPH, CHIEF (IN-MUT-TOO-YAH-LAT-LAT), "An Indian's View of Indian Affairs." *North American Review,* Vol. 128, pp. 415–433 (April, 1879).

KABOTIE, FRED, *Designs from the Ancient Mimbreños.* San Francisco, 1949.

KAH-GE-GA-GAH-BOWH, CHIEF (GEORGE COPWAY), *The Life, Letters and Speeches.* New York, 1850.

———, *The Ojibway Conquest: A Tale of the Northwest.* New York, 1850.

An epic poem on the origin of the Wendigo, or vampire spirit of the North.

———, *Organization of a New Indian Territory, East of the Missouri River*. New York, 1850.

———, *Running Sketches of Men and Places in Europe*. New York, 1851.

———, *Traditional History and Characteristic Sketches of the Ojibway Nation*. Boston, 1851.

KAHKEWAQUONABY, CHIEF (PETER JONES), *History of the Ojebway Indians*. London, 1861.

———, *Life and Journals*. Toronto, 1860.

An account of Kahkewaquonaby's travels among the Ojibway and other tribes.

KAONDINOKETC, CHIEF FRANÇOIS, *Récit de François Kaondinoketc, chef des Nipissingues*. Paris, 1877.

Not seen. Description from Pilling's *Bibliography of the Algonquian Languages*, p. 274.

KE-WA-ZE-ZHIG, *An Address Delivered in Allston Hall, Boston, February 26th, 1861*. Boston, 1861.

A vitriolic condemnation of the white man.

LA FLESCHE, FRANCIS, *The Middle Five*. Boston, 1900.

School days of an Omaha Indian.

———, *Osage Tribe: Rite of the Chiefs, Sayings of the Ancient Men*. Bureau of American Ethnology, 36th Annual Report. Washington, 1921.

———, *Who Was the Medicine Man?* Philadelphia, 1904.

[LEFT HANDED], *Son of Old Man Hat: A Navaho Autobiography*, recorded by W. Dyk. New York, 1938.

Letters of Eleazar Wheelock's Indians, ed. by James Dow McCallum. Dartmouth College Manuscript Series, No. 1. Hanover, N.H., 1932.

[LITTLE PINE], *Little Pine's Journal*. Toronto, 1872.

A pedestrian account of an uneventful trip.

LONG LANCE, CHIEF BUFFALO CHILD (SYLVESTER LONG), *Long Lance*. New York, 1928.

A description of Blackfoot life by a mixed-blood Croatan.

MCLAUGHLIN, MRS. MARIE L., *Myths and Legends of the Sioux*. Bismarck, N.D., 1916.

MAUNGWUDAUS [MAUNGWADAUS], *Remarks Concerning the Ojibway Indians by One of Themselves, Called Maungwudaus*. Leeds, 1847.

Maungwudaus (George Henry) was interpreter to several governors of Canada. Pilling (*Bibliography of the Algonquian Languages*, p. 228) describes a work by Maungwudaus entitled *An Account of the Chippewa Indians Who Have Been Travelling among the Whites* (Boston, 1848). This is probably a revised edition of the Leeds pamphlet.

Memorial of the Delegation of the Cherokee Nation. Washington, 1840.
A recital of Cherokee grievances and a plea for redress.

MOURNING DOVE (HUM-ISHU-MA), *Co-ge-we-a, the Half Blood.* Boston, 1927.
A romance by a mixed-blood Okanogan.

"Narrative of a Cheyenne Woman," ed. by T. Michelson. *Smithsonian Misc. Coll.*, Vol. 87, No. 5 (1932).

NICOLAR, JOSEPH, *Life and Traditions of the Red Man.* Bangor, Me., 1893.

OCCOM, SAMSON, *Sermon at the Execution of Moses Paul.* New Haven, 1788.

OHIYESA (DR. CHARLES A. EASTMAN), *From the Deep Woods to Civilization.* Boston, 1916.

———, *Indian Boyhood.* New York, 1902.

———, *Indian Heroes and Great Chieftains.* Boston, 1923.

———, *Indian Scout Talks.* Boston, 1914.

———, *The Indian Today.* New York, 1915.

———, "The North American Indian." *Universal Races Congress,* No. 1, pp. 367–376. London, 1911.
A brief analysis of the Indian's way of life and the effect of white civilization upon him.

———, *Red Hunters and the Animal People.* New York, 1904.

——— and ELAINE GOODALE EASTMAN, *Wigwam Evenings: Sioux Folk Tales Retold.* Boston, 1909.

OWEN, NARCISSA, *Memoirs* [Washington, 1907(?)].
Recollections of an old Cherokee woman.

PARKER, ARTHUR C., *The Code of Handsome Lake, the Seneca Prophet.* New York State Museum Bulletin 163. Albany, 1913.
The teachings of Handsome Lake (c. 1735–1815) are recorded in the Gai'wiio'.

———, *Life of General Ely S. Parker.* Buffalo, 1919.
General Parker was the "last grand Sachem of the Iroquois and General Grant's Military Secretary." His grandnephew, Arthur C. Parker, is State Archeologist of New York and the author of many valuable monographs on Iroquois life and culture.

PIERCE, CHIEF M. B., *Address on the Present Condition and Prospects of the Aboriginal Inhabitants of North America.* Philadelphia, 1839.
A Seneca chief and student at Dartmouth, Pierce opposed the removal of the Senecas from New York to beyond the Mississippi. The removal was favored by Chief N. T. Strong (see below).

[PITCHLYNN, COLONEL PETER], *Remonstrance of Col. Peter Pitchlynn, a Choctaw Delegate, Against the Bill to Unite Under One Government the Several Indian Tribes West of the Mississippi River.* Washington, 1849.

[PLENTY-COUPS], *American: The Life Story of a Great Indian*, ed. by Frank B. Linderman. New York, 1930.

Ploughed Under: The Story of an Indian Chief Told by Himself (by William J. Harsha?), with an Introduction by Inshta Theamba (Bright Eyes). New York, 1881.

POKAGON, CHIEF SIMON, *O-Gi-Maw-Kwe Mit-I-Gwa-Ki* (*Queen of the Woods*). Hartford, Mich., 1899.

An Indian romance. For a sketch of the author's life, see Winger's *Potawatomi Indians* (1939). A bibliography of Pokagon's periodical writings (in *Harper's*, *Forum*, etc.) will be found in Buechner's "Pokagons," *Indiana Historical Society Publications*, Vol. 10, No. 5 (1933).

———, *The Red Man's Greeting*. Hartford, Mich., 1893.

A birch-bark pamphlet. Reprinted in Buechner's "Pokagons."

POSEY, ALEXANDER L., *Poems*. Topeka, Kans., 1910.

Conventional verse. Posey (1873–1908), a mixed-blood, was secretary of the Sequoyah convention (1905), held when the principal tribes in the Indian Territory attempted to gain admission to the Union as the State of Sequoyah.

[PRETTY-SHIELD], *Red Mother*, ed. by Frank B. Linderman. New York, 1932.

The autobiography of Pretty-shield, a Crow medicine woman.

A Pueblo Indian Journal, 1920–21, ed. by E. C. Parsons. Memoirs of the American Anthropological Association, No. 32. Menasha, Wis., 1925.

[RED JACKET], *A Long Lost Speech of Red Jacket*, ed. by J. W. Sanborn. Friendship, N.Y., 1912.

"Reminiscences of a Cheyenne Indian," *Journal de la Société des Américanistes de Paris*. Paris, 1935.

RIDDLE, JEFF C., *The Indian History of the Modoc War*. [San Francisco], 1914.

A vindication of Captain Jack and the Modocs by the son of Winema, the heroine of the Modoc War.

RIDGE, JOHN R., *The History of Joaquin Murieta*, rev. ed. Hollister, Calif., 1927.

———, *Poems*. San Francisco, 1868.

Conventional verse, prefaced by an interesting autobiography.

[ROSS, CHIEF JOHN], *Letter from John Ross, the Principal Chief of the Cherokee Nation, to a Gentleman of Philadelphia*. Philadelphia, 1837.

A discussion of the question of the Cherokee removal.

———, *Memorial of a Delegation of the Cherokee Nation Remonstrating Against the Instrument of Writing (Treaty) of December, 1835*. Washington, 1838.

[Ross, Mrs. William P.], *The Life and Times of the Honorable William P. Ross.* Fort Smith, Ark., 1893.

She Watched Custer's Last Battle, interpreted by Thomas B. Marquis. [Custer Battle Museum, Hardin, Mont.], 1933.

[Sitting Bull], "Three Pictographic Autobiographies," ed. by M. W. Stirling. *Smithsonian Miscellaneous Collections,* Vol. 97, No. 5. Washington, 1938.

Pictorial record of Sitting Bull's "coups" counted on Crows, Rees, Assiniboins, and whites. The records cover the period *prior* to the Custer battle (1876).

Standing Bear, Chief Luther, *Land of the Spotted Eagle.* Boston, 1933.

———, *My Indian Boyhood.* Boston, 1931.

———, *My People, the Sioux.* Boston, 1928.

Strong, Chief N. T., *Appeal to the Christian Community on the Condition and Prospects of the New-York Indians.* New York, 1841.

———, *A Further Illustration of the Case of the Seneca Indians in the State of New York.* Philadelphia, 1841.

Swimmer, *Sacred Formulas of the Cherokees,* ed. by James Mooney. Bureau of American Ethnology, 7th Annual Report. Washington, 1891.

[Talayesva, Don C.], *Sun Chief: The Autobiography of a Hopi,* ed. by Leo W. Simmons. New Haven, 1942.

Two Paiute Autobiographies, ed. by J. H. Steward. Univ. of Calif. Publications in American Archaeology and Ethnology, Vol. 33, No. 5. Berkeley, 1934.

Warren, William W., *History of the Ojibways, Based upon Traditions and Oral Statements.* Collections of the Minnesota Historical Society, Vol. 5. St. Paul, 1885.

When Shall We Three Meet Again. A Ballad. The Poetry Written by an American Indian. Philadelphia, Pa. [c. 1815].

Conventional song lyrics of the period, possibly apocryphal.

White Horse Eagle, *We Indians: The Passing of a Great Race,* as told to Edgar von Schmidt-Pauli, transl. by Christopher Turner. New York, 1931.

Completely unreliable but very interesting.

Williams, Eleazar, *Life of Te-ho-ra-gwa-ne-gen alias Thomas Williams.* Albany, 1859.

Williams's life of his father. For an interesting but inaccurate account of Eleazar Williams, who claimed to be the "Lost Dauphin," see John H. Hanson's *Lost Prince* (New York, 1854).

———, *The Salvation of Sinners Through the Riches of Divine Grace.* Green Bay, Wisconsin Territory, 1842.

[Wooden Leg], *A Warrior Who Fought Custer*, interpreted by Thomas B. Marquis. Minneapolis, 1931.

"Xube: A Ponca Autobiography," ed. by William Whitman. *Journal of American Folklore*, 1939.

[Yellow Wolf], *Yellow Wolf: His Own Story*, ed. by L. V. McWhorter. Caldwell, Idaho, 1940.

Chief Joseph's retreat described by one of his warriors.

AMERICAN INDIAN PERIODICALS

This selected list of periodicals includes the most interesting magazines and newspapers published by or for American Indians. Certain short-lived periodicals, such as the *Chickasaw Intelligencer* (1854), *Choctaw Telegraph* (1848), *Oklahoma Chief* (1889) and others similar are omitted.

The American Indian Magazine. Tulsa, Okla., 1926–1931.

Edited by Lee F. Harkins. A valuable periodical containing much information on Indian history and customs written by Indians.

The Cherokee Advocate. Tahlequah, Cherokee Nation, 1844–1906.

Edited by William P. Ross and others. Consists mostly of news reprinted from other newspapers. About one-fourth of the *Advocate* was printed in Cherokee.

The Cherokee Phoenix. New Echota, Ga., 1828–1834.

Edited by Elias Boudinott. The first American Indian newspaper. A weekly, printed mostly in English. Mainly a collection of articles reprinted from other newspapers. Vol. I, No. 24, contains an interesting account of Sequoyah's invention of the Cherokee alphabet. No complete file of this periodical is known to exist.

Chickasaw and Choctaw Herald. Tishomingo City, Indian Territory, 1858–1859.

A weekly edited by J. T. Daviess.

Copway's American Indian. New York, 1851.

Published and edited by Chief Kah-ge-ga-gah-bowh (George Copway). Possibly only Vol. I, No. 1 (July 10, 1851), was issued. This newspaper, according to the editor, was "devoted entirely to subjects connected with the past and present history and condition of the people of his own race." No. 1 contains an account of Tecumseh's death by his aide, Shah-wah-wan-noo.

The Indian. Hagersville, Ont., 1885–1886.

Edited by P. E. Jones, an Ojibway.

The Indian Helper: A Weekly Letter. Carlisle, Pa., 1884?–1894?.

"*The Indian Helper* is printed by Indian boys, but edited by the man-on-the-band-stand, who is NOT an Indian." Contains very little material written by Indians.

Indian Journal. Muskogee, Indian Territory, 1876–1887.
Edited by William P. Ross and M. P. Roberts. See Pilling's *Bibliography of the Muskhogean Languages*, p. 46.

The Indian Speaking Leaf; Red Man's Journal. Carlisle, Pa., 1938–1949.
Published by the students at Carlisle.

Muskogee Phoenix. Muskogee, Indian Territory, 1888–1889.
Edited by Leo E. Bennett.

The Talking Leaf. Brooklyn, N.Y., 1945–1947?.
"A magazine of Indians by Indians, for Indians and their friends." Written and edited by Indians and devoted largely to Indian news items.

The Youth's Companion: A Juvenile Monthly Magazine. Tulalip Indian Reservation, Snohomish Co., Washington Territory, 1881–1886.
See Pilling's *Bibliography of the Algonquian Languages*, p. 542.

APOCRYPHA

ANONYMOUS, *Works of Sitting Bull*. 1878.
An unusual forgery, perpetrated shortly after Custer's defeat when many people believed that Sitting Bull was a graduate of West Point. The "works" are poems in various languages including Latin.

APES, WILLIAM, *Indian Nullification of the Unconstitutional Laws of Massachusetts*. Boston, 1835.
The ideas expressed are probably those of Apes, but according to Sabin the author was William J. Snelling.

BARRY, ADA L., *Yunini's Story of the Trail of Tears*. London, 1932.
Although the title indicates that this romance was written by an Indian named Yunini, the author (as stated on the title page) was Ada L. Barry.

DOMENECH, L'ABBE EM. (Ed.). *Manuscrit pictographique américain précédé d'une notice sur l'idéographie des peaux-rouges*. Paris, 1860.
An elegantly printed facsimile of a pictographic manuscript from the collection of the Marquis de Paulmy. Domenech divided the "pictographs" into fourteen chapters which, he claimed, described the introduction of Christianity among the Indians and the subsequent history of the Indians. After publication, it was found that the "pictographs" were actually a series of crude, very obscene drawings by a German settler's boy. The book was hastily withdrawn from circulation.

[HORNE, HENRY, JR.], *The Citizen of Nature, in a Series of Letters from an American Indian, in London, to His Friend at Home*. London, 1824.

THORPE, JAMES, and THOMAS F. COLLISON, *Jim Thorpe's History of the Olympics*. Los Angeles, 1932.
According to the title page, written in collaboration with Collison; but probably Thorpe merely gave his name to the book.

WAUBUNO, *The Traditions of the Delawares.* London [c. 1875].

Based on Chief Kahkewaquonaby's *History of the Ojebway Indians.* Names, places, and dates have been changed, but otherwise the text is almost identical with that of Kahkewaquonaby's *History of the Ojebway Indians.*

ANTHOLOGIES OF INDIAN WRITINGS

ASTROV, MARGOT, ed., *The Winged Serpent: An Anthology of American Indian Prose and Poetry.* New York, 1946.

CRONYN, GEORGE W., ed., *The Path on the Rainbow: An Anthology of Songs and Chants from the Indians of North America,* new and enl. ed. New York, 1934.

CURTIS, NATALIE, ed., *The Indians' Book: An Offering by the American Indians of Indian Lore, Musical and Narrative.* New York, 1907.

FLETCHER, ALICE C., *Indian Story and Song from North America.* Boston, 1900.

A SELECTED LIST OF BACKGROUND BOOKS ON THE INDIANS

A comprehensive list of books containing speeches and comments by Indians would extend to many hundreds of volumes and would include the narratives of most early explorers, traders, and missionaries. I have listed here only a few of the more important sources used in preparing this volume.

BEACH, WILLIAM W., ed., *The Indian Miscellany.* Albany, 1877.

Contains a translation of the *Walum Olum,* Delaware epic.

BLODGETT, HAROLD W., *Samson Occom.* Hanover, N.H., 1936.

CAMPBELL, WALTER S., comp., *New Sources of Indian History, 1850–1891.* Norman, Okla., 1934.

CAUGHEY, JOHN W., *McGillivray of the Creeks.* Norman, Okla., 1938.

Contains many letters of McGillivray.

COLDEN, CADWALLADER, *History of the Five Indian Nations.* New York, 1904.

DIXON, DR. JOSEPH K., *The Vanishing Race: The Last Great Indian Council,* 2nd ed. New York, 1914.

Includes many Indian eyewitness accounts of the Custer battle.

DODGE, COL. RICHARD I., *Our Wild Indians.* Hartford, 1883.

DRAKE, SAMUEL G., *Biography and History of the Indians of North America from Its First Discovery,* 11th ed. Boston, 1847.

FORSBERG, ROBERTA, ed., *Redmen Echoes.* Los Angeles, 1933.

A collection of letters and fugitive writings by Buffalo Child Long Lance.

HODGE, FREDERICK W., ed., *Handbook of American Indians North of Mexico.* Washington, 1907–1910.

JOHNSON, W. FLETCHER, *Life of Sitting Bull.* N.p., 1891.

JONES, ELECTA F., *Stockbridge, Past and Present.* Springfield, Mass., 1854.

KINGSTON, W. H. G., *Adventures Among the Indians.* Chicago, n.d.

LLEWELLYN, K. N., and E. A. HOEBEL, *The Cheyenne Way.* Norman, 1941.
Contains material dictated by Cheyenne informants.

LOVE, W. D. L., *Samson Occom, and the Christian Indians of New England.* Boston, 1899.

MCKENNEY, THOMAS L., and JAMES HALL, *The Indian Tribes of North America,* ed. Frederick W. Hodge. Edinburgh, 1933–1934.

MCLAUGHLIN, JAMES, *My Friend, the Indian.* Boston, 1910.

MCWHORTER, LUCULLUS V., *Tragedy of the Wahk-shum.* Yakima, Wash., 1937.
Includes an eyewitness account by Su-el-lil of the murder of Major Bolon, Sept., 1855, which touched off the Yakima War.

MALLERY, G., *Pictographs of the North American Indians.* Bureau of American Ethnology, 4th Annual Report. Washington, 1886.

———, *Picture-Writing of the American Indians.* Bureau of American Ethnology, 10th Annual Report. Washington, 1893.

Obsequies of Red Jacket at Buffalo. Transactions of the Buffalo Historical Society. Buffalo, 1885.

PIDGEON, WILLIAM, *Traditions of De-coo-dah, and Antiquarian Researches.* New York, 1852.

RADIN, PAUL, *The Winnebago Tribe.* Bureau of American Ethnology. 37th Annual Report, 1916. Washington, 1923.

SCHOOLCRAFT, H. R., *Information Respecting the History of the Indian Tribes.* Philadelphia, 1851–1857.

SCHULTZ, J. W., *My Life as an Indian.* New York, 1907.

THATCHER, B. B., *Indian Biography.* Akron, Ohio, 1910.

———, *Indian Life and Battles.* New York and Akron, 1910.

SELECTED BIBLIOGRAPHIES

[FIELD, T. W.], *Catalogue of the Library Belonging to Mr. Thomas W. Field.* New York, 1875.

———, *An Essay Towards an Indian Bibliography.* New York, 1873.

HARGRETT, LESTER, *Bibliography of the Constitutions and Laws of the American Indians.* Cambridge, 1947.

KLUCKHOHN, CLYDE, "The Personal Document in Anthropological Science," in L. R. Gottschalk and others, *Use of Personal Documents in History* (Social Science Research Council, Bulletin 53). New York, 1945.

PILLING, JAMES C., *Bibliography of the Algonquian Languages*. Washington, 1891.
———, *Bibliography of the Athapascan Languages*. Washington, 1892.
———, *Bibliography of the Chinookan Languages*. Washington, 1893.
———, *Bibliography of the Muskhogean Languages*. Washington, 1889.
———, *Bibliography of the Salishan Languages*. Washington, 1893.
———, *Bibliography of the Siouan Languages*. Washington, 1887.

INDEX